Lukas Sebastian Kaul

Human-Inspired Balancing and Recovery Stepping for Humanoid Robots

Karlsruhe Series on Humanoid Robotics

Edited by Prof. Dr.-Ing. Tamim Asfour

Vol. 05

Human-Inspired Balancing and Recovery Stepping for Humanoid Robots

by

Lukas Sebastian Kaul

KIT Scientific Publishing

Dissertation, Karlsruher Institut für Technologie
KIT-Fakultät für Informatik

Tag der mündlichen Prüfung: 23. Januar 2019
1. Referent: Prof. Dr.-Ing. Tamim Asfour
2. Referent: Prof. Dr.-Ing. Ralf Mikut

Impressum

KIT Scientific Publishing

Karlsruher Institut für Technologie (KIT)
KIT Scientific Publishing
Straße am Forum 2
D-76131 Karlsruhe

KIT Scientific Publishing is a registered trademark
of Karlsruhe Institute of Technology.
Reprint using the book cover is not allowed.

www.ksp.kit.edu

Print on Demand 2019 – Gedruckt auf FSC-zertifiziertem Papier

ISSN 2512-0875
ISBN 978-3-7315-0903-5
DOI 10.5445/KSP/1000091605

Human-Inspired Balancing and Recovery Stepping for Humanoid Robots

Zur Erlangung des akademischen Grades eines

Doktors der Ingenieurwissenschaften

von der KIT-Fakultät für Informatik
des Karlsruher Instituts für Technologie (KIT)

genehmigte

Dissertation

von

Lukas Sebastian Kaul

aus Trier

Tag der mündlichen Prüfung:	23. Januar 2019
1. Referent:	Prof. Dr.-Ing. Tamim Asfour
2. Referent:	Prof. Dr.-Ing. Ralf Mikut

Deutsche Zusammenfassung

Humanoide Robotik ist ein Teilgebiet der Robotik mit dem übergeordneten Ziel der Schaffung von Robotern, deren sensomotorische und kognitive Fähigkeiten denen des Menschen gleichen. Dieses Ziel motiviert sich aus zwei grundlegenden Überlegungen: Zum einen ist der Großteil der vom Menschen geschaffenen oder modifizierten Welt, von Handwerkzeugen bis zu Treppenhäusern, für die Interaktion mit dem menschlichen Körper ausgelegt. Roboter, die sich in dieser Welt so flexibel und zielgerichtet bewegen können wie Menschen und dadurch ein breites Spektrum an nützlichen und sinnvollen Aufgaben übernehmen können, müssen daher über einen humanoiden Körper und über die erforderlichen sensomotorischen und kognitiven Fähigkeiten verfügen. Zum zweiten erfordert die Nachahmung des Menschen im Rahmen der Robotik eine intensive Auseinandersetzung mit den menschlichen Fähigkeiten aus einer technischen Perspektive heraus. Diese Betrachtungsweise kann neue Erkenntnisse über den Menschen erbringen und damit andere, auch nicht technische Forschungsfelder, bereichern.
Eine Fähigkeit von fundamentaler Bedeutung für zweibeinige humanoide Roboter ist das Wahren der Balance, insbesondere unter dem Einfluss unvorhergesehener Stöße, welche reaktive Maßnahmen hierzu erfordern ("*Push Recovery*"). Ohne diese Fähigkeit sind humanoide Roboter ungeeignet für den Einsatz außerhalb von Forschungslaboren oder jenseits von bekannten Umgebungen. Trotz dieser immensen Wichtigkeit und erheblicher Forschungsanstrengungen im Bereich der humanoiden Robotik ist das Wahren der Balance unter dem Einfluss von Stößen weiterhin ein hochaktuelles und

in weiten Teilen ungelöstes Problem. Diesem Problem widmet sich die vorliegende Arbeit.
Eine wesentliche Schwierigkeit bei der Entwicklung geeigneter Methoden ist die Anforderung, entsprechende Balancierbewegungungen sehr schnell zu erzeugen, da die Zeitspanne zwischen einem Stoß und einem unausweichlichen Sturz des Roboters kurz ist. Da humanoide Roboter gleichzeitig vielfältige, rechenintensive Aufgaben erfüllen müssen, ist die verfügbare Rechenleistung für das Wahren der Balance beschränkt. Daraus ergibt sich die Erforderlichkeit von Methoden, die bei geringem Rechenaufwand sehr schnell zu dem gewünschten Roboterverhalten führen.
Der Stand der Forschung beinhaltet zahlreiche Ansätze, die sich dem Balance-Problem mittels der Lösung komplexer Optimierungsprobleme zur Laufzeit, innerhalb einer Regelschleife, nähern. Diese Ansätze sind prinzipiell sehr erfolgversprechend, da sich die Balance entweder als Zielgröße oder sogar Randbedingung solcher Optimierungsverfahren formulieren lässt, und damit bei hinreichender Modellgüte und Konvergenz der Optimierung gewährleistet werden kann. Bedingt durch die hohe Zahl an kinematischen Freiheitsgraden sowie Einschränkungen und Redundanzen sind diese Optimierungsverfahren im Allgemeinen jedoch sehr rechenaufwändig und widersprechen damit dem Ziel der Entwicklung effizienter Methoden.
Im Gegensatz dazu legt diese Arbeit besonderen Wert auf Effizienz. Dazu wird das zugrundeliegende Problem in drei Teilbereiche aufgeteilt, und zwar in (1) die sensorische Erfassung von Stößen und die Beurteilung der momentanen Stabilität des Roboters, (2) das Balancieren durch Ausgleichsbewegungen, und (3) das Wiedererlangen der Balance mittels eines Ausfallschritts. Bei der Interpretation von Sensordaten zur Stoßerfassung sowie der Erzeugung von Schrittbewegungen wird dabei das menschliche Vorbild herangezogen, um effiziente Methoden zu entwickeln. Zur Erzeugung von Ausgleichsbewegungen wird ein effizientes, lineares Verfahren angewendet, das mittels systematischer Optimierung von Hyperparametern verbessert

und für das komplexe, nichtlineare Ganzkörper-Balancierproblem nutzbar gemacht wird.
Die Beiträge zu den drei genannten Unterthemen lassen sich wie folgt zusammenfassen:

Erfassung von Stößen und Beurteilung der Stabilität Es wird an menschlichen Probanden untersucht, wie sich die Richtung und Stärke eines während des statischen Stehens erfahrenen Stoßes anhand eines am Torso angebrachten Inertialsensors ermitteln lassen, und entsprechende Methoden dazu werden eingeführt. Außerdem wird der Frage nachgegangen, wie sich das menschliche Verhalten (Balancieren oder Ausfallschritt) auf Basis der Inertialsensordaten prädizieren lässt, um es auf humanoide Roboter übertragbar zu machen. Weiterhin wird ein Verfahren vorgestellt und am humanoiden Roboter ARMAR-4 validiert, mit dem eine externe Kraft auf den Roboter an beliebiger Stelle allein anhand der Kraft/Momentensensorik in den Fußgelenken des Roboters rekonstruiert werden kann. Schließlich wird anhand eines umfangreichen Satzes menschlicher Bewegungsdaten untersucht, wie ein System mehrerer, am Körper verteilter Inertialsensoren genutzt werden kann, um die Erforderlichkeit von Balanciermaßnahmen auch während dynamischer Bewegungen zu erkennen. Die durchgeführten Untersuchungen legen nahe, dass schon wenige am Körper verteilte Inertialsensoren eine gute Abschätzung erfahrener Stöße und der momentanen Stabilität erlauben.

Balancieren durch Ausgleichsbewegungen Methoden zur Verbesserung der Erzeugung ausgleichender Ganzkörperbewegungen mittels lokal optimaler, linearer Zustandsregelung werden untersucht. Dazu wird der Raum der der Reglersynthese zugrundeliegenden freien Gewichtsparameter heuristisch eingeschränkt und die verbleibenden Parameter durch ein gradientenfreies Optimierungsverfahren verbessert, um einen linearen Balanceregler mit der besten Eignung zu erhalten. Diese Optimierung, in

Kombination mit neuen Methoden zur Linearisierung der Bodenkontaktes, wird auf einem Simulationsmodell des ARMAR-4 Roboters validiert und führt zu sehr gutem Balancierverhalten unter Einbezug der Robotergelenke in den Beinen, im Torso und in den Armen.

Reaktive Ausfallschritte Die grundlegenden Fragen zur Erzeugung reaktiver Ausfallschritte sind zum einen die Methode der Bewegungserzeugung selbst, und zum anderen die Wahl der Schrittparameter wie Weite, Richtung und Geschwindigkeit. Im Rahmen der vorliegenden Arbeit wird ein auf menschlichen Bewegungen basierender Schrittgenerator entwickelt, der durch die Nutzung dynamischer Bewegungsprimitive im Gelenkwinkelraum wesentlich weniger rechenaufwändig ist als vergleichbare Methoden der Bewegungserzeugung. Mit diesem Generator und einem Simulationsmodell des ARMAR-4 Roboters wird mittels bestärkendem Lernen eine Abbildung von sensoriell erfassbaren Stoßparametern auf Schrittparameter gelernt, die über ein weites Spektrum von Stößen zu erfolgreichen Ausfallschritten führt.

Acknowledgment

This thesis is the result of my research work at the High Performance Humanoid Technologies Lab (H^2T) of the Institute for Anthropomatics and Robotics (IAR), Karlsruhe Institute of Technology (KIT).

First and foremost I would like to thank my doctoral advisor Prof. Tamim Asfour for giving me the opportunity to become a „Humanoid“, to conduct research in the exciting and multi-faceted area of humanoid robotics and to contribute to many inspiring projects. I am particularly grateful for his strong support and trust during every phase of my thesis, for his continuous guidance, and for the great team and working environment he created. I would also like to extend my gratitude to Prof. Ralf Mikut who kindly co-supervised this thesis.

The Humanoids group at KIT is an exceptional environment full of bright and ambitious people whom I proudly call my colleagues and friends. I want to thank all past and present Humanoids for the inspiring discussions, critical questions and fruitful feedback, but also for the good times we had during lunch breaks, lab parties, retreat meetings, at conferences, or even when just wanting to get something done way past midnight. I would like to particularly thank Jonas Beil for being a great office mate, for our coffee break discussions, for the good times playing table tennis in summer (although he mostly won) and the weekend skiing trips in winter. Nikolaus Vahrenkamp and Christian Mandery for their guidance during the earlier stages of my thesis and during our work on the KoroiBot project. Peter Kaiser for the insightful discussions on robotics research and beyond, and Mirko Wächter for the help and guidance throughout my thesis, as well as for his contagious and seemingly inexhaustible enthusiasm for robotics. Samuel Rader, Pascal Weiner and Dmitriy Shingarey for the unforgettable times we had during the year we built ARMAR-6, and all the student assistants who helped us during this intense time.

I want to thank Robert Zlot for supervising my master's thesis at CSIRO's QCAT (Australia) and introducing me to the world of robotics research. Without his guidance, trust and enthusiasm I may have never decided to become a robotics researcher, and his example continues to guide me in many ways.

During my time at the Humanoids group I had the pleasure to supervise several student projects myself, and I gratefully acknowledge the contributions of Laura Steffan, Simon Bäuerle and Johannes Pankert to this thesis.

I want to thank my friends Fabian Sehn and Andreas Trenkle for their friendship from my very first days in Karlsruhe. In particular I want to thank Alexander Albrecht for the continuous support and reliable friendship, for the many adventures we had together, from hiking in China and rock climbing in sunny Spain and Italy to traversing alpine glaciers in the freezing cold, for the countless sessions at the climbing wall, and for the support in virtually any situation I ever needed him.

Most importantly I want to wholeheartedly thank my parents Helga and Martin for their guidance and unconditional support, my brother Matthias for being a mentor and a great friend, and my girlfriend Alice for her patience and ability to see even the most complicated of matters crystal clear. I would be nowhere near where I am today without all of you.

Karlsruhe, February 2019 *Lukas Kaul*

Contents

1 Introduction

Robotics is arguably one of the key technologies that will (continue to) have a transformative impact on society in the 21st century. Robots are, in a very general sense, machines that can perform certain physical tasks autonomously. Conceiving, designing and building these machines requires efforts in a variety of technological fields, most notably mechanical engineering, electrical engineering, and computer science. As many applications of modern robots require highly domain-specific knowledge, be it space or deep sea exploration, geological research, the automation of medical laboratories or elderly care, robotics often involves in-depth exchange between roboticists and the respective domain experts. This inherent interdisciplinarity of robotics research makes it a particularly attractive, stimulating, but also challenging field.
Robotics spans a wide area from application-proven solutions that have been in use for decades, such as part-handling in industrial car manufacturing, to areas of fundamental research that continuously push the boundaries of what is possible.

Humanoid Robotics One of the most captivating areas of fundamental robotics research might be the field of humanoid robotics. Humanoid robots are machines that strive to, at least partially, mimic the human body in its dimensions as well as in its sensorimotor and cognitive capabilities.
From a mere technological point of view, building humanoid robots is motivated by their prospective universal applicability, as well as by the enormous challenge that the imitation of the human body represents, oftentimes

forcing engineers and researchers to leave the beaten track and follow highly innovative approaches. The cultural world has not been designed with robots in mind, it has been optimized to be used by humans, possessing a human body with all its unique capabilities and constraints. If robots are to become truly flexible and universally applicable, they need to be able to interact with this world (and the people in it) just the way humans do, and this requires a human-like body and human-like capabilities. This is the core hypothesis that underlies humanoid robotics. There is no known alternative to humanoids for robots that combine human capabilities such as climbing stairs, working with tools, seamlessly interacting with people and helping the elderly in their daily activities, just to list a few illustrative examples.
The current state of robotic technology, however, is still far from realizing this vision.
The applications in which robots are successfully deployed typically consist of a well-defined task and little variation. Mowing the lawn, vacuuming the floor and repetitive material handling are amongst the few areas where commercial robots currently excel, and these robots are all different and specialized for their one task. This illustrates the large gap between the state of the art in robotics and the vision of truly humanoid robots, and gives one an idea of the research efforts that still lie ahead.
Another, less technical aspect of the motivation for humanoid robotics research is its use to serve to satisfy the inherent human desire to better understand the human body and its capabilities. The human body is the core inspiration for humanoid robotics, which is why researchers aim at understanding the human skills, in order to re-implement them on a humanoid robot. This process almost inevitably leads to a deep appreciation of the human capabilities, which far exceed all current technical solutions in their generality. While specific robots might be more precise, or able to move faster, or stronger, and some cognitive algorithms might be better at categorizing images or playing board games, the entirety of skills and capabilities enabled by the human body and brain are technologically unmatched.

Methodological Principles The challenges of closing the gap between what is currently technologically possible and realizing the vision of human-like robots is too large to address it all at once. One of the core principles underlying humanoid robotics research is therefore to investigate a certain skill, be it motor or cognitive, *in isolation*, and then, eventually, integrate these skills into an overall humanoid system.

Finding methods that are *efficient* in terms of the use of computational resources is especially important in humanoid robotics, as humanoids will have to possess and make use of a large number of skills (e. g. visual scene understanding, motion planning, and human-robot interaction) simultaneously. If these skills are not implemented in an efficient way, the fundamentally restricted on-board resources that allow the robot to act autonomously will quickly become a limiting factor, even with the advent of more and more powerful computation hardware. While efficiency is an important requirement in the majority of technical applications, it is a principle of paramount importance in humanoid robotics due to the high number of skills these robots are envisioned to possess, and due to the real-time constraints imposed by tasks such as dynamic locomotion.

Since the human is a direct role model for all the skills humanoid robots are envisioned to one day have, *exploiting the human expertise* is another common principle in humanoid robotics research.

1.1 Problem Statement and Contributions

Among the many capabilities that are required from humanoid robots, many are applicable to other robots as well, such as navigation, visual scene understanding, or grasping and manipulation. However, a few are, at least currently, unique to humanoids. Amongst these very humanoid-specific fields is the challenge of *balancing* on two legs. Although proven to be possible and highly useful by the human example, its technological challenges have yet prevented bipedal locomotion from seeing widespread use in robotics.

Instead, robots largely rely on wheels, or four or more legs, and bipedalism has remained a domain of few research groups focusing on humanoids. The work presented in this thesis represents a contribution to this area. More concretely, it tries to find new ways of answering the following question:

What does a bipedal humanoid robot need to perceive and to do in order to regain its balance after a forceful push?

In doing so it follows the above stated principles. It considers the problem of push recovery in isolation, as a building block for humanoid capabilities that will incrementally lead to ever more capable humanoid robots. It considers the human role model as a reference for decision making and motion generation and proposes a new method to transfer the human balancing expertise to humanoid robots. And lastly, it explicitly focuses on methods that can be implemented in an efficient manner, prioritizing efficiency over performance in order to find methods that can eventually find their application on humanoid robots that have to fulfill many concurrent tasks with limited computational resources.
In the context of bipedal humanoid robotics, balancing and push recovery is a particularly interesting topic because of its fundamental importance for the application of these machines in real-world scenarios. Disturbances will inevitably occur, be it from colliding with moving obstacles, getting into contact with people in crowded spaces or even from strong winds and other environmental influences in disaster scenarios. Given that the risk of damage to the robot and even its surroundings in case of a fall is high, the robot, just like a person, needs to be able to avoid those falls. It seems unlikely that humanoid robots that lack the capability to flexibly and efficiently react to balance disturbances will be suited for any appreciable real-world application.

However, detecting when balance recovery actions are required, choosing the correct strategy for balancing and then executing it in an efficient manner is a technologically challenging problem. The robot (1) has to infer from the abundance of sensory information, and despite the infinite amount of possible states it can be in, that its current state requires active balance recovery. It then needs to decide whether balance can be maintained by means of (2) coordinated whole-body motions in place, or if the situation requires (3) taking a step. Given the uni-lateral ground contact, the nonlinear, highly coupled nature of the robot's hybrid dynamics, its kinematic redundancy and the constraints on its state and its actions, generating appropriate motions efficiently is difficult.
This thesis contributes to the three above mentioned fields by investigating efficient methods for the decision-making from internal sensors, investigating improvements to highly efficient whole-body postural balancing methods, and proposing a novel method for efficient recovery step generation, leveraging human examples and simulation-based reinforcement learning.

Disturbance Estimation and Stability Classification The first contribution of this thesis is concerned with extracting the necessary information for reactive stepping in order to recover balance from a small number of internal sensors, i. e. answering the questions of when to step and where to step. To this end, studies with a human subject show that a small number of body-mounted inertial sensors can be an effective sensor setup in this context. Building on this result, a comprehensive study on stability classification with body-worn sensors based on a large dataset of human motion recordings is conducted, showing that stable states can be differentiated from unstable ones (i. e. states that require recovery action) by means of body-worn inertial sensors and supervised learning. Additionally, a method for extracting detailed information about a received push solely from a robot's fore/torque sensors in the ankles is presented.

Whole-Body Postural Balancing The second contribution of this thesis is concerned with performing balancing motions in the case when stepping is not required, with a strong focus on computational efficiency at runtime. The underlying hypothesis is that the balancing problem, despite the nonlinear robot dynamics, can be addressed successfully and efficiently with a linear balance controller when the differences between the linear model and the real robot are accounted for by means of hyperparameter optimization and novel ways of ground contact linearization. This hypothesis is systematically evaluated using a planar humanoid robot model and several thousand simulated push recovery experiments as part of an optimization cycle. The results are reproduced on a simulation model of the ARMAR-4 robot and the method is shown to be able to produce highly successful whole-body balancing motions, enabling the robot to mitigate frontal pushes.

Recovery Stepping The third contribution of this thesis is a novel method to generate recovery stepping motions to regain the robot's balance after a push that would otherwise lead to a fall. The proposed method leverages human motion recordings of push recovery steps by representing them as motion primitives on the joint level and encapsulating them in a highly efficient parametric stepping motion generator. Using systematically generated data from dynamics simulations of the ARMAR-4 robot, a mapping from push parameters that can be obtained with the robot's own sensors to the appropriate step parameters as input to the motion generator is learned. The entire system, consisting of the learned parameter mapping (policy) and the motion generator, is evaluated in a physics simulation environment and demonstrated to enable the ARMAR-4 robot to successfully recover from a wide range of pushes from different directions by means of reactive stepping.

1.2 Structure of the Thesis

This thesis is divided into seven chapters. After a general introduction to the topic, the core research questions and a general overview over the individual contributions in Chapter 1, an overview over the foundational concepts and methods that underlie the presented work is presented in Chapter 2. Chapter 3 presents a structured overview over related research in the three main areas covered by this thesis and explains the relation of the presented work to the current state of the art.

The following three chapters contain the main contributions of the thesis. In Chapter 4, the topic of stability estimation with body-mounted inertial sensors as well as disturbance estimation with the robot's internal force sensors is addressed. In Chapter 5, ways to optimize linear whole-body balance controllers by means of novel linearized ground contact models and iterative, simulation-based hyperparameter optimization are presented. A data-driven stepping motion generator based on motion primitives and a simulation-based learning method for its application to the ARMAR-4 robot are presented in Chapter 6. As these three contributions represent individual building blocks for the balancing and push recovery system of humanoid robots, each chapter includes an individual evaluation of the presented method.

Finally, Chapter 7 concludes the thesis with a summary and a discussion of the obtained results, as well as ideas for future research to address questions that remain unanswered or were newly raised by the presented work.

2 Fundamentals

The aim of this thesis is to contribute to the field of push recovery and dynamic stability of bipedal humanoid robots. To set the stage for the work presented in the later chapters, this chapter will briefly introduce core theoretical concepts as well as key methodological building blocks and tools. In Section 2.1, the fundamental concepts of *Rigid Body Dynamics*, i. e. the formal description of the motion of rigid bodies under the influence of forces and moments, will be introduced. After this general description, Section 2.2 will narrow the focus on the core concepts of static and dynamic *Stability* in the context of bipedal robots.
The subsequent sections introduce important tools that will be used in the presented work, starting with *Linear Quadratic Regulators* in Section 2.3, a concept used extensively in Chapter 5, and proceeding with a short description of *Dynamic Movement Primitives* in Section 2.4 that constitute a key method enabling the work presented in Chapter 6. *Learning* methods, i. e. techniques to fit input/output relations to given training data that are used in various parts throughout this thesis, are introduced in Section 2.5. Lastly, Section 2.6 highlights a few important robotics related aspects of *Dynamics Simulation*, an important tool for the work described in Chapter 5 and Chapter 6.

2.1 Rigid Body Dynamics

Rigid bodies are physical bodies that always keep their initial shape and mass distribution. All kinematic and dynamic models used throughout this thesis will be based on the assumption that a robot consists of rigid bodies connected by joints, an assumption that is found in almost all literature on balancing and push recovery of humanoids.

The dynamics of a rigid body describe the evolution of its position $x(t)$ and orientation $\phi(t)$ under the influences of forces $f(t)$ and moments $m(t)$[1]. Rigid bodies possess the important dynamic quantities *linear momentum p* and *angular momentum L*, both of which are conserved quantities and only changed by the forces and moments acting on the body with

$$\frac{dp}{dt} = f(t) \tag{2.1}$$

and

$$\frac{dL}{dt} = m(t) \tag{2.2}$$

The linear velocity $\dot{x}$ of a rigid body is directly proportional to its linear momentum p, with the inverse of its total mass m being the proportionality factor such that

$$\dot{x}(t) = \frac{1}{m}p(t). \tag{2.3}$$

Similarly, the rotational velocity ω of a rigid body is directly proportional to its angular momentum L with the inverse of its moment of inertia I being the proportionality factor such that

$$\omega(t) = \frac{1}{I}L(t). \tag{2.4}$$

Note that the moment of inertia in general depends on the axis about which the body rotates.

Planar equations of motion of a rigid body Based on these few preliminaries one can obtain the equations of motion of a rigid body that

[1] Forces and moments are in fact the only influences that determine the evolution of a body's motion.

describe the connection between its motion (i. e. linear and angular acceleration) and the forces and moments acting on it, which are generally time dependent:

$$m\ddot{x}(t) = f(t) \tag{2.5}$$

$$I\dot{\omega}(t) = m(t) \tag{2.6}$$

If $f(t)$ and $m(t)$ are known, double-integration of these equations yields the position and orientation trajectories $x(t)$ and $\varphi(t)$ as the solution of the equations of motion. A common way of organizing the equations of motion is to have all terms caused by the body's own motion (such as the inertial terms above) on the left side, and all external forces such as contact forces or gravity on the right side.

3D equations of motion of a system of rigid bodies A humanoid robot is usually modeled as a system of rigid bodies (called links), connected by joints. The most common joint type used in robots is the rotational joint, whose state can be described by the joint angle θ. Advancing from the description of a single rigid body's planar motion to the 3D motion of a *system of rigid bodies* such as a humanoid significantly increases complexity. The fundamental concepts outlined above still apply, but need to be extended and new concepts need to be introduced. A complete derivation of the equations of motion is out of scope for this section. The aim is rather to equip the reader with an intuitive understanding of the terms involved.
A powerful concept in multibody dynamics is that of *generalized forces* and *generalized coordinates* that allows to express the two equations 2.5 and 2.6 in one. As it is common in the robotics literature, the generalized coordinates describing linear and angular displacements will be denoted as vector $\mathbf{q}$, and the generalized forces describing forces and moments $\mathbf{f}$. Expressing equations 2.5 and 2.6 with generalized coordinates and forces, extending them to 3D and to a system of rigid bodies connected by joints described by

generalized coordinates $\mathbf{q}$ and actuated by joint torques τ yields the basic dynamic description of a robot[2]

$$\mathbf{H}(\mathbf{q})\ddot{\mathbf{q}} + \mathbf{C}(\mathbf{q}, \dot{\mathbf{q}}) = \mathbf{B}(\mathbf{q}, \dot{\mathbf{q}})\tau + \Phi(\mathbf{q})^T \lambda, \tag{2.7}$$

a matrix equation that describes the equilibrium of generalized forces. $\mathbf{H}(\mathbf{q})$ is the inertia matrix that depends on the system's configuration $\mathbf{q}$ and maps generalized accelerations $\ddot{\mathbf{q}}$ to generalized forces. $\mathbf{C}(\mathbf{q}, \dot{\mathbf{q}})$ is a matrix containing all forces that depend on the generalized coordinates and velocities, namely the Coriolis forces and gravity. $\mathbf{B}(\mathbf{q}, \dot{\mathbf{q}})$ maps the joint actuator torques τ to generalized forces, and $\Phi(\mathbf{q})$ maps all external forces λ (e. g. ground contact forces) to generalized forces[3]. Note that $\mathbf{B}(\mathbf{q}, \dot{\mathbf{q}})$ is the identity for a fully actuated system.

2.1.1 Underactuation

A humanoid robot with n actuated joints, in contrast to an industrial robot arm, is not fixed at one position but is free to move and change its pose in the world. It therefore has $n+6$ Degrees of Freedom (DoF), namely all its joint positions and the position and orientation of its base frame. The six degrees of freedom describing the general motion of the robot's base frame are not directly driven by actuators but influenced by the overall movement of the robot. Since the motion of the base frame is not actuated, the entire system is underactuated, meaning that it does not have direct control over all its DoFs. A common term for underactuated mechanical systems with base frames that are free to move is the notion of *floating base* systems. Figure 2.1 visualizes the six unactuated DoFs of a humanoid robot's floating base.

[2] Notation based on [Featherstone 2008](Equation 1.1) with extensions adapted from [Kuindersma et al. 2014].

[3] $\Phi(\mathbf{q})$ in this context is referred to as the *Contact Jacobian*.

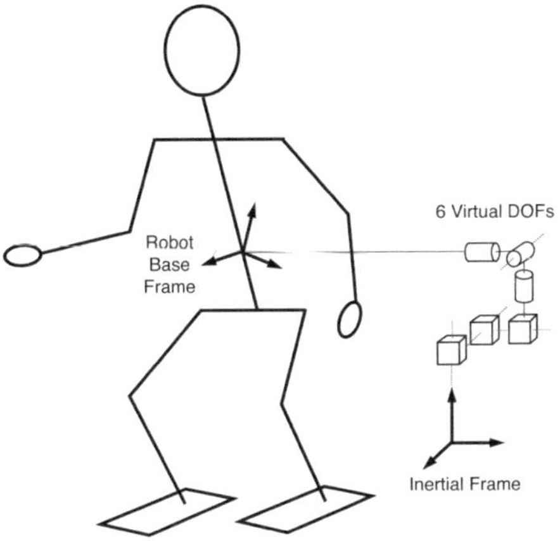

Figure 2.1: The six unactuated degrees of freedom (or virtual DoFs) of a humanoid robot's floating base frame make the entire system underactuated (taken from [Mistry et al. 2010], © 2010 IEEE).

Describing the dynamics of underactuated floating base systems requires modifications to Equation 2.7 since the term $\mathbf{B}(\mathbf{q},\dot{\mathbf{q}})\tau$ contains zeros for the six unactuated joints. One way is to interpret $\mathbf{B}$ as a selection matrix $\mathbf{S}$ that selects the actuated joints from the vector of joint torques τ with $\mathbf{S} = [\mathbf{I}_{n\times n} \quad \mathbf{0}_{n\times 6}]$, as for example noted in [Mistry et al. 2010]. Another way is to split the dynamics (Equation 2.7) into two parts, an actuated part (subscript a) and a floating base part (subscript f)[4]:

$$\mathbf{H}_f\ddot{\mathbf{q}} + \mathbf{C}_f = \Phi_f^T \lambda \tag{2.8}$$

$$\mathbf{H}_a\ddot{\mathbf{q}} + \mathbf{C}_a = \mathbf{B}_a\tau + \Phi_a^T \lambda \tag{2.9}$$

[4] Notation based on [Featherstone 2008](Equation 9.11) with extensions adapted from [Kuindersma et al. 2014].

This notation can be especially useful when the dynamics are incorporated in the formulation of an optimization problem, as will be exemplified in Section 3.3.1.
A comprehensive way of deriving the dynamics of floating base systems with a focus on arbitrary parameterization (e. g. changing contact situations) with simulation-based applications to humanoids has been described in [Bouyarmane and Kheddar 2012].

2.1.2 Hybrid Dynamics

Humanoid robots pose special requirements on their description as multi-body dynamic systems not only due to the fact that they are underactuated, but also due to their dynamics being inherently *hybrid.* A hybrid system in this case refers to a system whose dynamics are governed by different equations of motions at different times, with discrete transitions in between. *"A hybrid dynamical system can thus be regarded as a set of dynamical systems together with their initial and final states, so that every time a certain final state is reached, a jump occurs. Hence, a jump represents a transition to a (generally different) initial state appurtenant to a (generally different) dynamical system from the set."* [Karer and Škrjanc 2012]
For humanoids, these 'jumps' arise from making and breaking contact between the end-effectors and the environment, e. g. between the feet and the ground during walking. An exhaustive taxonomy of contact poses for the human and humanoid body that also distinguishes between *planar* (unilateral) and *hold* (multilateral) contacts, each of which constitutes a different dynamical system, is presented in [Borras and Asfour 2015]. Since contacts pose kinematic and dynamic constraints, they are regarded in the derivation of most components of the equations of motion (see Equation 2.7), and an altered contact situation requires altered equations of motion. Examples of different contact situations encountered by humanoid robots are depicted in Figure 2.2. The hybrid nature of the dynamics make bipedal humanoid

motion generation an especially challenging problem for Model Predictive Controllers (MPC) (e. g. [Ishihara and Morimoto 2015; Griffin and Leonessa 2016]), since the model changes happen at potentially unknown times.

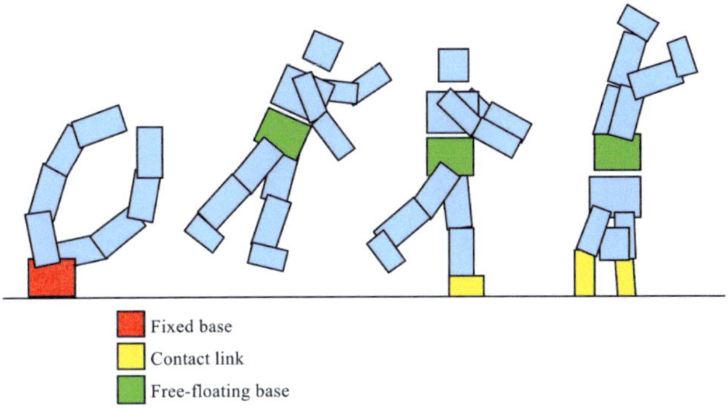

Figure 2.2: A humanoid robot is a floating base system (as opposed to fixed base) with hybrid dynamics due to changing contact situations (taken from [Bouyarmane and Kheddar 2012], © 2012 IEEE).

2.1.3 Velocity and Torque Control

The rigid body dynamics of a humanoid robot (see Equation 2.7) that underlie the majority of robot control approaches is formulated in the space of generalized forces. These generalized forces translate to torques on the robot joint level. Many stabilizing balancing controllers that influence the robot dynamics in a desired way are therefore naturally formulated in the torque domain, and their computed outputs are joint torques. However, it is technologically challenging to design and build a physical robot whose actuators readily accept and are able to execute torque commands. This is predominantly due to high cost and complexity of in-actuator torque sensing (two recent approaches are compared in [Kashiri et al. 2017]) and the required high control bandwidth for precise and stable torque control of a stiff multi-body mechanism with ground contacts. It is therefore a relatively recent development that full-body humanoid robots with torque control capabilities such as KIT's ARMAR-4 [Asfour et al. 2013], DLR's Toro [Englsberger et al. 2014b], NASA's Valkyrie [Radford et al. 2015] or the Boston Dynamics Atlas [Boston Dynamics 2018] have become available.

(a) HRP-2 (b) TORO (c) ARMAR-4

Figure 2.3: (a) The velocity-controlled HRP-2 (taken from [Kaneko et al. 2004], © 2004 IEEE), (b) the torque-controlled TORO (adapted from [Englsberger et al. 2014b], © 2014 IEEE) and (c) the torque-controlled ARMAR-4 humanoid robot.

In contrast, the majority of humanoid robots to date rely on velocity control on the joint level, where the high-level controller can command desired velocities that will be enforced by high-gain PD or PID servo controllers. Prominent examples for full-body velocity-controlled humanoids are the HRP robots developed within the Japanese Humanoid Robotics Project (HRP) [Hirukawa et al. 2004]. Especially HRP-2 [Kaneko et al. 2004] and HRP-4 [Kaneko et al. 2011] have had significant impact on the research on humanoid locomotion and balancing as hardware platforms for validation experiments. This type of robots typically requires a computational middle-layer between the balance control, operating on the dynamics in the torque domain, and the low-level controllers, relying on joint velocity commands, to translate desired torques to desired velocities. This bridge can be built by computational forward dynamics that computes the joint accelerations which would arise from a set of desired joint torques. Time-integration of these accelerations yield the desired velocities that are issued to the joint-level servo controllers. For the purpose of walking and balancing, more specialized schemes with lower computational demands have been introduced such as the 'Posture/Force control layer' described in [Kajita et al. 2010] that achieves desired foot contact forces by a damping control law implemented on the velocity-controlled HRP-2 robot. Figure 2.3 shows the HRP-2 as an example for velocity-controlled humanoids and the TORO and ARMAR-4 as examples for torque-controlled humanoid robots.

2.2 Stability and Balance

To formalize the goal of enabling robots to maintain their balance under nominal conditions and to regain their *stability* under the influence of external disturbances, it is necessary to define the term stability in the context of bipedal systems and to discuss its different aspects and implications.

2.2.1 Static Stability

By definition, the state of a mechanical system is statically stable when the velocity and all its derivatives are zero, meaning that the system is at rest and the equilibria of forces and moments do not require any non-zero accelerations. This state can, without external influence, persist infinitely. A statically stable state therefore satisfies the conditions

$$\sum_{i=1}^{n} \mathbf{f}_i + \mathbf{G} = 0 \tag{2.10}$$

and

$$\sum_{i=1}^{n} \mathbf{f}_i \times \mathbf{c}_i + \mathbf{G} \times \mathbf{r}_{CoM} = 0 \tag{2.11}$$

where n is the number of ground contacts, $\mathbf{f}_i$ and $\mathbf{c}_i$ are the contact forces and locations, $\mathbf{G}$ is the overall gravitational force and $\mathbf{r}_{CoM}$ is the location of the center of mass (see Equation 2.12). For a humanoid robot standing on the ground, static stability requires it to be at rest and have the vertical floor projection of the center of mass within the boundaries of the support polygon.

Since static stability forbids the movement of a robot, this concept has little applicability to mobile robotics. It is instead often synonymously used with the term *quasi-static stability*, describing a state-trajectory in which velocities are small and the effects of accelerations are negligible. Quasi-static walking is thus a slow walking motion in which the center of mass is above the support polygon at all times and accelerations are negligible. Consequently, the motion can be paused at any time, without compromising stability. In contrast, this is in general not true for walking in the dynamically stable regime where pausing the motion induces unplanned accelerations that disturb the robot's dynamic stability. Despite this added complexity and risk, dynamic motion is prevalent in many biological system, such as in humans.

The terms *Center of Mass* and *Support Polygon* will be briefly clarified in the following sections.

Center of Mass

A robot's center of mass, commonly abbreviated as CoM, is the spatially weighted sum of the masses of all its mechanical components (links) computed as

$$CoM = \frac{1}{M} \sum_{i=1}^{n} m_i \mathbf{r}_i \tag{2.12}$$

where M is the overall mass, n is the number of mechanical components considered and m_i and $\mathbf{r}_i$ are the masses and locations of the individual components, respectively.
The CoM plays an important role in stability considerations and often, together with the overall mass, even serves as a (heavily) simplified surrogate model for the entire robot, such that only its location, velocity and acceleration are considered instead of those of the individual robot components. Commonly used simplified dynamic models such as the linear inverted pendulum in its 2D formulation [Kajita and Tani 1991] and 3D extension [Kajita et al. 2001], its extension by a flywheel to include angular momentum (which a point mass located at the CoM alone cannot possess) [Pratt et al. 2006] or the cart-table model originally proposed in [Kajita et al. 2003] are based on CoM-centered considerations and simplifications.

Support Polygon

The support polygon of a legged system is the convex hull of all its ground contacts. It is one of the most important geometric concepts in stability considerations, where the area of the support polygon as well as its centroid and its edges might be of interest. In most applications, the support polygon is assumed to be oriented horizontally. In the case of uneven terrain, the support polygon can be defined as the *horizontal projection* of the actual contact pattern [McGhee and Iswandhi 1979].

2.2.2 Dynamic Stability

For modern approaches in legged robotics research, requiring static stability is far too restricting, as it forbids dynamic motions and thereby the exploitation of a robot's full capacity. Push-recovery, which is the core problem of this thesis, is almost always a dynamic action as the external disturbance in form of a push generally induces a non-negligible acceleration. While the definition of static stability provided in Section 2.2.1 is very intuitive, defining *dynamic* stability is more involved. The concept of a *Zero Moment Point* has gained significant importance and applicability in the field of legged robots and will be briefly introduced in the following section.

Zero Moment Point

The Zero Moment Point, commonly abbreviated as ZMP, is in some sense the dynamic equivalent of the floor projection of the CoM, taking into account dynamic forces caused by accelerations and inertia. It was initially introduced under the name ZMP in the context of legged robotic research by Vukobratović and Stepanenko in the early 1970s [Vukobratović and Stepanenko 1972] while the underlying ideas and formulation were presented as early as the late 1960s [Vukobratović and Juričić 1969]. An overview over the evolution and applications of the ZMP formalism within the 35 years after its initial formulation is provided by the original authors in [Vukobratović and Borovac 2004].

Every force acting on the robot, either caused by external contacts, gravity or inertia, induces a moment around *any* point on the ground. If there exists a point on the ground where all horizontal components of these ground reaction moments $\tau_{GR}|_h$ cancel out and hence the net horizontal moment is zero, this point is called the Zero Moment Point $\mathbf{r}_{ZMP}$ with

$$\tau_{GR}(\mathbf{r}_{ZMP})|_h = 0. \tag{2.13}$$

If the ZMP is located within the support polygon of the legged system, the system is said to be dynamically stable, i. e. it fulfills the *ZMP-criterion* for dynamic stability. In this case, the ZMP coincides with the Center of Pressure (abbreviated CoP), the point on the ground through which the force vector resulting from the ground contact forces passes. The authors in [Vukobratović and Borovac 2004] clarify that a ZMP outside the support polygon, i. e. not coinciding with the CoP (then called the *fictitious* ZMP or FZMP) indicates a disturbance, and that its *"distance from the foot edge represents the intensity of the perturbation"*. Such a perturbation does not necessarily indicate dynamic instability, rendering the ZMP-criterion a sufficient, but not a necessary criterion for dynamic stability, as summarized in [Diehl and Mombaur 2006](p.305).

If the CoP can be measured during motion execution, e. g. with a 6-axis F/T sensor in the robot's ankles, it can be used as a feedback signal for a balancing controller. In a simple balancing controller, the position of the ZMP can be directly influenced using the robot's ankle torques, even though the limited size of the feet severely limits the application of ankle torque-based dynamic balance control in practice.

Based on Equation 2.13 and following the derivation in [Popovic et al. 2005] the horizontal position of the ZMP for a flat ground can be computed from the robot kinematics and dynamics as follows:

$$ZMP_x = \frac{\sum_{i=i}^{n} \{r_i \times m_i(a_i - g) + [d(I_i \omega_i)/dt]\}_Y}{M(\ddot{Z}_{CoM} + g)} \tag{2.14}$$

$$ZMP_x = \frac{\sum_{i=i}^{n} \{r_i \times m_i(a_i - g) + [d(I_i \omega_i)/dt]\}_X}{M(\ddot{Z}_{CoM} + g)} \tag{2.15}$$

where n is the number of rigid links in the robot's body, r_i and m_i are those links' position vectors and masses, a_i are the linear accelerations of all links, g is the gravitational acceleration and I_i and ω_i are the inertia tensors and rotational velocities of all links. M is the robots overall mass and $\ddot{Z}_{CoM}$ is the height of the CoM. Using this formulation, the ZMP can be computed during a robot's motion and used to assess and verify its dynamic stability. If kinematic and dynamic measurements are available, this formulation can also be used to compute the ZMP and therefore assess the dynamic stability of a robot or human body in motion.

Another important application of the ZMP formalism is dynamically stable motion planning, and there exists a significant body of work that describes the ZMP-based generation and execution of walking motions. e. g. [Huang et al. 2001; Kajita et al. 2010]. In this case, a set of future foot steps is initially provided. A ZMP-trajectory is then generated that connects all these footsteps in their temporal order. Using conceptual tools such as the cart-table model, the ZMP-trajectory can be converted to a CoM trajectory based on which the actual walking motion can be synthesized and stabilized [Kajita et al. 2003]. Figure 2.4 shows a planned footstep pattern, a (measured) ZMP-trajectory as well as the synthesized and controlled CoM-trajectory for a walking experiment.

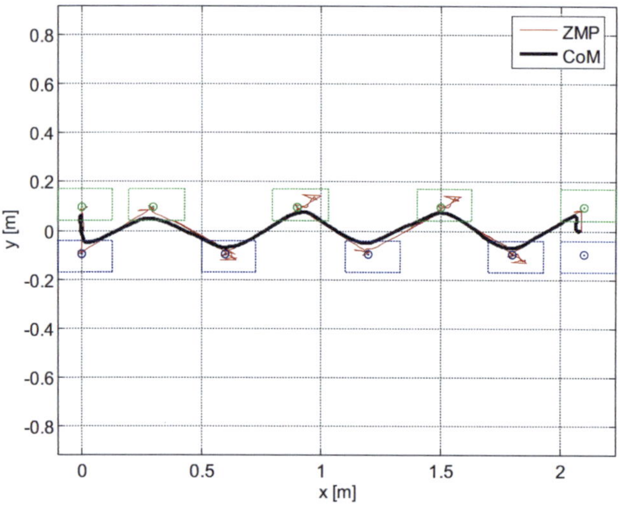

Figure 2.4: Planned footsteps as well as measured ZMP- and CoM-trajectory during a walking experiment with a biped robot (taken from [Kajita et al. 2006], © 2006 IEEE).

2.2.3 Linear Inverted Pendulum Dynamics

It has oftentimes proven useful to use simplified models for the rigid body dynamics rather than the complex dynamics of a humanoid robot for controller synthesis and analysis. One of the most fundamental surrogate dynamics models is the *Linear Inverted Pendulum* (LIPM). The conceptual LIPM consists of a massless telescopic leg with a point-mass representing the robot's CoM at the hip, depicted in Figure 3.7(a). The telescopic leg ensures that the hip stays at a constant height at all times, which leads to the following one-dimensional equation of motion

$$\ddot{x} = \frac{g}{z_0} x \tag{2.16}$$

where x is the horizontal position of the CoM, g is the gravitational acceleration and z_0 is the constant hip height. Note that this is a linear differential equation, hence the name LIPM.

The LIPM has been a pivotal concept for many works in humanoid walking and balance control, and extensions that capture more aspects of the robot dynamics while maintaining its conceptual simplicity will be briefly described in Section 3.4.

2.3 Linear Quadratic Regulators

Linear Quadratic Regulators (LQR) are a subfield of optimal control theory for linear systems. An LQR state-feedback controller controls a dynamical system (described by a set of linear equations of motion) optimally, in the sense that it minimizes a quadratic cost functional. The linear system in state space formulation takes on the form

$$\dot{\mathbf{x}}(t) = \mathbf{A}\mathbf{x}(t) + \mathbf{B}\mathbf{u}(t) \tag{2.17}$$

$$\mathbf{y}(t) = \mathbf{C}\mathbf{x}(t) + \mathbf{D}\mathbf{u}(t) \tag{2.18}$$

and is characterized by the four time-invariant coefficient matrices **A**, **B**, **C** and **D**. To drive the system to its desired state, a linear state-feedback controller produces an output signal $\mathbf{u}(t)$ proportional to the system state $\mathbf{x}(t)$ with feedback gain matrix **K**:

$$\mathbf{u}(t) = \mathbf{K}\mathbf{x}(t) \tag{2.19}$$

Generally, $\mathbf{x}(t)$ in the state-feedback Equation 2.19 denotes the state error, i. e. the deviation $\mathbf{x}_0 - \mathbf{x}_{act}$ of the actual state $\mathbf{x}_{act}$ from the initial state (of linearization) $\mathbf{x}_0$. This error is denoted $\mathbf{x}$ only for brevity.

The LQR method is essentially a formalism to algorithmically find the entries of the feedback matrix $\mathbf{K}$ that makes the controller optimal under a problem-specific cost, considering the system's open loop dynamics characterized by $\mathbf{A}$ and $\mathbf{B}$. For the infinite horizon LQR formulation[5] the cost J to be minimized is formulated as the integral

$$J = \int_0^\infty (\mathbf{x}(t)^T \mathbf{Q}\mathbf{x}(t) + \mathbf{u}(t)^T \mathbf{R}\mathbf{u}(t))dt. \tag{2.20}$$

The cost function within this integral is quadratic in the state error $\mathbf{x}(t)$ and in the controller output $\mathbf{u}(t)$, meaning that an LQR controller simultaneously aims at minimizing both, the state error and the control input. The cost on the state error is influenced by the weight matrix $\mathbf{Q}$ which will be called the *state cost* matrix, and the cost on the output is influenced by the *control cost* matrix $\mathbf{R}$. A controller minimizing Equation 2.20 with a symmetric positive semi-definite weight matrix $\mathbf{Q}$ and symmetric positive definite $\mathbf{R}$ can be found by solving the resulting algebraic Riccati equation and is guaranteed to stabilize the underlying linear system. With the LQR formalism, the design choices are thus shifted from the gain matrix $\mathbf{K}$ (which is found algorithmically) to the weight matrices $\mathbf{Q}$ and $\mathbf{R}$. The space of entries of $\mathbf{Q}$ and $\mathbf{R}$ forms the *design weight space* of the controller. A more in-depth introduction to LQ regulators is provided e. g. in [Boyd and Barratt 1991] and [Anderson and Moore 2007].

Designing a controller in the design weight space rather than directly designing the state-feedback gains can have several advantages for multi-DoF systems with coupled dynamics, such as humanoid robots with multiple

[5] There also exist finite horizon formulations that consider a terminal cost term which can be omitted in the infinite horizon case.

actuated joints. For one, the appropriate control action $\mathbf{u}_i(t)$ for joint i typically depends on multiple (if not all) entries in the state vector. Those inter-DoF couplings are generally non-intuitive and encoded in the off-diagonal elements of $\mathbf{K}$. In contrast, the entries of the design weight matrices can be interpreted intuitively: Entries in $\mathbf{Q}$ penalize deviations from the desired state and entries in $\mathbf{R}$ penalize the action of a specific actuator. Any objective that can be represented as a linear combination of states can be encoded in $\mathbf{Q}$ to turn the controller into a task-specific one[6]. Furthermore, designing the cost matrices and deriving the feedback matrix $\mathbf{K}$ with the LQR-formalism by solving the Ricatti equation is guaranteed to produce a stable controller, a guarantee that can generally not be given for any directly designed $\mathbf{K}$.

2.4 Dynamic Movement Primitives

Describing complex whole-body motions of humans, animals and robots in a mathematically elegant and concise way is an active area of research in the biomechanics, the neuroscience and the robotics communities. One approach that has gained popularity in all of these fields is to regard complex motions such as walking or reaching as being constructed out of temporarily concatenated movement primitives[7]. The existence of movement primitives in biological systems has been experimentally studied in frogs in [Giszter et al. 1993] and mathematically formalized using virtual force fields in [Mussa-Ivaldi 1997]. The concept of movement primitives has resonated with roboticists, as it can greatly simplify the generation and adaptation of complex movements.

---

[6] Balance control objectives for whole-body LQR can be found in [Mason et al. 2014] and [Mason et al. 2016] and will be detailed in Chapter 5.

[7] Periodic movements (such as walking) can be encoded with a single periodic movement primitive, and there even exist techniques to encode a periodic movement and its initial transient in a single primitive [Ernesti et al. 2012]. However, only discrete DMPs without periodic characteristics are utilized in this thesis.

One of the formalizations of movement primitives that has gained a certain prevalence in robotic application is the concept of *Dynamic Movement Primitives* (DMPs) which is based on methods for trajectory representation as the solution to a forced nonlinear differential equation presented in [Ijspeert et al. 2002] and [Ijspeert et al. 2003]. The term DMP was introduced in [Schaal 2006] and updated and exemplified in [Ijspeert et al. 2013]. The notation used in this chapter is taken from this latter publication. A DMP is essentially a one-dimensional trajectory approximator. In the context of motion generation, this dimension can, for example, be the angle of one of the robot's joints. DMPs have a number of desirable properties which make them popular for motion representation:

- The trajectory is guaranteed to end up in the specified goal, independent of the characteristics of the path it is taking.
- Changing the goal and the execution speed of the trajectory is possible and computationally efficient.
- The qualitative appearance of the trajectory is preserved even if the goal and the execution speed are changed.
- Coupling multiple DMPs to encode e. g. the coordinated motion of multiple joints is straightforward.

Formal definition

The underlying idea of DMPs is to encode a trajectory $y(t)$ as the solution to a differential equation. This differential equation represents a forced linear dynamical system with point attractor dynamics[8]:

$$\tau \ddot{y} = \alpha_z(\beta_z(g-y)-\dot{y})+f \tag{2.21}$$

[8] The physical equivalent of this point attractor can be thought of as a damped spring-mass system.

This system is called the *transformation system* with positive constants α_z and β_z, scaling factor τ, the eventual goal state g and the forcing term f (note that time dependencies of y and f are omitted in the notation). In the literature, the transformation system is often written in its first-order notation with the newly introduced variable z:

$$\tau\dot{z} = \alpha_z(\beta_z(g-y)-z)+f \tag{2.22}$$

$$\tau\dot{y} = z \tag{2.23}$$

To obtain an time-independent system, the evolution of the transformation system is controlled by the phase variable x, that in turn is the solution to another linear differential equation:

$$\tau\dot{x} = -\alpha_x x \tag{2.24}$$

This system, monotonically converging to zero with positive constant α_x, is called the *canonical system*.
The key to encoding arbitrary trajectories in the evolution of the transformation system is to appropriately shape the forcing term f that, by directly influencing the acceleration of the transformation system, indirectly influences its trajectory. In DMPs, the forcing term is represented by a superposition of weighted Gaussian kernel functions $\Psi(x)$ with

$$\Psi_i(x) = exp\left(-\frac{1}{2\sigma_i^2}(x-c_i)^2\right), \tag{2.25}$$

where c_i and σ_i are the center and the width of each kernel. The trajectory is thus ultimately encoded in the number and parameters of these Gaussian kernels.
To encode the forcing term in N Gaussian kernels Ψ_i and obtain the desired temporal and spatial scaling properties listed above, the forcing term is formalized as

$$f(x) = \frac{\sum_{i=1}^{N} \Psi_i(x) w_i}{\sum_{i=1}^{N} \Psi_i(x)} x(g - y_0). \tag{2.26}$$

Figure 2.5 shows an example input trajectory (blue) and three different DMPs with weight vectors **w** optimized to reproduce it, obtained using the H^2T DMP library (see Section A of the appendix). The presented DMPs differ only in the number of kernel functions and, consequently, in the weights of the kernels. As one would expect, a higher number of kernels enables the DMP to reproduce the input trajectory more accurately. Especially the two sharp bends in the center of the original trajectory are difficult to capture for the Gaussian kernel-based DMPs, and only the DMP using 500 kernels (dark purple) can capture the shape of this section at least qualitatively.

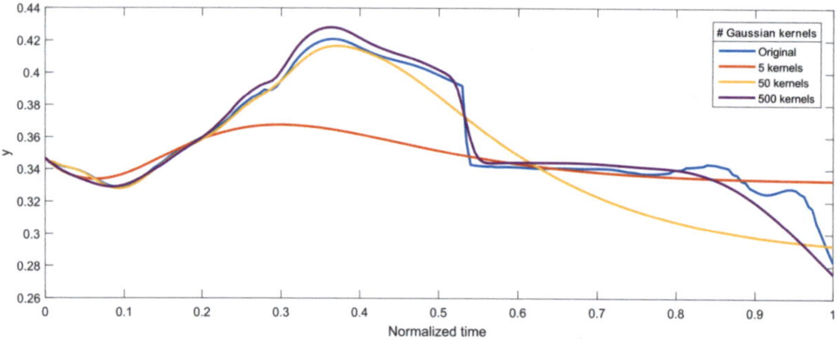

Figure 2.5: Dynamical Movement Primitive reproductions of a trajectory using different numbers of Gaussian kernel functions. It can be seen that a higher number of kernels enables the DMP to reproduce the original trajectory more accurately. The data for this graph was produced using the H^2T DMP library.

The fact that DMPs are better suited to reproduce smooth rather than jerky trajectories is arguably not a significant shortcoming in the context of encoding and imitating human motions, as humans have been observed to strongly prefer minimal jerk motions (at least in the unconstrained case) [Flash and Hogan 1985].

Shaping and adapting DMPs

The goal of choosing the parameters y_0, g and w_i is to let the transformation system $y(t)$ follow a demonstrated trajectory $y_d(t)$ as closely as possible. The weight parameters w_i are responsible for the qualitative shape of the trajectory, whereas y_0 (the start-point of the trajectory), g (the end-point of the trajectory) and τ (the temporal scaling factor of the canonical system) can flexibly adapt the trajectory to new high-level requirements.

Shaping Given an input trajectory as a triplet $(y_d(t), \dot{y}_d(t), \ddot{y}d(t))$, first y_0, g and τ are chosen to match this trajectory. Finding the weight parameters w_i then amounts to an optimization problem with the aim of minimizing the difference between the demonstrated trajectory and that reproduced by the DMP. While virtually any optimization technique could be used for this problem, the authors in [Ijspeert et al. 2013] strongly advocate the use of locally weighted regression for several reasons, including its „*very fast one-shot learning procedure*", meaning that learning the parameters can be achieved in a non-iterative process. By learning w_i for multiple demonstrations and averaging over the obtained parameters, learning from multiple demonstration trajectories $y_{d,i}$ can be achieved in an easy manner, a property that is especially interesting for learning from human demonstrations. A method to include information about the style of the motion into an attractor landscape rather than a single transformation system was introduced in [Matsubara et al. 2011].

Adapting Once the weight coefficients w_i are learned, the DMP can reproduce the qualitative shape of the demonstrated trajectory to the extent that the chosen number of kernel function N allows. If this trajectory describes a motion, e. g. the path of an end-effector or a joint trajectory, it can be regarded and used as a motion pattern or primitive. The power of the DMP formulation is revealed when the learned motion primitive is to be applied to a *similar* task, characterized by the same overall motion characteristic and shape but different execution speed, start- and end-point (such as stepping to a slightly different location). One can simply change y_0, g and scale τ to match the new requirements. Solving the transformation system by means of forward integration yields a new trajectory that fulfills the new requirements.

DMPs for multiple DoFs

A single DMP encodes a 1-dimensional trajectory. To encode a multidimensional trajectory, e. g. a 6D end-effector trajectory, six individual DMPs are needed, one for each DoF. In this case it is critical to coordinate the produced trajectories in order to retain the overall motion characteristics. One way of achieving this is to have individual transformation systems and nonlinear forcing terms for each DoF but only one *shared* canonical system, meaning that all transformation systems evolve depending on the same phase variable x. This coupling mechanism results in a dynamical system for multiple DoFs.

When using DMPs to generate end-effector (i. e. task space) motions, it remains necessary to calculate the corresponding joint angle trajectories using an inverse kinematics (IK) solver. This process can cause significant computational overhead, especially when the IK is subject to constraints, such as the fixed position of the stance foot during a step. However, since a DMP's dimensionality only depends on the number of transformation systems and forcing terms, they can equally well be used directly in the joint space of a robot. In this case an IK solution is only necessary to convert a task-space goal into goals for the joint-level DMPs, and no computation other than the forward integration of the transformation systems is needed subsequently.

2.5 Learning Methods

In the classical approach to computational problem solving, the human programmer has to specify the solution to a problem as a sequence of conditional instructions, a control law, or any other algorithmic representation.
Broadly speaking, the premise of *machine learning* is to automate as much as possible of the process of finding a computational solution to a problem by taking the human designer out of the loop and replacing it by what might synonymously be called learning, training or optimization. While the learning algorithm is still specified by the programmer, a single learning method can potentially generalize to a large number of problems, albeit at the cost of requiring large amounts or training data for each individual problem. A popular way to implement learning of an arbitrary Input/Output relation is to use a very generic class of models for this relation, such as Artificial Neural Networks (ANN) or Hidden Markov Models (HMM), and optimize them to solve the problem at hand based on available training data. To this end, the training data needs to contain examples of Input/Output pairs of the relationship to be learned. In the learning process, a set of free model parameters are optimized, whereas hyperparameters of the model (e. g. the number of layers in an ANN or the number of states in a HMM) are mostly pre-defined by the human designer[9]. The algorithm for training the model is called the *learning method.* As machine learning is concerned with finding optimal parameters for a model, it is closely related to, and shares many methods and terms with, the field of optimization.
While machine learning is a broad and currently extraordinarily active line of research with numerous rapidly evolving branches, one can distinguish machine learning methods based on the origin of the data that is used to train the model:

[9] Hyperparameters can also be optimized automatically. Several methods are presented in [Bergstra et al. 2011]

1. Suitable training data might be readily available for the learning method in the form or labeled pairs of input and correct/desirable output. Training a model to predict the output for new input data on such labeled training data constitutes the problem of *supervised learning*. A comprehensive introduction into this topic in general and into deep learning in particular is provided in [Goodfellow et al. 2016].

2. In a different setting, where the goal is to learn the optimal behavior of an agent (e. g. a robot), none or very limited training data might be available. In this case, the *agent* needs to interact with the environment to generate more training data (experience), not obtaining labels but receiving rewards depending on the success of its actions. This setting constitutes the problem of *reinforcement learning*. A comprehensive introduction to reinforcement learning with a focus on the special requirements imposed by the application to robotics is provided in [Kober et al. 2013].

Both areas have different fields of application and requirements, e. g. sample efficiency in the case of reinforcement learning for robotics where experiments on actual hardware are expensive. In contrast, supervised methods widely used in the computer vision domain typically have access to vast amounts of labeled training data.

3. The third major field of machine learning, *unsupervised learning*, is concerned with extracting information from raw data without neither labels nor feedback through interaction. Typical problems are clustering of data to identify some underlying structure or, anomaly detection in a stream of data. In this thesis, methods of unsupervised learning will not be used and the field is mentioned here only for the sake of completeness. An overview over common methods in unsupervised learning is provided in [Hastie et al. 2009].

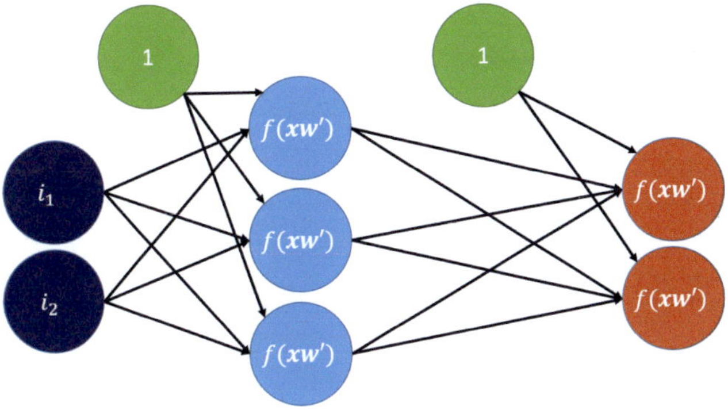

Figure 2.6: Schematic depiction of a fully connected neural network used for supervised learning. The dark blue neurons form the input layer to which the data is fed. The light blue neurons form the hidden layer, and the orange neurons form the output layer from which the result is computed. The green circles are bias units. All edges transport a scalar value x and have a weight w (labels omitted for legibility). Hidden and output neurons compute a nonlinear function f of the weighted sum of their input x, i. e. of the scalar product of x and w represented as vectors.

These three sub-fields provide a common yet very rough structuring of the vast field of machine learning research, and many branches at lower and higher levels of abstraction as well as intermediate approaches (e. g. semi-supervised learning) exist. The following subsections give a more detailed account of selected aspects of *supervised learning*, which plays a key role for stability estimation in Chapter 4, and of *reinforcement learning*, which will be used to find suitable step parameters in Chapter 6.

2.5.1 Supervised Learning

Supervised learning is concerned with automatically finding an initially unknown functional mapping from an input to an output. For example, the input might be an image of a hand-written digit and the output might be the number this digit is representing. Finding this mapping is achieved by learning from labeled training examples that constitute tuples of input and outputs (both of which might be multidimensional), e. g. an image of the digit 5 with the semantic label five. The outputs might belong to discrete classes, as in the example of digit recognition. In this case, the supervised learning aims to solve a *classification* problem. The output can also be continuous, e. g. when predicting a temperature that cannot be directly measured from other sensory information, in which case the specific problem is a *regression*.

Currently, a large part of supervised learning approaches rely on ANNs as very generic models for the function to be learned. A feed-forward neural network consists of layers of computational neurons: An input layer, an output layer and any number of hidden layers in between (see Figure 2.6). The number of hidden layers and the number of neurons in the hidden layers are design choices.

The data processing within a feed-forward neural network is implemented as follows: The input layers feed the input data to all neurons of the subsequent hidden layer. Each neuron performs a nonlinear function on the weighted sum of all its inputs and a bias, and then feeds its output to the neurons of the next layer. The type of nonlinear function used in the neurons is a high-level design choice, with the hyperbolic tangent or the rectified linear unit (ReLU, [Nair and Hinton 2010]) being popular choices. The output of the last layer is converted into a label (for classification) or a continuous number (for regression).

Training these networks amounts to tuning the weights in the weighted summation that takes place within the neurons. For training on labeled training data, input of a training example is fed to the input layer of the network and the output is computed. From the computed output and the ground-truth label of the training sample, an error, or *loss* is derived. The gradient of this loss with respect to all weights is then computed in a backward-pass through the network with backpropagation. Using stochastic gradient descent (or another optimization technique), all weights are tuned in a way that decreases the training loss.

Supervised learning with deep neural networks (DNN), i. e. neural networks that have many hidden layers, is called *Deep Learning*. Deep learning has recently proven to be highly successful for many applications, provided that a large amount of training data is available. A discussion of achievements and limitations of deep learning in robotics with a focus on visual data processing is presented in [Sünderhauf et al. 2018]. In the context of push recovery, supervised learning has been used for stability estimation and fall prediction (see Section 3.1.1), to which this thesis also contributes. However, for motion generation and control, (deep) reinforcement learning currently seems to be the more promising approach.

2.5.2 Reinforcement Learning

In the setting of reinforcement learning (RL), an agent gets to interact with an environment through its actions and receives rewards for the results of these interactions. The agent and the environment are both characterized by their states which are partially or entirely observable by the agent. The agent essentially learns by trial-and-error how to achieve a given goal with the set of actions it can perform (see Figure 2.7). More formally, the goal of reinforcement learning is for the agent to find a mapping of its state to an action that maximizes the sum of all rewards it will gain in the future. This mapping is called the policy and is commonly denoted as

$$a = \pi(s) \tag{2.27}$$

with a being the action, π the policy and s the observable agent state[10]. A comprehensive introduction to reinforcement learning is given in [Sutton and Barto 1998]. Reinforcement learning methods that directly find an explicit policy π are called *policy-based* reinforcement learning. In contrast,

[10] This represents a deterministic policy. Probabilistic policies that model a probability distribution of a set of actions over the state space are another common approach.

value-based reinforcement learning methods model a state-value function for a given policy over the agent's state space that represents the expected future reward for being in a particular state s and operating under a policy π:

$$V_{\pi}(s) = E(R|s) \tag{2.28}$$

where E denotes the expectation of all future rewards R. Similarly, an action-value function can be defined for a given policy over the agent's state-action space, representing the expected future reward for taking a particular action a in state s, referred to as the Q-function:

$$Q_{\pi}(s,a) = E(R|s,a). \tag{2.29}$$

Value function based methods offer deeper theoretical insights and even optimality guarantees if the setting the agent operates in is modeled as a Markov process, but have proven to be challenging in the application to problems with the high number of dimensions typically found in robotics [Kober et al. 2013]. Both the policy and the value function can be modeled using deep neural networks (see Section 2.5.1). The resulting methods belong to the field of deep reinforcement learning, which has achieved some remarkable successes such as surpassing the performance of human players in computer games [Mnih et al. 2015], beating world-class human players at complex board games [Silver et al. 2016], or realizing controlled in-hand object manipulation with a robotic hand [Andrychowicz et al. 2018].
To improve a policy $\pi(s)$, an agent has to interact with the environment. The environment will provide the agent with a scalar reward signal for its action, and the agent can then update the policy according to this feedback. As the agent's goal is to maximize future rewards, it is driven to improve its policy by trying out new actions on previously seen states. This aspect of reinforcement learning is called *exploration*. However, out of the same motivation, the agent is driven to apply its current policy when it knows that it will lead

to some reward, no matter if that reward is optimal or not. This part, applying a known policy that will lead to some (likely sub-optimal) reward, is called *exploitation*. Balancing exploration and exploitation is an intrinsic dilemma in reinforcement learning and has been extensively researched, with *ε-greedy* and *Softmax* being two of the more popular algorithms to address it (a brief introduction to both is given in [Tokic and Palm 2011]). Probabilistic policies, as opposed to deterministic policies outlined in Equation 2.27, can be used to provide an intrinsic motivation for the agent to explore new strategies.

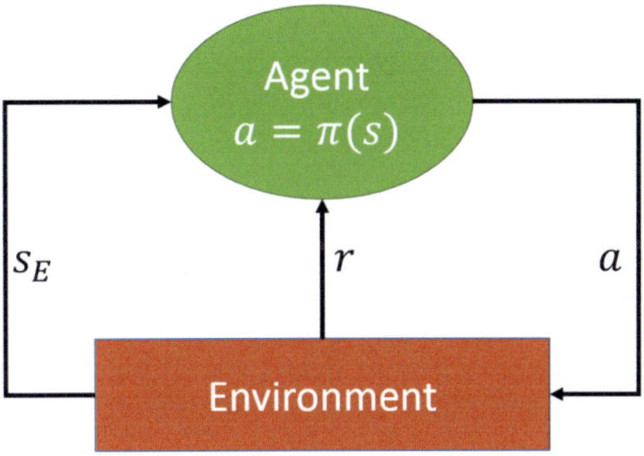

Figure 2.7: Schematic depiction of the reinforcement learning setting: The agent applies a policy to the current state (consisting of its own and the state of the environment) to compute an action a which it uses to influence the environment. The environment updates its state s_E accordingly and provides some reward feedback r to the agent that it can use to update its policy. Note that time-step indices were left out for legibility.

Many problems in robot control can be formulated as reinforcement learning problems. However, due to the difficulties of gathering sufficient training data on real robots, especially in the domain of balance control and push recovery where a failed trial can lead to substantial damage, the majority of these studies is confined to simulation.

2.6 Dynamics Simulation

Both the evaluation of control methods as well as iterative learning methods to find suitable controllers, such as reinforcement learning, rely on robot experiments. Experiments on actual robot hardware are expensive due to availability constraints, necessary robot maintenance, the risk of damage and the fact that they can only take place in real-time, which can make them very time consuming. It is therefore often favorable to perform experiments in a simulation environment that does not suffer from these disadvantages, and that can be sped-up or even parallelized to gather much more data than experimenting in the real world would allow.
For the results acquired in simulation to be useful it is necessary that the simulation environment accurately represents the real-world physics and the robot dynamics. This is achieved by the use of an accurate robot model and a dedicated physics engine. The engine solves the numerical equations of motion, respecting constraints, external forces and contact effects. In essence, simulation engines solve the dynamic equations of motion of a multibody dynamic system by numerical forward integration. These equations are generally not altered on making and breaking contacts to account for the hybrid nature of the system. Instead, contacts are individually modeled as forces arising from local spring-damper systems, where the spring provides the repulsive contact force and the damper provides friction and ensures numerical stability.
Most physics engines currently used for robotics were initially designed for physically plausible motion generation in 3D-games or virtual reality applications. Their design focus therefore lies more on plausibility, computational efficiency and numerical stability rather than on accuracy or reproducibility. However, by tuning the engines' parameters, they can be adjusted to deliver highly accurate simulation results that are suitable for robotics research. The most important parameter that determines the trade-off between accuracy and computation speed is the size of the integration timestep. The

smaller this timestep the more computations are performed per time interval (i. e. the slower the simulation runs), but the higher the physical accuracy will be (see Figure 2.8).

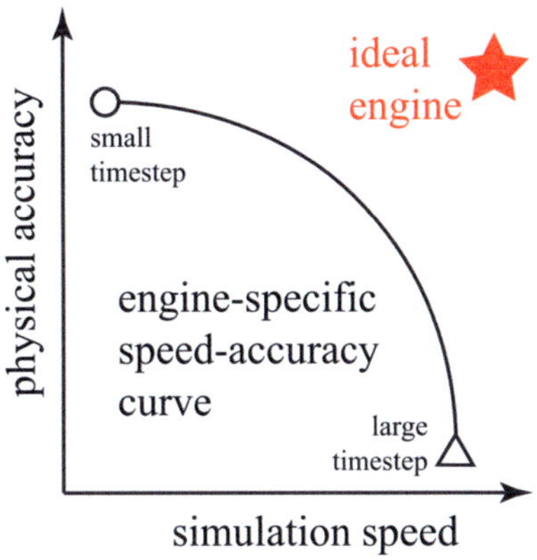

Figure 2.8: Conceptual depiction of the influence of the integration timestep on the trade-off between physical accuracy and simulation speed in physics simulations (taken from [Erez et al. 2015], © 2015 IEEE).

A number of recent works in the literature have evaluated the suitability of commonly used physics engines for robotics research in terms of accuracy, repeatability and predictability. In [Erez et al. 2015], the authors compare five physics engines, including *Bullet* [bulletphysics 2018] which is the engine used in this thesis and *MuJoCo* [Todorov 2018], the engine developed by the authors themselves[11] against a number of performance criteria. They conclude that all tested engines are capable of delivering good results over a wide variety of applications, as long as their parameters are tuned appropriately, and sufficiently small integration timesteps are used. In [Chung and Pollard 2016], the authors examine four simulation engines, also including

[11] MuJoCo has recently gained large popularity as a simulator for research on robotic reinforcement learning.

Bullet and MuJoCo, on benchmark tests designed to quantify predictability. They define predictability as the ability to produce plausible changes of the simulation results in response to small changes in the initial conditions (e. g. rolling farther when pushed a bit harder). Their work comes to a similar conclusion as Erez et al., assessing all four tested engines as capable of producing plausible results as long as the parameters are tuned in favor of physical accuracy. Both works include the Bullet physics engine, which is consistently assessed as a viable option for physically accurate robot simulation. The Bullet engine is integrated into the ArmarX software framework (see Section C of the appendix) and will be used for extensive simulation-based learning and evaluation in this thesis.

The second tool for simulated experiments that will be used in this thesis is the proprietary *Matlab/Simulink* dynamics simulation environment *SimMechanics* [MathWorks 2018]. SimMechanics was specifically designed for physically accurate simulations of multibody systems and has the ability to chose both the most suitable solver and integration timestep automatically to ensure high simulation accuracy.

3 Related Work

This thesis is a contribution to the wide research area of humanoid robot balancing. The following chapter aims at giving a structured overview over this area and at showing where the subsequently presented work expands it. The structure of this overview is aligned with the three main contribution of this thesis, i. e. *stability classification and disturbance estimation*, *postural whole-body balancing*, and *recovery stepping*. In Section 3.1, works from the literature on humanoid robotics and human movement sciences are presented that address the problem of deciding whether a robot or human is currently stable, unstable, or falling. These methods are based on either external or internal sensors, and use specifically engineered features or machine learning to assess the current state of stability.

In close relation to stability estimation, Section 3.2 gives an overview of methods for disturbance estimation for humanoid robots, i. e. ways for the robot to measure or infer where, in which direction, and how strongly it was pushed. This body of work is broadly categorized into the two classes of methods that either directly rely on contact force sensors or on internal force and torque sensing.

Balancing as reaction to a push can be achieved either by balancing in place or by taking a step. In Section 3.3, methods for stabilizing a robot without initiating a step, either around a predefined pose or along a predefined motion, are presented. These methods are divided into those that are based on computationally expensive online optimization on the one hand, and on efficient yet less versatile linear controllers on the other.

Methods for stepping for push recovery are summarized in Section 3.4. These methods can be classified into those that adjust preplanned steps of a walking pattern by altering the step location or the step timing (be it by engineered controllers or through learning methods), and into those that consider push recovery the sole purpose of the step and freely decide where and how to step.
A concluding summary of this overview is presented in Section 3.5.

3.1 Stability Classification

Estimating the current stability of a bipedal system is a crucial component of effective balance and push recovery mechanisms. Stability estimation can be implemented as a process that outputs a continuous feedback signal to a balance controller, such as the Zero Moment Point (ZMP). It can also be implemented as a classifier that maps the current observable state of the system to a discrete signal, for example to indicate that a change of control policy is needed [Yi et al. 2011a], that a fall is inevitable and damage-minimizing measures have to be taken [Kalyanakrishnan and Goswami 2010] (see Figure 3.1), or that a fall has already occurred [Zigel et al. 2009]. In the case that a fall is inevitable, the research question becomes how to minimize damage caused by the impact. A study on leveraging motion capture data from human trials for motion generation aimed at reducing impact forces has recently been presented in [Ding et al. 2018].
Since this work is of high relevance both in the context of humanoid robotics as well as in the context of human movement science with applications to wearable robots and elderly care, a broad body of work has been established in both communities, and similar concepts have emerged under different names.

Figure 3.1: Stability estimation and classification gives the robot the ability to distinguish between different states of (in-) stability, for example to let it know when to brace for an inevitable fall. Reproduced from [Kalyanakrishnan and Goswami 2010], © 2010 AAAI (www.aaai.org).

3.1.1 Stability Classification for Humans

In the context of biomechanics, human stability estimation is of special importance to improve fall prevention by assistive devices such as (partial) exo-skeletons, and to accelerate post-fall treatment of elderly or otherwise weakened patients. This work can be split into methods based on measurements by external sensors such as cameras, acoustic microphones or floor vibration sensors, and methods based on body-worn sensors such as accelerometers, gyroscopes or inertial measurement units (IMUs).

Methods based on external sensors such as vibration sensors [Zigel et al. 2009] or cameras [Stone and Skubic 2015] are typically confined to controlled and appropriately sensorized indoor environments and thus do not translate well to real-world robotic applications. Methods based on the data of body-worn sensors on the other hand are very similar in their requirements to robotic applications, especially when they make use of IMUs that are easy to integrate and readily found on many humanoid robots. These works generally focus on detecting an inevitable fall as early as possible and can be subdivided by the type and number of sensors they consider, and by the complexity of the action classifier. For the use with accelerometers, it was shown that even conceptually simple and intuitive features like

threshold violations of the absolute acceleration can be used to reliably infer the *occurrence* of a fall [Doughty et al. 2000; Karantonis et al. 2006]. However, triggering the fall-signal based on acceleration peaks that are high enough to prevent excessive false positives only happens when either a very significant disturbance was applied or a fall has already occurred, rendering this approach impractical for the purpose of fall *prevention*.
Features in the sensor signals that are detectable with significant lead-time prior to a fall are much more subtle and can more successfully be captured by data-driven machine learning models such as Support Vector Machines (SVM) [Zhang et al. 2006], Decision Trees [Ojetola et al. 2011], k-Nearest Neighbor (kNN) [Erdogan et al. 2010] or Hidden Markov Models (HMM) [Tong et al. 2013].

3.1.2 Stability Classification for Humanoid Robots

In robotic applications there is typically more internal sensor data available than in the previously described context of human motion monitoring. In addition, the motion plan of the robot can be known to a stability estimator and thus be used to differentiate between planned motions and disturbances. Based on this insight, the authors in [Kalyanakrishnan and Goswami 2010] train a rule-based machine learning system to identify whether a dynamic robot state belongs to either the classes *Balanced*, *Falling* or *Fallen*. They train and validate their approach on simulated data form an 'Asimo-like' robot and are able to detect upcoming falls with at least 700 ms of lead time. A similar classification had previously been proposed in [Wieber 2008], where the author defines a 'Viability Kernel' formed by all states from which a stable state can be reached by the robot's control system. If the current robot state is outside this kernel, a fall is inevitable.
In applications where frequent falls are to be expected, such as in small humanoid soccer robots, stability estimation, fall prediction and *damage prevention* when falling are especially important. [Moya et al. 2015] address

this problem by fusing torso attitude sensing and joint-level position sensing into a combined stability signal on which they perform thresholding to quickly detect states that will lead to a fall, enabling the robot to trigger a bracing routine. A similar approach that senses the discrepancy between attitude sensors attached to a walking robot and attitude predictions of a feed-forward model had previously been introduced by [Renner and Behnke 2006]. In their work, the authors use the magnitude of this discrepancy to trigger one of two fall avoidance strategies, either slowing down the gait or completely stopping the robot.

3.2 Disturbance Estimation

For effective push recovery strategies on humanoid robots, the robot oftentimes needs to be aware of the disturbance itself, i. e. the external forces it is subjected to. Estimating these disturbances is therefore an important capability in the context of active balance control, and has consequently been addressed by the scientific community working on humanoid robots[1]. The estimation of the external force includes its magnitude, its spatial direction and the point on the robot's body where it is applied.

3.2.1 Using Contact Force Sensors

The most straight-forward way to identify contact forces and force application points along the robot structure is by means of force sensors, sensor arrays or even tactile skin on the outside of the robot. Advanced examples of such sensor systems include the tactile skin developed for the iCub humanoid robot [Cannata et al. 2008] and the HEX-O-SKIN [Mittendorfer and Cheng 2011]. While these distributed sensors can directly measure the magnitude and application point of the contact force, they only measure the force

[1] It should be noted that passivity based balancing approaches such as the one reported in [Hyon et al. 2007] do not require an estimate of the external contact force.

component normal to the robot's body and therefore cannot be used to determine the actual direction of the contact force. For higher-level cognition, such as the awareness of the robot's immediate surroundings (the *peripersonal space*), distributed contact sensors can be conceptually coupled with information from cameras [Roncone et al. 2015].

Sensors that can resolve the 3D force direction include the camera-based approaches proposed in [Kolker et al. 2016], the optical tactile sensors proposed in [Yamaguchi and Atkeson 2016] or the optical sensor array presented in [De Maria et al. 2012]. Due to the use of cameras and optical components, sensors of this type are generally too large to be used along the outside of a humanoid robot, and their applications are restricted to highly specific use-cases such as tactile sensing in custom, non-humanoid end-effectors. 3D force resolution can also be achieved with magnetometer-based sensors such as the ones proposed in [Tomo et al. 2016], where magnets embedded into an elastic material (e. g. silicone) allow the magnetometers to resolve the material's spatial, force-induced deformation. All these 3D measuring methods have the drawback of complicated calibration processes due to the non-linear deformation behavior of the elastic materials involved. Generally, using arrays of tactile sensors on the outside of a robot for contact force estimation has the disadvantage of requiring additional hardware, necessitating additional wiring and increasing overall cost and weight of the robot.

3.2.2 Using Internal Proprioceptive Sensors

To mitigate the problems that come with additional sensing, it has been proposed to estimate external contacts between the robot and its environment with the use of internal proprioceptive sensing alone, most commonly with joint torque sensors [Haddadin et al. 2017; Manuelli and Tedrake 2016]. Using the internal joint torque sensors alleviates the need for contact-specific sensing. However, using internal torque sensors raises a number of additional methodological challenges: Firstly, even under ideal conditions, the exact point of force application cannot be reconstructed, only the line in space it acts along (the *line of force action*). It is therefore necessary to resort to methods based on a geometric robot model to project the line of force action onto the robot's surface and handle the arising ambiguities, which in itself poses several interesting questions. Alternatively, exteroceptive sensing can be used to identify the force application point, which has been implemented for a single robot arm using an externally mounted RGB-D camera in [Magrini et al. 2014]. Secondly, the force application point needs to lie sufficiently far away from the robot's ground contact point, i. e. with enough (six) torque-sensing joints between the application point and the ground to allow reconstruction of the force action line. In other cases, or in singular configurations even if the aforementioned criterion is fulfilled, reconstruction of the force action line becomes impossible. Adding 6 DoF force/torque sensors (F/T sensors) along the kinematic structure of the robot can under certain conditions alleviate these problems, as has been recently shown in [Vorndamme et al. 2017]. Internal F/T sensors can also be used to estimate the internal joint torques in the absence of joint torque sensors [Fumagalli et al. 2010] and for computing external contact wrenches if the force application point is known [Ivaldi et al. 2011].

Thirdly, the internal joint torque and F/T sensors do not only measure the effects of an external contact from which the contact force can be reconstructed, but also the effects caused by gravity and, in the case of non-static situations, the dynamic forces acting on the robot. In order to accurately compute the external forces, the internal measurements have to be compensated for those effects. Several ways of achieving this compensation have been proposed, ranging from early works that directly observe the motor currents to identify unexpected contacts for assuring safe human-robot coexistence [Suita et al. 1995] to residual-based methods leveraging the concept of *generalized momentum* [De Luca and Mattone 2003, 2005]. An extension

to this approach for floating base systems (such as humanoid robots) was recently presented in [Flacco et al. 2016].
Lastly, contact estimation can rely on measuring the contact forces and moments between the robot and its surroundings alone, as has been shown e. g. in simulation for a simple fixed-base manipulator in [Ott and Nakamura 2009]. The work presented in this thesis extends this idea to the double contact situation for the application in humanoid robots.

3.3 Postural Balancing in Place

A popular classification of balancing actions is the subdivision into three strategies, namely the *Ankle Strategy* (i. e. using the ankle joints to adjust the CoP location), the *Hip Strategy* (i. e. bending the hip to generate angular momentum) and the *Stepping Strategy* when the ankle or hip strategy are not sufficient. Figure 3.2 depicts a small robot exemplarily executing the ankle and hip strategies. These three terms were initially introduced in the biomechanics literature in [Horak and Nashner 1986] and adopted in the robotics community, e. g. in [Stephens 2007; Hyon et al. 2009; Yi et al. 2011b]. However, researchers both from the biomechanics community as well as from the robotics community have noted that the ankle and hip strategy of balancing are fundamentally combined both in the human postural control and in modern robot control algorithms [Hyon et al. 2009; Hettich et al. 2014]. The method developed in this thesis also includes the torso and shoulder joints in the balancing, without explicitly treating the different joints individually. All balancing approaches that do not involve taking a step, regardless of the exact joints they are using, will therefore be summarized under the term *Postural Balancing in Place*.
Balancing in place requires that the foot contact state does not change during the balancing action, i. e. none of the feet breaks its ground contact. This requires the balance control to be realized as compensatory motion of the entire body, dynamically changing the body posture. Balancing in place

is therefore also referred to as *Whole-Body Balancing* [Henze et al. 2016] or *Postural Balancing* [Hyon et al. 2009]. As the method developed in this thesis involves all major body joints, i. e. the legs, the torso and the shoulder in the postural balancing process, it will be referred to as *Whole-Body Postural Balancing*.

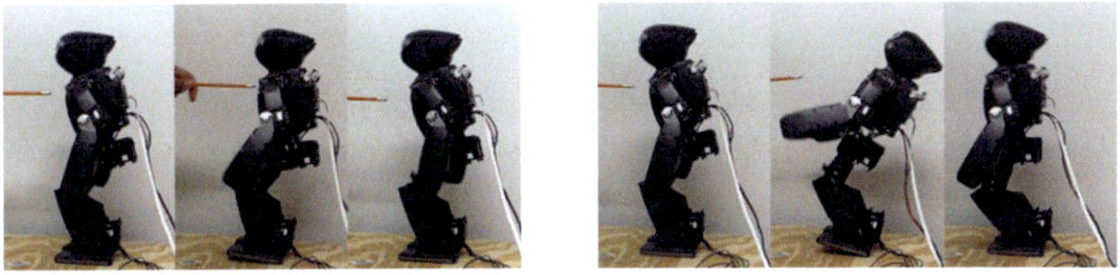

(a) Ankle Strategy (b) Hip Strategy

Figure 3.2: A DARwin-OP humanoid robot reacting to a push from the front by (a) actuating its ankle joints (ankle strategy) and (b) bending its hip (hip strategy). Adapted from [Hyon et al. 2009], © 2009 IEEE.

3.3.1 Online Optimization Methods

A powerful way of addressing the postural balancing problem that has received significant attention in humanoid robotics research over the past years is the formalization of balancing as constrained optimization problem. The different goals of postural balancing, e. g. maintaining a certain body pose and staying within a ZMP-based stability margins, are encoded in the cost function. Constraints arise from physical limitations of the robot (e. g. on the joint angles, torques and velocities and from self-collision avoidance) as well as from the ground contact, where the interaction forces need to remain within the friction cone to avoid slipping of the feet.

Optimization based balance controllers have the ability to generalize well over a wide range of the state space of the robot and are thus suitable to stabilize complex motions. They are therefore often coupled with capable (oftentimes also optimization based) off-line motion planners that generate a whole-body trajectory, subject to the same above mentioned constraints that is then executed and stabilized online by the motion controller (e. g. [Feng et al. 2013; Kuindersma et al. 2016]). As such, the applicability of optimization-based motion controllers reaches beyond balancing in place, and they are more generally applied to stabilizing pre-computed trajectories. However, since these methods do not have the ability to initiate and execute a step and the problem of balancing in place is essentially a sup-problem of trajectory stabilization, these methods will be covered in this section.

Both motion planners and motion controllers that rely on model-based optimization are necessarily based on kinematic and dynamic models of the robot. All of these models lie on a spectrum of simplified abstractions that spans from simple and highly abstract to complex and accurate. On this spectrum, the LIPM (see Figure 3.7) model with its point mass at the hip and massless leg represents the far end on the simplification side, whereas a detailed multi-body robot model with equations of motions that contain all DoFs of the robot represents the other, highly complex end.

Motion Generation Taking into account both the full kinematics and the full dynamics model of the humanoid robot for motion generation can naturally produce highly accurate results, but can come at the cost of very long computation times, especially when applied to highly dynamic motions. [Mombaur 2009] and [Posa et al. 2014] are examples of this approach, and computation times on the order of an hour for finding an optimal periodic running motion with a Sequential Quadratic Program (SQP) were reported in the latter. The majority of recent robotic applications of optimization based motion generation are therefore located somewhere between the two extremes of model abstraction, aiming at striking a balance between the ability to leverage as much of the robot's physical capabilities as possible on the one hand and computational tractability on the other. In [Kuindersma et al. 2016], the authors describe a whole-body motion generator that takes into account the detailed kinematics of the robot to be able to fulfill the challenging tasks of the DARPA Robotics Challenge [Pratt and Manzo 2013] but reduces the dynamics to the mere total linear and angular momenta of the robot, controlled by the interaction forces between the robot and the environment, similar to the approach in [Feng et al. 2013] (see Figure 3.3). This approach is shown to be sufficiently accurate for locomotion tasks, but the simplification of the dynamics to the total momenta makes it impossible for the planner to reason about the internal torques applied at the joint level. The authors of [Kuindersma et al. 2016] argue that this can either be mitigated by using a very strong robot (like the Boston Dynamics Atlas), or by feeding the solution as a seed into a subsequent trajectory optimization process that in turn reasons over the full dynamics and considers limitations on the joint level.

Figure 3.3: A simulated Atlas robot walking over uneven terrain under torque-based QP control, following a previously generated trajectory (taken from [Feng et al. 2013], © 2013 IEEE).

A motion generation technique that solves the inverse dynamics under multiple unilateral contact constraints inside a hierarchical optimization was introduced in [Saab et al. 2013], and it has been proposed that the same method could be used as real-time controller if the computation time could somehow be decreased and sensor feedback could be included.

Motion Control Optimization based motion control formulated as Quadratic Program (QP) is currently one of the most prominent whole-body control techniques for humanoid robots. The goal of a QP is to minimize a quadratic cost defined over the system state and the outputs of the QP under a set of linear equality and inequality constraints. The objectives encoded either in the cost or the constraints of the optimization can be viewed as *tasks* that the QP is designed to accomplish, and deciding which task to include in the cost and which to include in the constraints is a choice left to the designer. An interpretation often found in the related robotic literature that can help to address this design choice is the idea of a *hierarchy*: The objectives of the cost function are subject to optimization, the QP will 'try its best' to meet them. In contrast, the constraints *must* be met or otherwise the QP inevitably fails. In this two-level hierarchy, the tasks encoded as constraints therefore have higher priority than the ones encoded in the cost function. It is further common to include a set of slack variables η in the equality constraints to somewhat 'soften' them, increasing the solution space for the QP and the chances to find a viable solution. In this case, the slack variables η are included in the cost function, ensuring that they remain small and the equality constraints are not violated drastically. This addition of slack variables in the equality constraints leads to a hierarchical order among them, with the inequality constraints (without slack variables) taking priority over the equality constraints (with slack variables) [Kanoun et al. 2009], ultimately leading to a three-level hierarchical optimization with the levels in decreasing priority:

1. Inequality Constraints (no slack variables)
2. Equality Constraints (with slack variables)
3. Components of the Cost Function (optimization objectives)

Example QP To illustrate the complexity of a dynamic balancing QP in the joint acceleration domain with torque constraints (in contrast to the linear control approach in the torque domain pursued in Chapter 5), the respective work presented in [Kuindersma et al. 2014] will be addressed here in more detail. The optimization problem in [Kuindersma et al. 2014], required to be solved at high frequencies at runtime, is posed as follows:

$$\underset{\ddot{q},\beta,\lambda,\eta}{\text{minimize}} \quad V(\bar{x},\bar{u},t) + w_{\ddot{q}}||\ddot{q}_{des} - \ddot{q}||^2 + \varepsilon \sum_{ij} \beta_{ij}^2 + ||\eta||^2 \tag{3.1}$$

subject to

$$H_f \ddot{q} + C_f = \Phi_f^T \lambda \tag{3.2}$$

$$J\ddot{q} + \dot{J}\dot{q} = -\alpha J\dot{q} + \eta \tag{3.3}$$

$$B_a^{-1}(H_a\ddot{q} + C_a - \Phi_a^T \lambda) \in [\tau_{min}, \tau_{max}] \tag{3.4}$$

$$\forall_{j=\{1\ldots N_c\}} \lambda_j = \sum_{i=1}^{N_d} \beta_{ij} v_{ij} \tag{3.5}$$

$$\forall_{ij} \beta_{ij} \geq 0 \tag{3.6}$$

$$\eta \in [\eta_{min}, \eta_{max}]. \tag{3.7}$$

V is a cost function representing a ZMP feedback controller based on the CoM dynamics and therefore encodes the dynamic balancing objective. The second term in the objective, $w_{\ddot{q}}||\ddot{q}_{des} - \ddot{q}||^2$, encodes the trajectory tracking of the controller with $\ddot{q}$ being the end-effector accelerations. The desired acceleration $\ddot{q}_{des}$ can be derived from a reference trajectory, e. g. by a PD control law. β_{ij} are the coefficients that form the ground contact forces as linear combinations of the edges of a polyhedral friction cone approximation (see Equation 3.5). The third term (with normalizing coefficient ε) therefore aims at minimizing the contact forces. The last term's objective is to minimize the slack variables in 3.3.

Constraints 3.2 and 3.4 ensure consistency with the actuated and underactuated parts of the robot dynamics and enforce the adherence to joint torque limits. Constraints 3.3, 3.5 and 3.6 are dedicated to the foot contacts and enforce that all contact forces comply to friction constraints (3.5), that the robot does not aim to pull on the ground and thus respects the unilateral nature of the contact (3.6), and that any slipping motion is damped (3.3). Lastly, the bounds of the slack variables to limit the possible violation of 3.3 are enforced in 3.7.
Efficient solvers for this class of problems are a research topic in their own right.

Applications In one of the early works in which QP optimization was applied to postural balancing, the authors set up the QP in the joint acceleration space [Kudoh et al. 2002]. The objective of the optimization is to minimize the joint acceleration vector $\ddot{\theta}$ and to maximize the horizontal component of the CoM acceleration $\ddot{s}_y$ that drives the CoM back to the center of the support polygon. The cost to be minimized thus takes on the form

$$\ddot{\theta}^T C_\theta \ddot{\theta} - \ddot{s}_y, \tag{3.8}$$

where C_θ is a weighting term. Note that $\ddot{s}_y$ is a function of the joint angles, velocities and accelerations. The constraints considered in this work are the physical limitations of the robot on the joint level (upper and lower boundaries on θ, $\dot{\theta}$, $\ddot{\theta}$), CoM acceleration boundaries, a symmetry constraint on the leg motions, and, to ensure dynamic stability, a constraint on the ZMP location that forces it to remain within the boundaries of the support polygon. Since the optimization does operate on joint acceleration, neither limitations on the joint torques nor on the ground interaction forces are considered. However, a simulation based evaluation shows successful push recovery behavior and a qualitative similarity to human recovery motions.

In [Feng et al. 2013] the authors describe their combined motion planning and trajectory control framework that was used for their entry in the DARPA Virtual Robotics Challenge [Agüero et al. 2015]. After planning the motion with a *Differential Dynamic Programming* method (DDP, [Jacobson and Mayne 1970]) that reasons about the point mass abstraction of the robot dynamics, they use a QP-based motion controller to generate the torque commands for the robot joints. In contrast to the earlier work by Kudoh et al. they formulate the optimization in the torque-domain, enabling direct application to the torque controlled Atlas robot. The equations of motion act as equality constraints on the optimization and ensure dynamic feasibility of the QP solution. Torque limits in the joints and friction restrictions on the feet act as inequality constraints to prevent torque saturation of the joints and slipping of the robot's feet. In this formulation of the QP, the horizontal friction restrictions can be efficiently formulated as

$$|F_{x,y}| \leq \mu F_z \tag{3.9}$$

without the polyhedral approximation to the friction cone used in e. g. [Koolen et al. 2016; Kuindersma et al. 2014] (see Equation 3.5).
QP-based approaches operating on simplified dynamics models were also successfully applied to humanoid robots competing in the DARPA Robotics Challenge (e. g. [Johnson et al. 2015]).

3.3.2 Linear Balancing Control

Due to the generally non-linear hybrid dynamics discussed in Chapter 2, whole-body balance control of humanoid robots does not naturally lend itself to the application of linear control theory. However, since linear control methods are well studied, well understood and typically have much lower computational demands than non-linear and/or optimization based control such as QP-based methods, significant efforts have been made in the robotics literature to apply linear control to the non-linear problem of humanoid balancing. The work presented in Chapter 5 of this thesis is based on this premise and expands this line of work.

Linear CoM and ZMP tracking

In [Kajita et al. 2010], the authors proposed and demonstrated a linear tracking controller for the CoM and ZMP position of the LIPM (see Section 2.2.3) on the position-controlled HRP4-C humanoid robot that stabilizes a walking trajectory and shows robustness against uneven ground, using the LIPM as a linear surrogate for the non-linear robot dynamics. To achieve balance control, they split the control problem into three sub-parts: A '*Body posture controller*' that maintains the upright posture of the robot and ensures that only minimal changes of the CoM-height occur. A '*Floor reaction force controller*' to control the location of the center of pressure within the support polygon (a similar problem that was addresses for torque-controlled robots in [Hyon 2009]) which provides the control action for the higher level '*Linear Inverted Pendulum tracking*' controller. Splitting the complex control problem of walking stabilization into smaller subproblems is one way of making it amenable to comparatively simple linear controllers[2]. This tracking controller is formulated as a linear state feedback controller with a static gain matrix K, and the state being the position x and velocity $\dot{x}$ of the CoM as well as the position of the center of pressure p. The output u of the controller is the desired position of the center of pressure denoted p^{d*}:

$$u = p^{d*} = K(x^d - x) + p^d. \tag{3.10}$$

The pre-computed motion provides reference values for all three state variables, and the feedback gain matrix K together with a feedforward pass of

[2] This *divide and conquer* approach is in noteworthy contrast to the methods described in paragraph 3.3.1 that aim at capturing the entire problem in one comprehensive optimization, at the cost of higher complexity and typically much higher computational cost per timestep.

p^d turns them into reference values for the floor reaction force controller (see Figure 3.4).

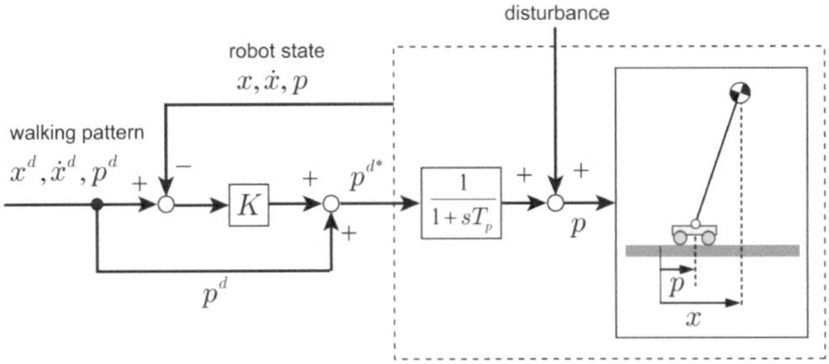

Figure 3.4: Block diagram of a linear control scheme for walking stabilization. x denotes the horizontal position of the CoM and p that of the center of pressure. The dashed box represents the robot together with the *Body posture* and *Floor reaction force* controllers (taken from [Kajita et al. 2010], © 2010 IEEE).

LQR Balancing

LQR controllers are a control concept for linear time-invariant (LTI) systems that can be represented in linear state-space form according to Equation 2.17 and Equation 2.18, as introduced in Section 2.3. The dynamics of a humanoid robot do not naturally fall into the LTI category, as they are non-linear and, due to the hybrid nature of the dynamics, can be time-variant. Applying LQR-methods to the problem of humanoid balancing is therefore not straight-forward, and there broadly exist two approaches to mitigate this apparent incompatibility: One is to use a fundamentally linear abstraction of the robot dynamics (such as the Linear Inverted Pendulum) and design an LQR-controller for that case, possibly embedding it in a higher-level controller such as a QP-optimization that generates full-body control commands. The other approach is to linearize the entire, non-simplified dynamics of the *full* robot (including the ground contacts) and design a linear LQR controller for that case. Both approaches are active areas of research.

LQR for reduced models Based on the popular Linear Inverted Pendulum model, the centroidal dynamics of a humanoid robot can be formulated as a linear differential equation constituting an LTI system. This system can be stabilized by a standard LQR controller. The controller generates force commands that need to be applied to the CoM in order to track a desired CoM-trajectory, which in turn is designed to let the ZMP follow a specific trajectory that ensures dynamic stability.
Due to the inevitable gap between the LIPM and the actual robot dynamics, additional measures need to be taken in order for this method to result in a successful balancing controller. In [Kajita et al. 2003] the authors combine a LIPM-based centroidal LQR state feedback controller with a feedforward preview controller [Sheridan 1966] and an integral controller for the CoM position tracking error to dynamically stabilize a walking trajectory. In [Kuindersma et al. 2014], the authors embed the LQR formulation within the higher-level QP-controller to encode the balancing objective and let the QP compute joint commands that fulfill them. They use a linear time-varying form of the LIPM and specify a cost function similar to Equation 2.20, but for the finite time case and without implicit constraints on the control inputs (i. e. $\mathbf{R} = \mathbf{0}$). They then embed the resulting solution of the Riccati equation in the objective function of a whole-body QP which is thereby enabled to obey the objective of the balancing LQR while minimizing the control input (i. e. actuator torque).

Full dynamics LQR Other than using LQR for designing stabilizing balancing controllers for the linear LIP model, one can linearize the entire full-body dynamics of a humanoid robot and design an LQR for this linearized system. This concept, called 'Full Dynamics LQR', was proposed and validated both in simulation and in a robotic push recovery experiment on a hydraulically actuated humanoid robot in [Mason et al. 2014]. The authors considered the case for a torque-controlled humanoid robot in double support, both while standing and while performing a squatting motion. The controller was designed for the dynamics that were linearized around the standing position (see Figure 3.5). However, it was noted that the very same controller could be used for stably tracking the squatting trajectory without re-linearization of the dynamics at any other point, despite the deviation from the state of linearizaion[3]. The authors also noted that push recovery performance of the Full Dynamics LQR was comparable to that of much more intricate control schemes that take the time-varying non-linearities of the dynamics into account.

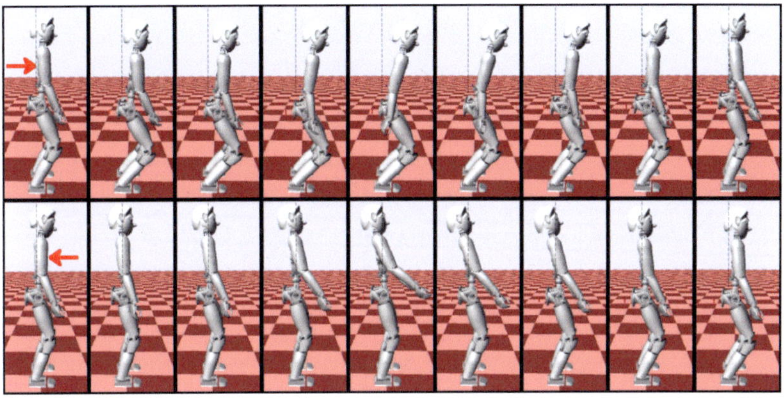

Figure 3.5: Simulation results of full dynamics LQR control for recovery from a 15 Ns push in dynamics simulation (taken from [Mason et al. 2014], © 2014 IEEE).

The authors extended this line of work in [Mason et al. 2016] in order to address the question of how far the functionality of the LQR controller extends from the original state of linearization. The key result from this work was that for the considered tasks (balancing and walking), only one re-linearization per contact state is necessary. In fact, no performance gain was measurable for higher numbers of linearizations. Each linearization constitutes a linear model in the sense of hybrid dynamics: One model

[3] This is in contrast to LQR controllers using iterative re-linearizations (*iLQR*).

represents the double contact case, one the right foot contact and one the left foot contact case. Those three models and the resulting three optimal LQR controllers were sufficient to stabilize a walking trajectory while the contact switching was enabled by smoothly transitioning from one controller to another.

Periodic LQR updates One of the questions that arises when using LQR control for linearized non-linear systems is how well the controller generalizes beyond the state of linearization. Although it is reported in [Mason et al. 2014] and [Mason et al. 2016] that the used controller for the task of whole-body balancing generalized well without further measures, this is in general not to be expected. A common method to cope with the growing gap between the linear model and the real system as it moves through the state space is the iterative re-linerization of the changing dynamics and the re-synthesis of a new gain matrix [Bryson 1999; Li and Todorov 2004]. This intuitive approach shows very good performance over a large part of the state space, since it is not tied to the initial state of linearization. The downside is a significant computational demand, depending on the frequency of the update. Another way of periodically updating the linear controller is by means of Differential Dynamic Programming, a technique that has been shown to be real-time capable in a simulation of a 36 DoF humanoid [Tassa et al. 2014].

Optimization-based LQR tuning A different way of mitigating the gap between the linear model and a non-linear system is to systematically tune the LQR for the envisioned application. Since the LQR formalism automatically finds the entries of the feedback gain matrix $\mathbf{K}$, the tuning takes place in the weight space spanned by entries of the matrices $\mathbf{Q}$ and $\mathbf{R}$ of the cost function (design weights) introduced in Equation 2.20. The process of tuning is generally an iterative one, with the aim of finding design weights that lead to a controller that minimizes the actual cost or maximizes a performance measure in a specific evaluation experiment. For the case of non-linear balancing systems, it has been shown in [Trimpe et al. 2014] that stochastic parameter optimization can lead to LQR controllers that successfully stabilize a double inverted pendulum after iterative tuning. Further extending this work, Entropy Search is used as an optimizer in [Marco et al. 2016] to tune an LQR controller for stabilizing an inverted pendulum without the need for periodic re-linearization. The authors here use a parametric description of the design weights to lower the dimensionality of the search space. They perform successive trials on the actual plant, consisting of a humanoid robot balancing an inverted pendulum (see Figure 3.6), to update the controller using global optimization. As Entropy Search formulates an explicit belief of the cost function as Gaussian Process, taking into account all previous experiments, the authors argue that such an approach yields good controllers faster (i. e. after lower numbers of experiments) than the technique proposed in [Trimpe et al. 2014].

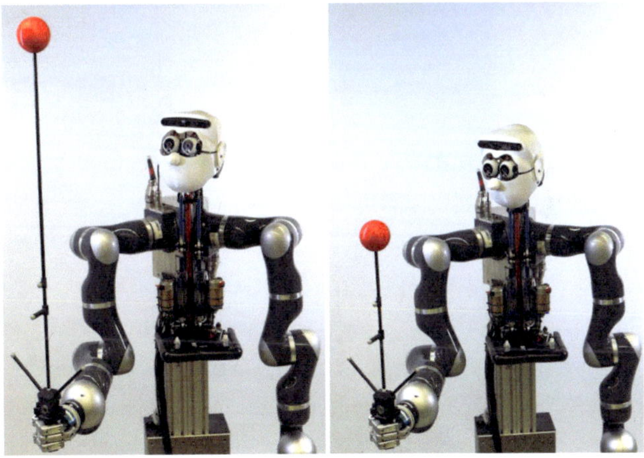

Figure 3.6: The humanoid robot Apollo balancing two different inverted pendulums using weight-optimized LQR control (taken from [Marco et al. 2016], © 2016 IEEE).

3.4 Balancing by Stepping

If a push disturbance to a legged robot exceeds a certain level of intensity, the only way to compensate this disturbance and remain upright is to take a step, as a new foot location can allow for different, more effective ground reaction forces. All methods for balancing that rely on stepping to change the foot location will be summarized here under the term *Balancing by Stepping*.

3.4.1 Step Location Adjustments

A step that is suited to let the robot regain static stability after a push disturbance is called a *capture step*, and the point on the floor the robot has to place its foot is called a *capture point*.
"A Capture Point is a point on the ground where the robot can step to in order to bring itself to a complete stop." [Pratt et al. 2006]
In general it is difficult to accurately determine when to step, where to step an how to step for a humanoid robot due to the high number of DoFs and the coupled dynamics of the robot's limbs. Principled approaches to the question of how to determine a suitable capture point have therefore only been developed for simplified dynamic models and then heuristically amended for their application on more complex models or robots.
The initial formulation presented in [Pratt et al. 2006] is based on the Linear Inverted Pendulum Model (LIPM, see Section 2.2.3 and Figure 3.7(a)). Following their derivation based on the requirement of zero orbital energy one can formulate a point on the floor where, for a given horizontal CoM velocity $\dot{x}$, the LIPM (i. e. the robot) has to position its foot in order for the CoM to come to rest over exactly this location. This point is called the capture point with coordinate $x_{capture}$ defined as

$$x_{capture} = \dot{x}\sqrt{\frac{z_0}{g}} \tag{3.11}$$

with the constant CoM height z_0 and the gravity acceleration g. For $x_{capture}$ to be the capture point it is required that the change of contact from the current foot location x to $x_{capture}$ happens instantaneously, which has motivated subsequent works in this area to call it *Instantaneous Capture Point* (ICP), e. g. in [Koolen et al. 2012]. Different names for the same concept have emerged in the related literature, such as the *Extrapolated Center of Mass* in [Hof 2008] after its derivation was introduced in the biomechanical context in [Hof et al. 2005], as well as the *Divergent Component of Motion* (DCM) in [Takenaka et al. 2009], which has later been extend into a 3D formulation in [Englsberger et al. 2015].

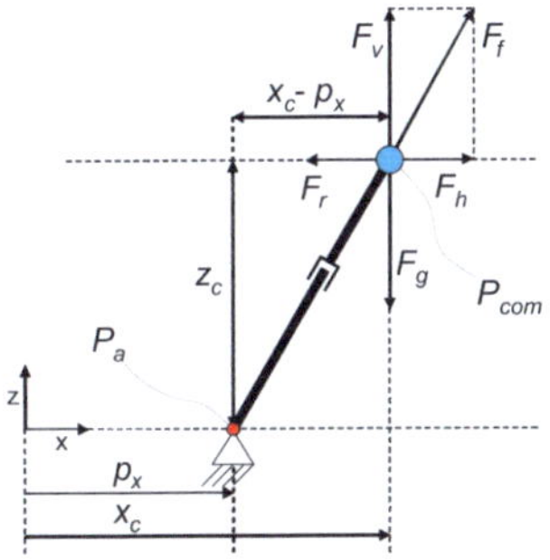

(a) LIPM

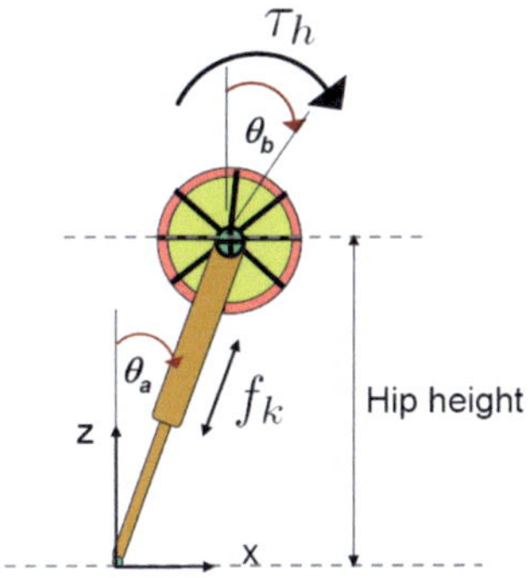

(b) LIPM with flywheel

Figure 3.7: (a) The standard Linear Inverted Pendulum Model (LIPM, taken from [Englsberger et al. 2011], © 2011 IEEE) and (b) the Linear Inverted Pendulum Plus Flywheel model, incorporating centroidal angular momentum (taken from [Pratt et al. 2006], © 2006 IEEE).

In their work from 2006, Pratt et al. extend the fundamental LIPM by a flywheel at the hip, enabling the model to incorporate angular momentum around the CoM (i. e. centroidal angular momentum). The authors call this model *Linear Inverted Pendulum Plus Flywheel Model*, depicted in Figure 3.7(b). The ability to generate angular momentum enables this model to better approximate the dynamics of a real robot, and it expands the capture point formulated in Equation 3.11 to a convex capture region containing an infinite number of capture points. The relation between the capture region and the support polygon can serve as a basis to determine if the robot needs to step. When taking the specific kinematic constraints of the robot into account, it can also be decided whether one step is sufficient or multiple steps need to be taken to place the CoP within the capture region. Those three different cases (no step, one step, multiple steps) are depicted in Figure 3.8.

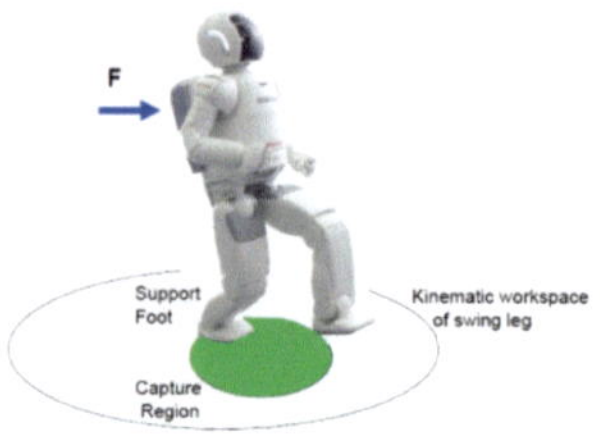

(a) Capture region and Support polygon overlapping

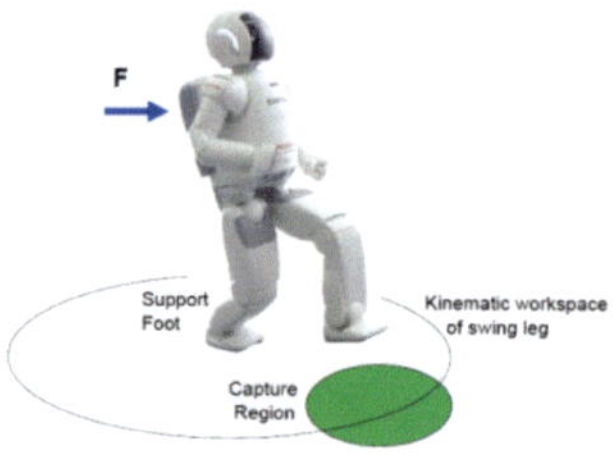

(b) Capture region outside the support polygon but partially inside the leg's kinematic workspace

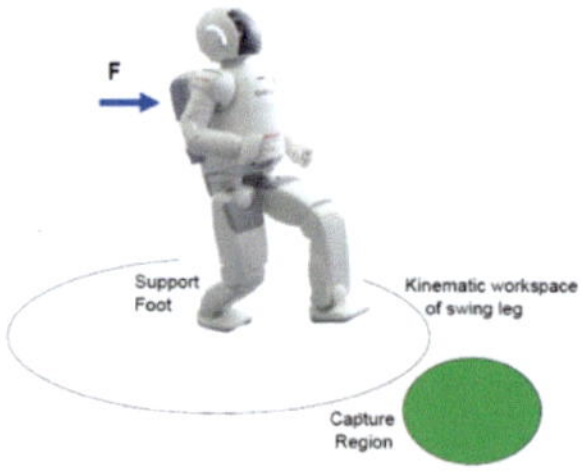

(c) Capture region outside the legs' kinematic workspace

Figure 3.8: Different locations of the capture region (green) for which the robot has to (a) take no step, (b) take one step, (c) take multiple steps (adapted from [Pratt et al. 2006], © 2006 IEEE).

The model assumptions and conceptual simplifications considered in the LIPM model as well as the instantaneous switch of contact locations assumed in the derivation of the ICP make it challenging to apply this concept directly to real robots. In [Rebula et al. 2007], the authors have attempted to bridge the gap between model-based calculation and the dynamics simulation of a simple bipedal robot with distributed mass by a sampling-based learning method. They learn state-dependent offsets to the model-based capture point and show that this significantly improves push recovery performance for a robot with segmented legs and an upper body (see Figure 3.9). [Pratt et al. 2012] present a capture point based push recovery method for the humanoid robot M2V2 (that resembles the simulation model used in [Rebula et al. 2007]), which shows good performance for balance recovery when pushed from a statically stable initial pose. The relatively large feet of the robot with respect to the step size, together with the actuated ankles, enable their push recovery controller to account for the model errors in the capture point computation.

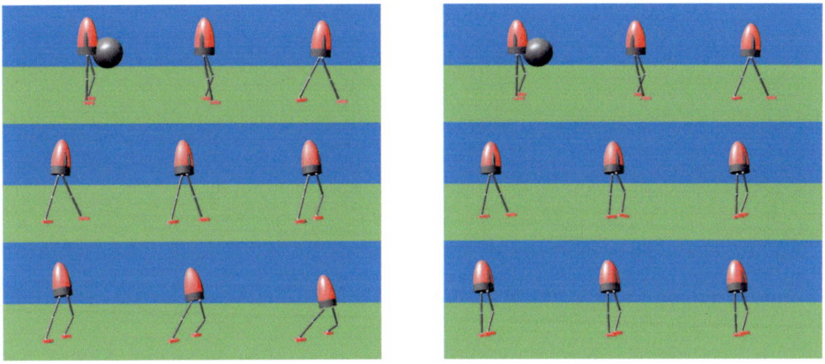

Figure 3.9: A simulated humanoid robot reacting to a push from the front by stepping before (left) and after (right) learning adaptations to the Capture Point. Before learning, the robot steps too far and the recovery fails. After learning, the robot successfully recovers. Temporal order of the images from left to right, top to bottom (taken from [Rebula et al. 2007], © 2007 IEEE).

Since walking for a number of n steps can be interpreted as n-step push recovery with a sequence of n capture steps, the concept of capture points has found numerous applications in the area of humanoid walking control.

Stepping into a capture point by definition lets the robot come to a full stop. However, a slightly shorter step lets the robot maintain or even increase its walking speed, while taking a longer step eventually lets the robot reverse its walking direction. Based on these considerations, a 2D walking controller with velocity control capabilities can be derived. As the connection between push recovery and walking controllers is so close, some of the above mentioned papers include contributions in both fields [Koolen et al. 2012; Pratt et al. 2012] or even entirely focus on walking control or walking trajectory generation [Englsberger et al. 2011, 2014a, 2015].

One way of achieving stable walking control via step location selection is by Model Predictive Control (MPC). In [Diedam et al. 2008] and [Herdt et al. 2010] the authors describe a linear MPC scheme based on the LIPM dynamics. The authors demonstrate how the control scheme presented in [Kajita et al. 2003], that was used for walking generation along pre-defined footsteps, can be used more generally for online adaptation of the footsteps during walking in order to satisfy the ZMP stability criterion. While the authors do not explicitly mention the capture point, the ZMP-based optimization in the MPC implicitly computes effectively the same quantity, but taking into account the actual (yet still simplified) system dynamics. In contrast, the MPC step location controller presented in [Griffin and Leonessa 2016] directly operates on the DCM dynamics to optimize step locations. The MPC is formulated as a quadratic program (see Section 3.3.1) that considers kinematic reachability constraints as well as desired foot rotations. Although a successful evaluation was performed in simulation, the authors acknowledge that their method is not always able to find feasible solutions due to the computational demand, and is therefore not ready to be applied to a real robot.

3.4.2 Step Time Adjustments

In the balance control approaches outlined in Section 3.4.1 the step location is adjusted, whereas the step timing, i. e. the duration of the step, is kept constant. An alternative approach is to modify the step timing and follow the pre-planned footsteps of the nominal walking trajectory, or to adjust step timing and step locations simultaneously.

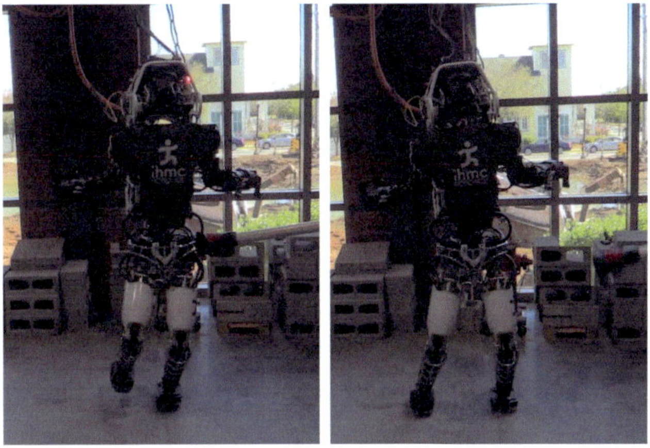

Figure 3.10: An Atlas humanoid robot reacting to a lateral push by quickly stepping to the side (taken from [Griffin et al. 2017], © 2017 IEEE).

In [Griffin et al. 2017], the authors argue that by adjusting the step timing, the necessary adjustments to the step location can be significantly decreased and validate this hypothesis through experiments on an Atlas humanoid robot (see Figure 3.10). Step timing adjustment is especially beneficial when the goal is to follow a pre-defined stepping trajectory under the influence of disturbances. The authors point out that adjustments to the step timing alone are only effective when the planned step direction and the current ICP trajectory coincide (for example when the robot is pushed forward while stepping forward), presenting a limitation to practical applications. In general it is therefore necessary to adjust both, step timing and step location. In [Kryczka et al. 2015] the authors develop a control framework that integrates with a walking trajectory generator and simultaneously optimizes the step location and step timing ('gait pattern regeneration') to enable walking motions that are robust to push disturbances. The non-linear gait pattern optimization takes less than 40 ms, which is sufficiently fast for the targeted application. The found trajectory is tracked with a ZMP-based CoM feedback controller. Their approach and implementation are validated through experiments on the COMAN humanoid robot [Tsagarakis et al. 2013]. Related to the work presented in [Herdt et al. 2010], the authors of [Aftab et al. 2012] show an extended MPC controller to include the ankle, hip and stepping strategy in one unified non-linear optimization. In contrast to previous works, step timing adjustments are considered and implicitly handled by the optimization that minimizes a cost function containing the constrained linear swing foot acceleration.

A conceptually similar approach of optimizing both step location and step time simultaneously is presented in [Khadiv et al. 2016]. In contrast to the other methods, the authors consider the linearized CoM dynamics of the LIPM as the basis for the optimization rather then the non-linear robot dynamics, allowing them to use fast convex linear optimization techniques. Stable walking is achieved by specifying a desired offset between the DCM and the CoM at the end of each step. They compare the performance of their technique to the one detailed in [Herdt et al. 2010] which does not include step timing optimization and find significant stability improvements on the task of stabilizing a 3D LIPM walking under lateral disturbances. Successful simulation results for the Athena humanoid robot with unactuated ankle joints walking and enduring a lateral push are also presented, indicating that step time adjustment is suited for addressing the special requirements of this class of robots that cannot exert moments at the ground contact.

3.4.3 Learning How to Step

To overcome the gap between the LIPM-based capture point concept and the application to real robots with their kinematic constraints and complex dynamics, machine learning and reinforcement learning in particular, can be used.

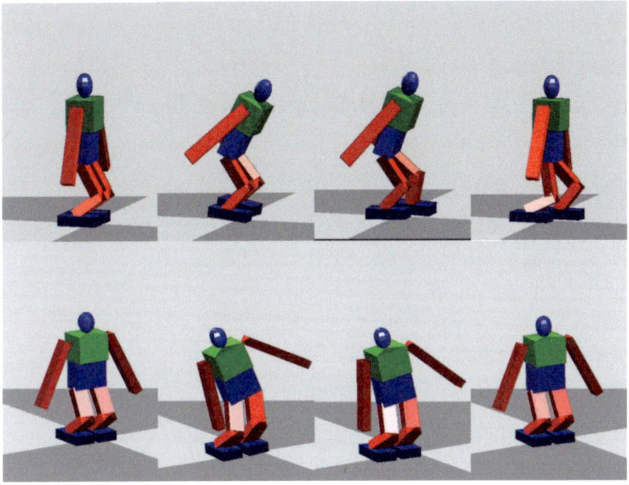

Figure 3.11: A simulated small humanoid robot applying push recovery methods that were optimized using reinforcement learning (taken from [Yi et al. 2011a],© 2011 IEEE).

In [Yi et al. 2011a] the authors use simulation-based stochastic policy gradient reinforcement learning to optimize a highly pre-structured controller for whole-body balancing of a small humanoid robot (see Figure 3.11). In [Levine and Koltun 2014] the authors simulate a simple 2D bipedal walking robot and use direct policy search reinforcement learning to let it learn how to walk under disturbances. Their algorithm develops a variety of successful push recovery strategies that enable the simulated robot to recover from strong lateral pushes.

Recent examples of simulation-based applications of reinforcement learning to dynamic biped locomotion include the work presented by [Peng et al. 2017] that uses deep reinforcement learning to realize walking controllers that show a certain robustness to pushes, albeit relying on very large amounts of simulated training data. A follow-up study presented in [Peng et al. 2018] combines a similar method with input from human motion capture to let a humanoid robot mimic highly dynamic human motions in a dynamics simulation.

The work that will be presented in Chapter 6 is in line with these works, as it uses input from motion capture and policy gradient reinforcement learning to turn produce viable stepping motions for push recovery.

3.4.4 Recovery Stepping with DMPs

The previously described methods were mostly concerned with finding appropriate step parameters in terms of step location and step execution time. The question remains how to generate stepping motions that realize these parametric requirements. One way of addressing this question is to use parametric motion generators based on Dynamics Movement Primitives (DMPs, see Section 2.4).

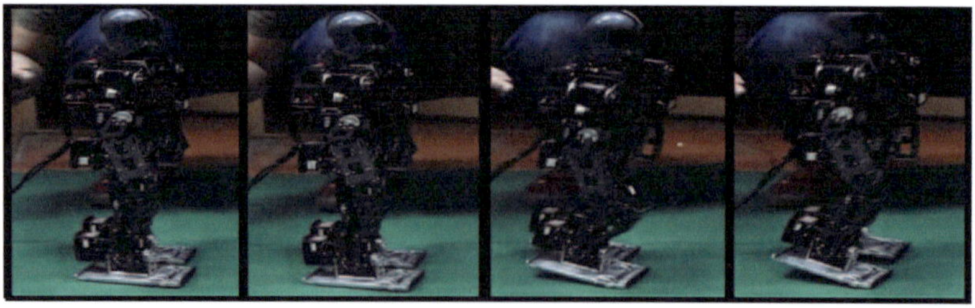

Figure 3.12: Validation experiments of a recovery step encoded as task-space DMP on a PKU-HR5 kid-sized humanoid robot (taken from [Luo et al. 2015], © 2015 IEEE).

Once a trajectory is encoded as a DMP, adaptation of the start and goal positions as well as of the execution speed can be achieved in a very efficient manner by changing the according high-level parameters and integrating over the dynamics of the transformation system. DMP-encoded trajectory representations are therefore well-suited for high-dimensional motion generation in time-critical applications, such as stepping for push recovery of humanoid robots. Some initial research into this direction has been presented in [Luo et al. 2015]. The authors encode a recovery stepping foot trajectory as DMP and conceive a simple control law that adapts the step length proportionally to the push intensity. They consider pushes only in the frontal direction and do not provide details on how they tune their control law. The motion is encoded as a foot trajectory in the task-space, and hence it remains necessary in their approach to explicitly compute joint angles for each time step by solving the Inverse Kinematics (IK) problem, not exploiting the potential of direct joint-level trajectory encoding. One of their validation experiments conducted on a PKU-HR5 robot is shown in Figure 3.12. While the approach appears to be promising and is reported to be successful, a number of interesting aspects remain unclear and a quantitative evaluation is not presented.

The work presented in Chapter 6 will bring together reinforcement learning for estimating correct step parameters and joint-level DMPs for efficient motion generation.

3.5 Summary

This chapter gave an overview of the most relevant literature in the three sub-fields where this thesis contributes to humanoid balancing and push recovery. The presented literature review contains the works this thesis builds on as well as alternative, competing and complementary approaches. A visual overview over the presented concepts and methods that summarize the related literature for each of the three areas is presented in Figure 3.13, Figure 3.14 and Figure 3.15.

Figure 3.13 summarizes the literature on stability classification and disturbance estimation. Stability classification can be categorized into methods relying on external sensors (e. g. cameras or microphones) or on internal sensors (e. g. IMUs). To find and evaluate descriptive features for the current state of stability in the internal sensor data, either heuristics (e. g. thresholding) or data-driven learning methods (e. g. neural networks) can be applied. The work presented in this thesis falls into the latter category. A similar categorization an be applied to method for disturbance estimation, where common methods either rely on contact force sensors (e. g. sensorized skin) or internal sensors. Methods based on data from internal sensors either employ joint torque sensors, IMUs or F/T sensors. This thesis will focus on leveraging IMUs and F/T sensors.

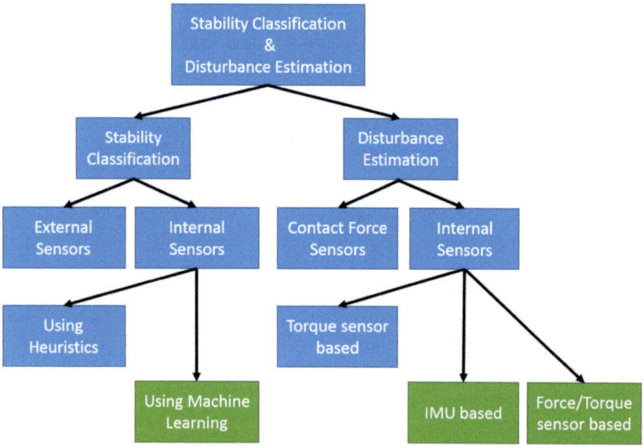

Figure 3.13: Structured summary of the reviewed methods for stability classification for humans and humanoid robots as well as for disturbance (i. e. push force) estimation on humanoid robots. Areas in which this thesis contributes are highlighted in green (see Chapter 4).

Figure 3.14 presents an overview over the related literature on postural balancing, where the main division is into methods that perform computationally expensive online optimization and methods that leverage efficient linear control theory. Online optimization methods can be divided into model predictive control (MPC) and quadratic programming (QP) approaches, and QP formulations can be further divided by considering whether the optimization is formulated in the acceleration or torque domain. Linear control methods on the other hand are either based on simplified or even inherently linear dynamics models (such as the point mass abstraction or the Linear Inverted Pendulum), or on a locally linearized full dynamics model. Controlling the linearized dynamics model can either be achieved with a linear quadratic regulator (LQR) using naive weight terms in the cost function, or by systematically optimizing the LQR-weights for the balancing task. This thesis investigates the latter approach.

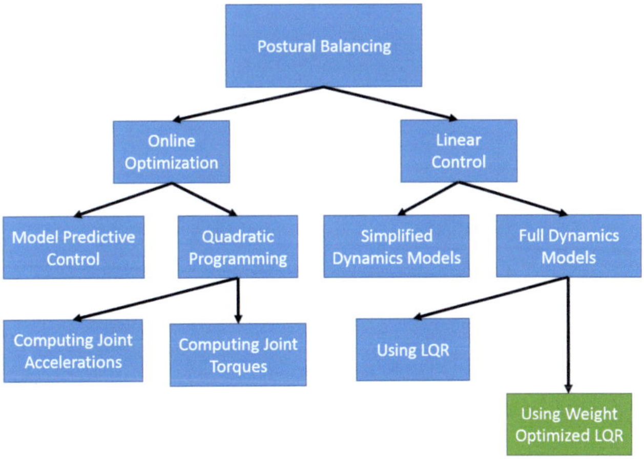

Figure 3.14: Structured summary of the reviewed methods for balancing in place (postural balancing). The area in which this thesis contributes is highlighted in green (see Chapter 5).

The related work on balancing by stepping is summarized in Figure 3.15 and can be subdivided into approaches that make adjustments to steps of a nominal pre-palnned walking pattern by altering the step location or the step time, and into approaches that consider recovery stepping from an initial standing pose. The two main questions for recovery stepping from standing are how to efficiently generate the motion, and how to find the right step parameters for a specific disturbance. One way to address motion generation is by making use of Dynamic Movement Primitives (DMPs) that can either be applied in the task space (Cartesian DMPs) or on the joint level, alleviating the computational requirements associated with iteratively solving the Inverse Kinematics (IK) problem. The parameters of the recovery step (e. g. step location and step duration) can either be determined heuristically or by data-driven learning methods. This thesis proposes the use of joint-level DMPs for parametric motion generation, and reinforcement learning (RL) for finding appropriate step parameters w. r. t. the push.

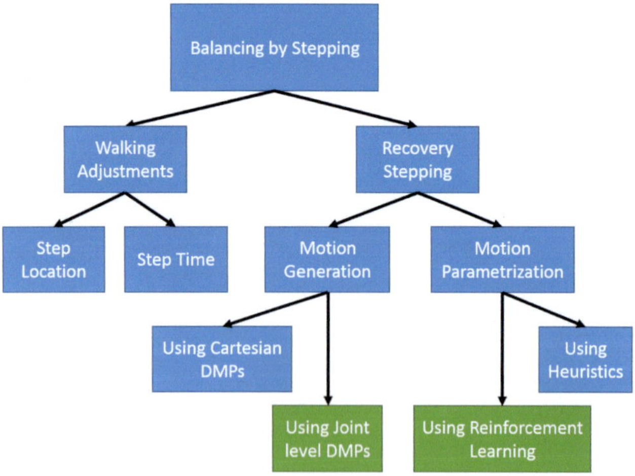

Figure 3.15: Structured summary of the reviewed methods for push recovery by stepping. Areas in which this thesis contributes are highlighted in green (see Chapter 6).

4 Disturbance Estimation and Stability Classification

Every form of closed-loop control requires feedback from the control system to estimate the *current* system state. This information, together with the *desired* system state, allows a controller to compute the appropriate control action. State, however, is a term that is used in a variety of contexts and with varying meanings. In [Rotella et al. 2014], the authors give an introduction to state estimation in mobile robotics in general, and explain how state estimation for humanoid robots is a special case, due to the hybrid system dynamics and geometric constraints in the foot contact.

A humanoid robot's state in the sense of classical control theory contains the spatial orientation, position and velocity of its floating base together with its joint angles and velocities. This state description can be referred to as the *low-level* state. This form of state information is typically required for continuous control tasks such as whole-body balancing. The measurement of each of the quantities in the low-level state on a real humanoid robot is a challenging task, and a large amount of research work has been carried out to identify and address this challenge. Thc joint angle measurement for example can be adversely affected by actuator backlash, and feed-forward computation of end-effector poses can be impeded by the robot's elasticity. Both of these problems have been reported for the Atlas humanoid in [Johnson et al. 2015] and were addressed with computational elasticity compensation and backlash estimation. In [Rotella et al. 2016], the authors explore how the estimation of joint velocities can be improved by adding IMUs to each robot link in order to mitigate differentiation noise that arises when computing the joint velocities from position encoders alone. In contrast to real hardware, simulated environments provide accurate information about the robot's low-level state.

Discontinuous control decisions on the other hand might rely on other state representations. In the context of this thesis, such discontinuous decisions are whether to take a step, and how to perform this step. Answering these questions calls for more specific, *higher-level* descriptors of the robot state. This work therefore aims at finding descriptors for the disturbance (i. e. push) the robot is subjected to, and the degree of its current dynamic stability, facilitating fast and informed decision making about whether and were to step. To circumvent some of the difficulties that come with traditional state estimation and to make the proposed methods more generic (i. e. applicable to a wide range of systems, including robots and wearable assistive devices such as robotic exoskeletons), a focus is put on a reduction of the number of sensors that are used. High-level state estimation with few sensors is a field far less researched than low-level state estimation, and even simulators cannot readily provide the desired information.

The methods introudced in Section 4.1 and Section 4.2 focus on the *static* case, in which a human or humanoid robot is initially at rest, relying on a single IMU or internal F/T sensors for disturbance estimation, respectively. In Section 4.3, an IMU based method for classifying the dynamic stability while in *dynamic motion* will be developed. Parts of the methods for disturbance estimation and stability classification have been published in [Kaul and Asfour 2016] and [Steffan et al. 2017].

4.1 Push Intensity Estimation with a single IMU

People are extremely adept at reacting to various kinds of disturbances without falling over. To this end they employ a range of balancing strategies that can be categorized into those that require taking a step, and those that are performed in place, i. e. without changing the foot placement. Being both very capable at push recovery and physically similar to humanoid robots, the human role model is a grounded source of inspiration for methods of humanoid push recovery. By equipping a human subject with a single body-worn IMU, subjecting it to pushes and analyzing the push as well as the human's reaction, the work presented in this section aims at validating the hypothesis that

1. the occurrence of a push (*push detection*)
2. the need to take a step (*strategy selection*)
3. and the direction of push (*push direction*)

can all be inferred from a minimal body-worn sensor setup. It thereby lays the foundation for subsequent work presented in this chapter that exploits this hypothesis.

4.1.1 Experimental Setup

The core of the experimental setup is a human subject equipped with a body-worn IMU sensor attached to the torso[1]. The torso is the part of the human body that most closely resembles the CoM prevalent in many simplified dynamics models for humanoid robots. It is furthermore comparatively easy to attach an IMU to the torso both on a humanoid robot as well as on a human body. These reasons led to the choice of this sensor location.
The IMU measures the spatial acceleration along its own coordinate axes. It furthermore computes its absolute spatial orientation (aligned with gravity and Magnetic North) by additionally using its integrated gyroscope and magnetometer, which also enables it to compute the gravity-compensated acceleration. This 3-dimensional gravity-compensated acceleration vector

[1] In some of the experiments, the subject was also wearing a light-absorbing suit with reflective markers for optical motion capture (see Figure 4.1(a)). However, the collected motion data was not used in the study presented in this chapter, only the data from the IMU.

is the sensory output used in the presented study. The subject and the location of the IMU are shown in Figure 4.1(a).

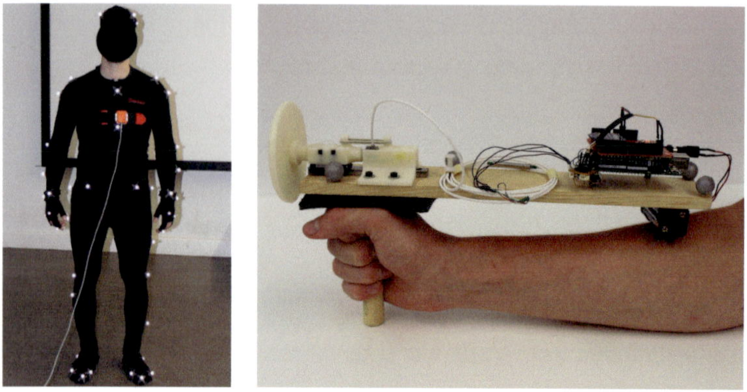

(a) Human subject with IMU attached to the torso

(b) Sensorized push device

Figure 4.1: Human subject equipped with a body-worn IMU sensor (orange) attached to the torso (a) and a sensorized device to measure the applied push force (b) (taken from [Kaul and Asfour 2016], © 2016 VDE).

For this study, a research-grade *xSens MTi* IMU was used, but low-cost consumer grade sensors provide equivalent functionality for this application. The IMU generates the data from which the strategy (stepping or no stepping), the direction of the applied push and its magnitude are to be reconstructed. The reaction of the subject provides the ground truth for the appropriate strategy. The person applying the pushes is doing so along one of four pre-specified directions (from the front, the back, the left or the right), which is recorded and forms the ground truth for the direction. A force-measuring device is used to apply these pushes in order to record the applied push force and provide ground truth data for the correlation of force and acceleration signals. This custom-made device accurately measures the force transmitted between the person who pushes and the subject that is being pushed, using a 1D load-cell, a 14 Bit ADC and a wireless connection to a laptop PC for data collection (see Figure 4.1(b)). Table 4.1 summarizes the collected data and data collection methods used during the trials.

4.1.2 Experimental Protocol

The aim of the experiments is to collect a dataset that contains information about the push, the subject's reaction to it, and the IMU data. Since any experiment that involves a human subject is susceptible to variances in the outcome caused by unpredictable influences on the human behavior, an experimental protocol was devised to standardize the experiments and to make them as reproducible as possible: At the beginning of each experiment, the subject wearing the IMU is instructed to stand upright with feet in parallel and placed at shoulder-width, eyes closed (see Figure 4.1(a)). It is further instructed to take a recovery step only when necessary, and to resort to postural in-place balancing whenever possible. After a waiting time, which is randomized to avoid premature reactions, the second person pushes the subject at shoulder height either from the front, the back, the right or the left side, provoking a push recovery reaction. The strategy chosen by the subject in reaction to the push (stepping or no stepping) is noted. During the entire experiment, the gravity-compensated linear torso acceleration measured by the IMU as well as the push force measured by the push device are synchronously recorded at a rate of 100 Hz.
Overall, 78 experimental trials were conducted with a single subject, covering reactions to pushes of a wide variety of intensities and from all four directions.

4.1.3 Methods and Results

This section will introduce the methods used to validate the initial hypotheses regarding push detection, strategy selection and push direction, and report on the obtained results.

Information	Measurement Modality	Data
Push force	Force-sensing push device (see Figure 4.1(b))	Continuous stream of 1D force information, sampled at 100 Hz
Push direction	Predefined	Label: Right, Left, Front, Back
Torso acceleration	Body-worn IMU (see Figure 4.1(a))	Gravity-compensated linear acceleration, sampled at 100 Hz
Strategy	Observed	Label: Stepping/no stepping (binary)

Table 4.1: Sensing modalities and recorded data during single-IMU human push recovery trials.

Push Detection The most intuitive sensor modality for push detection is the push force itself. However, the push force at arbitrary locations is difficult to measure by a robot (or human assistive device) and was therefore measured during the experiments with an external sensorized tool. The first part of the initial hypothesis thus states that a push can be detected using a single body-mounted IMU, measuring the absolute linear torso acceleration. In the early stages of the push, the push force and the torso acceleration show very close correspondence in accordance with the proportionality

$$\mathbf{f} = m\mathbf{a} \tag{4.1}$$

of the force $\mathbf{f}$ and the acceleration $\mathbf{a}$ governed by the subject's mass m. This correspondence, prevalent in all of the recorded trials, can be seen exemplary in Figure 4.2 in the section between the dashed vertical lines[2]. The only notable qualitative difference between the signals in this stage is a higher level of noise in the acceleration measurement.

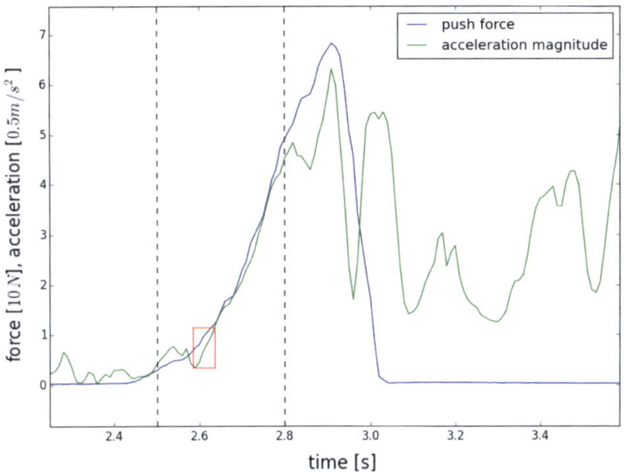

Figure 4.2: Push force (blue) and absolute torso acceleration (green) during an experiment in which the human subject, initially standing at rest, is pushed from the back and performs a recovery step in reaction to the push. Force and acceleration are highly correlated at the beginning of the push (between the dashed lines). The red rectangle visualizes the window-based push detector (adapted from [Kaul and Asfour 2016], © 2016 VDE).

In later stages of the trial, when the human begins to react, its motions introduce additional accelerations that make the acceleration signal deviate from the vanishing push force.

[2] The scaling of force values in the original publication was falsely denoted as 0.1 N. The figure printed here was corrected.

Since an acceleration-derived method for push detection should work equally well for pushes from all directions, the 3-dimensional gravity-compensated acceleration vector

$$\mathbf{a} = (a_x, a_y, a_z)^T$$

is expressed by means of its scalar magnitude

$$a = \sqrt{a_x^2 + a_y^2 + a_z^2}$$

to yield a direction-invariant feature.

From this initial correspondence between torso acceleration and push force it can be concluded that the absolute torso acceleration is an equally good signal for detecting the onset of a push disturbance. The most straightforward way of detecting a push based on this feature is to constantly compare it against a certain threshold. However, as the acceleration magnitude exhibits significant noise during a typical trial, this would require a comparatively high threshold value to avoid false positives, which in turn would delay the detection of the push.

A better detector was derived by using a sliding window with fixed window size n, containing the most recent and the last $n-1$ acceleration magnitude samples. The difference between the largest and the smallest value within this window becomes the detection feature, and a push is detected by comparing this difference against a fixed reference threshold[3]. The free parameters in this detector are the window size n and the threshold d. By

[3] Considering that all experiments start with the subject at rest, the push detector also requires that the largest acceleration occurs after the smallest. Occurrences that do not fulfill this requirement are considered noise.

systematically testing possible combinations of n and d on the entire dataset, it was found that the set

$$(n,d) = (5, 0.4\,\mathrm{m/s^2}),$$

i. e. a sliding window of sample size 5 (corresponding to a time span of 50 ms) and an acceleration difference of $0.4\,\mathrm{m/s^2}$ correctly identifies all beginnings of pushes without false positives. An example of a detecting sliding window is depicted as red rectangle in Figure 4.2.
These parameters were fitted to the dataset of 78 recorded push trials to initially validate the hypothesis that an external push can be quickly and reliably detected with a single body-worn IMU.

Strategy Selection Once a push is detected, the primary questions is whether or not a recovery step has to be performed. The hypothesis states that this question can be answered from a single body-mounted IMU by extracting a measure of push intensity. High push intensities are expected to result in the subject performing a recovery step, whereas low intensities would result in in-place postural balancing. Similar to the considerations of a direction invariant feature for push detection, the same input (absolute torso acceleration) can be used for intensity estimation. While an intuitive feature would be the the peak acceleration, acceleration evolutions like the one depicted in Figure 4.2 show that it can take as much as 0.5 s for this peak to occur after the beginning of the push. Waiting for this peak to occur would thus substantially delay the reaction.
To address the challenge of early push detection, a different indicating feature of the push intensity that can be evaluated earlier on is proposed here, namely the slope with which the torso acceleration increases (i. e. the torso *jerk*). However, as the acceleration is already a noise-afflicted signal, numerical differentiation increases the noise level even further, making a sample-wise jerk calculation based on finite differences an unsuitable

option. Instead, a linear approximation to the acceleration can be computed for the first m samples and the slope of the resulting regression model can serve as a time-averaged estimate of the jerk. This process is illustrated in Figure 4.3. In the implementation used for this study, the parameters of the linear approximation were found by least squares linear regression. The regression is based on the earliest sample in the push detection window and the subsequent $m-1$ absolute acceleration samples.

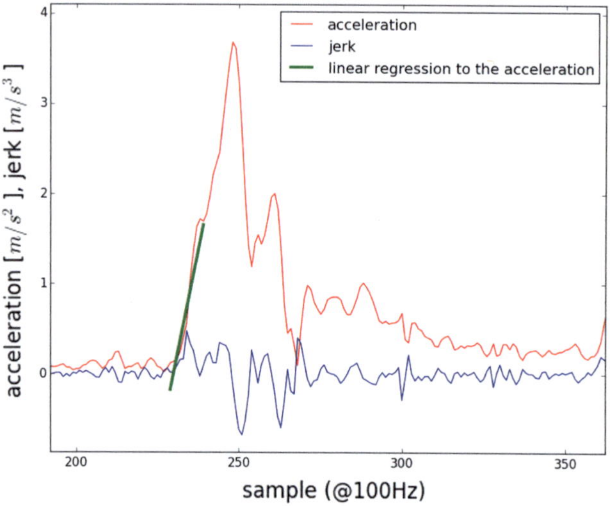

Figure 4.3: Torso acceleration (red) and its numerical derivative (blue) for one of the human trials. As the jerk itself is highly noise-afflicted, the slope of the linear regression to the acceleration (green) over the first 180 ms after the onset of the push serves as scalar push intensity estimate (adapted from [Kaul and Asfour 2016], © 2016 VDE).

Choosing a small value for m makes the jerk estimation faster, but more susceptible to noise in the acceleration signal. A large m makes the estimation more robust to the signal noise but increases the delay. Different values for m in the range from 5 samples (i. e. 50 ms of data) to 20 samples (i. e. 200 ms of data) were tested for their ability to generate a jerk estimate that correctly divides the trials into two halves, namely the trials in which the human subject took a step, and those in which it resorted to balancing in place.

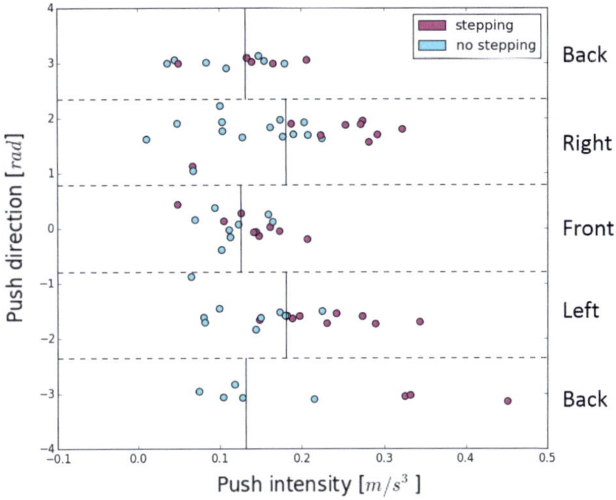

Figure 4.4: All 78 human push recovery trials colored by the observed strategy, with the push direction, the estimated push intensity (jerk) and the optimal decision boundaries for the respective push direction based on jerk approximation over 180 ms (adapted from [Kaul and Asfour 2016], © 2016 VDE).

The push intensity that can be endured by a human or humanoid robot without having to take a step varies with the direction of the push. The width of the stance leads to a higher inherent resilience against pushes from the side, whereas the limited length of the feet limits resilience against pushes from the back and the front. To account for this, different optimal decision boundaries between stepping and no-stepping with respect to the estimated torso jerk were allowed for the four directions front, back, left and right (with left and right having the same value due to symmetry considerations). On the reference dataset of 78 trials, $m = 18$ (i. e. 180 ms of IMU-data) is the parameter that results in a jerk (i. e. push intensity) estimate with the best ability to divide the trials into those that involved stepping and those in which the human resorted to balancing in place. Figure 4.4 illustrates that division by depicting all trials colored by the actual recovery strategy along with the direction of the push and the intensity, estimated over the first 18 acceleration samples, corresponding to the first 180 ms after the push was detected. With the optimal decision boundaries, 79% of the recovery strategies in all trials could be classified correctly. Table 4.2 presents the detailed results split into the four directions.

Push Direction	Strategy Prediction Accuracy
Front	14 out of 18 (78%)
Left and Right	33 out of 40 (83%)
Back	15 out of 20 (75%)
Overall	62 out of 78 (79%)

Table 4.2: Correct recovery strategy prediction from a single IMU.

This analysis reveals that the proposed method of push intensity estimation by approximating the torso jerk has the potential to predict the recovery strategy that a human would use, and hence the strategy a robot should use. This substantiates the hypothesis that a minimal set of body-worn IMU sensors are a viable method for estimating the applied disturbance. However, the obtained training accuracy of 79% and the distribution of trials in Figure 4.4 suggest that even an ideal method might not be able to perfectly predict the human's reaction. There certainly exists a range of push intensities in which both reactions, stepping and no stepping, are feasible reactions. Additional considerations like energy expenditure, concerns about the stability of the ground, or spatial constraints might be deciding factors in those cases.

Push Direction The direction of the push determines the direction of the recovery step, should one be necessary, where e. g. a push from the left necessitates a step to the right, and vice versa. Since the direction is a very important parameter for generating and executing a step, it is necessary for a humanoid robot or an assistive exoskeleton to be aware of the direction in which it was pushed as early on as possible. Given the initial close correspondence of the push force and the body acceleration observable in Figure 4.2, grounded in Equation 4.1, the force direction can be inferred from the torso acceleration vector. Since the push direction is a purely horizontal quantity, it is sufficient to consider the two horizontal acceleration components a_x and a_y. Computing the resulting direction $\mathbf{d}_h$ of the horizontal body acceleration $\mathbf{a}_h$ from these two vector components can, in principle, be achieved by element-wise evaluation of the two-argument arctangent

$$\mathbf{d}_h = atan2(a_x, a_y). \tag{4.2}$$

However, due to the noise in the raw acceleration signals, this form of direction computation is also highly noisy. In order to generate a more robust direction estimate, a similar technique to the one used for push intensity estimation is proposed here: The jerk of the horizontal acceleration components can be found as the slope of their linear regression lines, and instead of computing the direction from the noise-afflicted acceleration measurements, it can be computed from these regression-based scalar jerk estimates $\dot{a}_{xr}$ and $\dot{a}_{yr}$:

$$\mathbf{d}_h = atan2(\dot{a}_{xr}, \dot{a}_{yr}). \tag{4.3}$$

Using the same 18 acceleration samples that are used for the intensity estimation, a reliable classification into the four directions front, back, right, and left can be achieved. This result is visualized in Figure 4.5.
These findings substantiate the third part of the hypothesis, namely that the direction of an applied push disturbance can be estimated from a small number of body-mounted IMU sensors (in this case even from a single one).

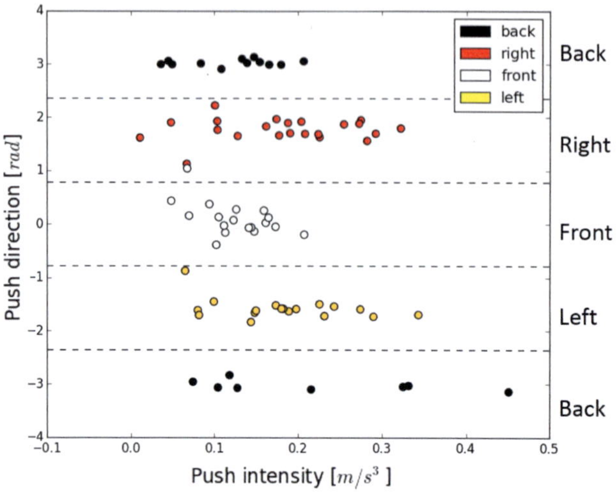

Figure 4.5: All 78 human trials, colored by the actual direction of the applied push, along with the estimated push intensity and push direction estimate computed with Equation 4.3 (adapted from [Kaul and Asfour 2016], © 2016 VDE).

4.2 Disturbance Estimation with F/T Sensors

As it was shown in Section 4.1, even a single IMU mounted at the torso of a human can reveal substantial information about the occurrence, the intensity and the direction of a push that requires push recovery. Body mounted inertial sensors are an appealing sensor modality, as they can be easily integrated both in humanoid robots and in wearable assistive devices for the augmentation of human locomotion. However, the previously presented results also indicate a remaining level of uncertainty in the parameters of the push, which makes it still challenging for a push recovery controller to generate the optimal recovery action. This motivates the consideration of an additional sensor modality for disturbance estimation that improves those estimations.

Figure 4.6: Detailed view of the F/T sensors of ARMAR-4. The sensors are the highlighted cylindrical elements mounted between the feet and the ankle joints.

A type of sensor that can be used for this purpose and that is commonly found in full-size humanoid robots such as the ARMAR-4 are 6 DoF force/torque sensors (F/T sensors in short) mounted between each foot and the ankle joints (see Figure 4.6). With two of these sensors (one at each foot), the robot is able to perceive the forces and torques that act between its body and the ground, which constitute the six elements of the contact wrench $\mathbf{w}_c$ with

$$\mathbf{w}_c = [(f_c^x, f_c^y, f_c^z)^T, (m_c^x, m_c^y, m_c^z)^T]$$

In the case of ground contact wrenches, the torque is commonly referred to as moment. In the static case, the forces and moments measured by the sensors are the sum of gravity-induced effects and external forces, i. e. pushes. After subtracting the effects of gravity from the sensor signal, the force measurements can therefore be regarded as reflections of the external

push forces, and similar methods to those introduced in Section 4.1 can be applied.
In addition to the force, F/T sensors also provide a measurement of the ground reaction moment. With the force and moment combined, additional information, namely the line in space along which the external force acts, can be computed.

4.2.1 Line of Force Action

If the 3D force vector and the 3D moment vector in the interaction point between the static robot and the ground are known, if gravity-induced effects are known and can be subtracted, and if the assumption holds that only one external force other than the ground interaction forces is acting on the robot, then the line along which this force is acting (the *line of force action*) can be computed. This line encodes the direction of the force and every possible force application point in 3D space.

Single Ground Contact The line of push force action can be determined by solving the fundamental relation between the contact moment $\mathbf{m}_c$, the contact force $\mathbf{f}_c$ and the force application point $\mathbf{r}_f$

$$\mathbf{m}_c = \mathbf{r}_f \times \mathbf{f}_c \tag{4.4}$$

for the force application point, yielding

$$\mathbf{r}_f = -[\mathbf{F}_c]_\times^+ \mathbf{m}_c. \tag{4.5}$$

$[\mathbf{F}_c]_\times$ is the skew-symmetric matrix representation of the cross product $\times\mathbf{f}_c$ (see [Featherstone 2008], Table A.2) with

$$[\mathbf{F}_c]_\times = \begin{bmatrix} 0 & f_c^z & -f_c^y \\ -f_c^z & 0 & f_c^x \\ f_c^y & -f_c^x & 0 \end{bmatrix},$$

and $[\mathbf{F}_c]_\times^+$ is its Moore-Penrose pseudo-inverse (see [Ben-Israel and Greville 2003]).

Since one has to resort to pseudo-inversion to solve Equation 4.4, it is impossible to retrieve the exact application point. Instead, Equation 4.5 yields the point on the line of force action that is closest to the sensor location[4]. The entire line of force action, consisting of all points $\mathbf{r}_{fa}$, can then be described parametrically, using the measured force vector $\mathbf{f}_c$ and the point $\mathbf{r}_f$ in

$$\mathbf{r}_{fa}(\lambda) = \mathbf{r}_f + \lambda|\mathbf{f}_c| \tag{4.6}$$

with a scalar parameter $\lambda \in \mathbb{R}$.

Extension to Dual Contacts In the case of a humanoid robot with two feet and hence two ground contacts, the resulting virtual contact wrench components $\mathbf{m}_v$ and $\mathbf{f}_v$ in a virtual contact frame $\mathscr{F}_v$ first need to be computed from the individual sensor readings. Assuming a flat ground and coplanarity of the feet, the transformation between the two foot frames $\mathscr{F}_1$ and $\mathscr{F}_2$ can be described with three parameters, namely a 2D displacement vector in the horizontal ground plane and a rotation around the vertical axis. While any point could be chosen as location of the virtual sensor frame $\mathscr{F}_v$, a reasonable choice that is both intuitive and computationally advantageous

[4] All spatial computations for the single contact case are implicitly expressed in the coordinate frame of the F/T sensor.

is the mid-point on the connection of the two foot frames. Under these preconditions, expressing the two contact wrenches in the virtual frame can be formulated as a two-step process: First, the y-axes of frames $\mathscr{F}_1$ and $\mathscr{F}_2$ are aligned with the line connecting the feet by rotating them around the vertical z-axis by suitable angles φ_1 and φ_2, respectively. These rotations lead to the aligned foot frames $\mathscr{F}_{1,\varphi_1}$ with the contact wrench

$$\mathbf{w}_{1,\varphi_1} = [(f^x_{1,\varphi_1}, f^y_{1,\varphi_1}, f^z_{1,\varphi_1})^T, (m^x_{1,\varphi_1}, m^y_{1,\varphi_1}, m^z_{1,\varphi_1})^T]$$

and $\mathscr{F}_{2,\varphi_2}$ with the contact wrench

$$\mathbf{w}_{2,\varphi_2} = [(f^x_{2,\varphi_2}, f^y_{2,\varphi_2}, f^z_{2,\varphi_2})^T, (m^x_{2,\varphi_2}, m^y_{2,\varphi_2}, m^z_{2,\varphi_2})^T].$$

With the scalar foot distance d_f as parameter, the virtual contact wrench

$$\mathbf{w}_v = [\mathbf{f}_v, \mathbf{m}_v] \tag{4.7}$$

can be derived by computing its two components $\mathbf{f}_v$ and $\mathbf{m}_v$ as

$$\mathbf{f}_v = \mathbf{f}_{1,\varphi_1} + \mathbf{f}_{2,\varphi_2} \tag{4.8}$$

and

$$\mathbf{m}_v = \frac{d_f}{2}(\mathbf{f}^T_{1,\varphi_1}\mathbf{S}_f - \mathbf{f}^T_{2,\varphi_2}\mathbf{S}_f) + \mathbf{m}^T_{1,\varphi_1}\mathbf{S}_m + \mathbf{m}^T_{2,\varphi_2}\mathbf{S}_m, \tag{4.9}$$

where

$$\mathbf{S}_f = \begin{bmatrix} 0 & 0 & 1 \\ 0 & 0 & 0 \\ 1 & 0 & 0 \end{bmatrix}, \qquad \mathbf{S}_m = \begin{bmatrix} 0 & 0 & 0 \\ 1 & 0 & 0 \\ 0 & 0 & 0 \end{bmatrix}$$

are $\mathbb{R}^{3\times 3}$ geometric selection matrices that have particularly simple structures thanks to the location of the virtual sensor frame. Figure 4.7 visualizes the described transformations.

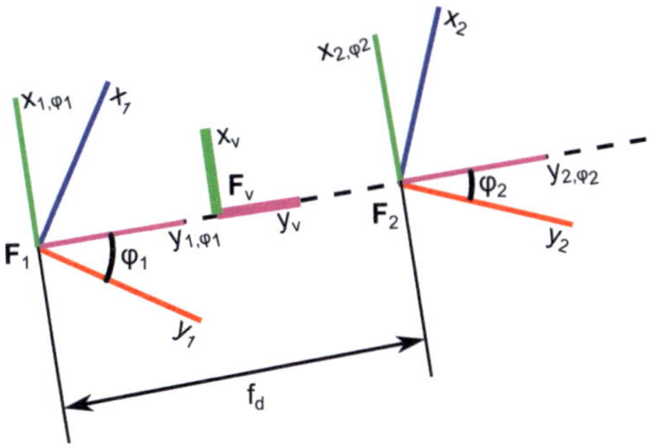

Figure 4.7: Visualization of the coordinate transformation for the dual contact case. Red and blue axis denote the actual sensor-aligned coordinate frames $\mathscr{F}_1$ and $\mathscr{F}_2$ in which F/T-measurements are taken. Those measurements are rotated by $\varphi_{1,2}$ and subsequently translated into the virtual sensor frame $\mathscr{F}_v$ at the center point between the two feet. The virtual wrench $\mathbf{w}_v$ in $\mathscr{F}_v$ is then computed by Equation 4.8 and Equation 4.9 and used as input for the force action line computation.

With the so obtained virtual contact wrench (Equation 4.7), the methodology for the single contact case using Equation 4.5 and Equation 4.6 can be applied to compute the line of push force action.
The following section will show how this method can be used to enable the humanoid robot ARMAR-4 to sense the line of force action of an external contact at an arbitrary point along its body.

4.2.2 Validation on the ARMAR-4 Humanoid Robot

In order to validate the presented dual contact extension of the computation of the line of force action, experiments with the ARMAR-4 robot were carried out. This constitutes an advancement over the related literature, where similar methods have been proposed for humanoid robots but remained purely theoretical or confined to simulation. In the here presented experiments, the robot stood on both feet and was pushed at various locations with the sensorized push tool depicted in Figure 4.1(b). The readings of the ankle F/T sensors were simultaneously recorded. Using Equation 4.8

and Equation 4.9, the gravity-compensated force and torque components of the virtual wrench at the midpoint between the feet were computed. Figure 4.8 shows the six elements of the virtual wrench, as well as the total force measured by the F/T sensors (red). The externally applied force measured by the push tool is shown in blue. The close correlation of these two curves serves as a validation of the correct functioning of the measurement setup as well as the data processing.

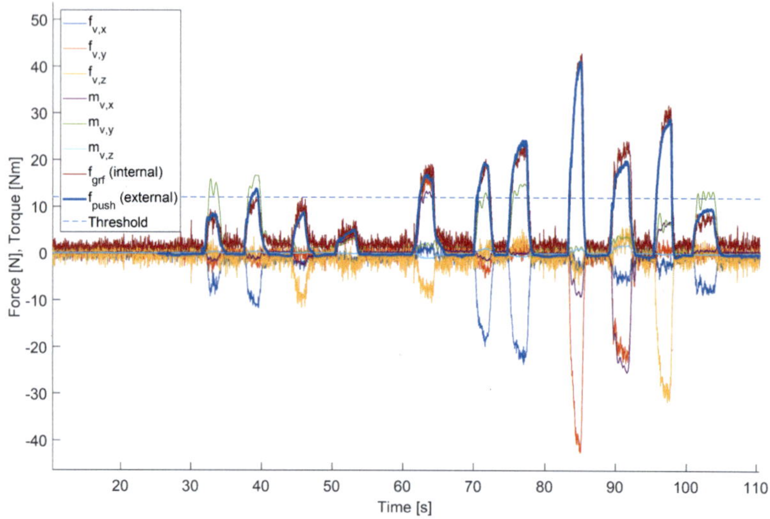

Figure 4.8: Virtual wrench force $\mathbf{f}_v$ ($f_{v,x}$, $f_{v,y}$, $f_{v,z}$) and moment $\mathbf{m}_v$ ($m_{v,x}$, $m_{v,y}$, $m_{v,z}$) together with the absolute ground reaction force (internal) and measured push force (external).

An external contact is assumed when the total gravity-compensated ground contact force exceeds a magnitude of 12 N (dashed horizontal line in Figure 4.8). For the seven time intervals where this criterion was met, the lines of force action were computed for every sample of ankle-F/T measurements. Figure 4.9 shows the resulting bundles of force action lines, colored by the time of their occurrence as overlays over a 3D-model of the ARMAR-4 robot. The correspondingly colored spheres represent the ground truth push locations, and the red points found on every line mark the solutions of Equation 4.5.

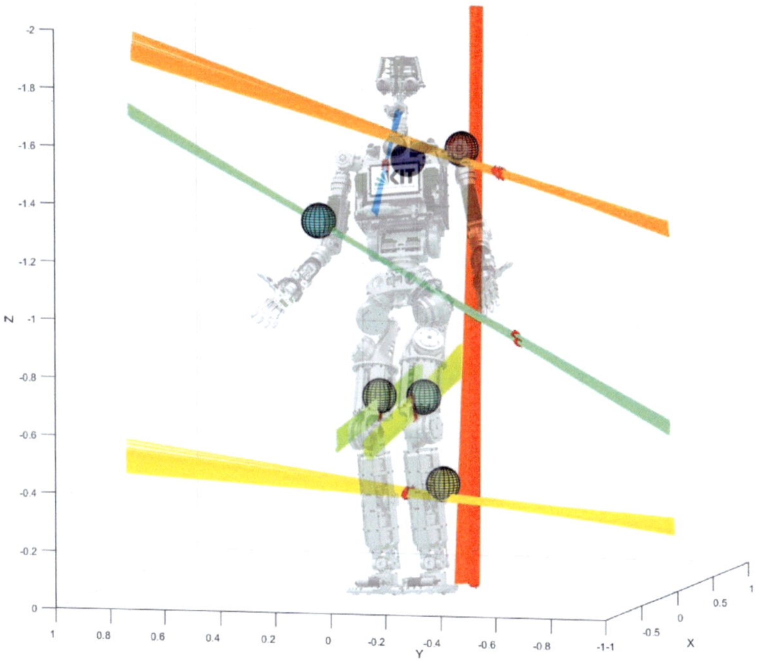

Figure 4.9: Lines of force action computed from the virtual contact wrenches shown in Figure 4.8, visualized on a model of ARMAR-4 together with the actual force application points, colored by time.

To validate the online capability of the method it was implemented in the ArmarX robot control framework (see Section C of the appendix) and executed on the ARMAR-4 robot in real-time for live visualization. Figure 4.10

shows images of the running system, where the robot is (1) pushed against the ankle and (2) pulled down on its right arm, with the visualization of the force lines in the background.

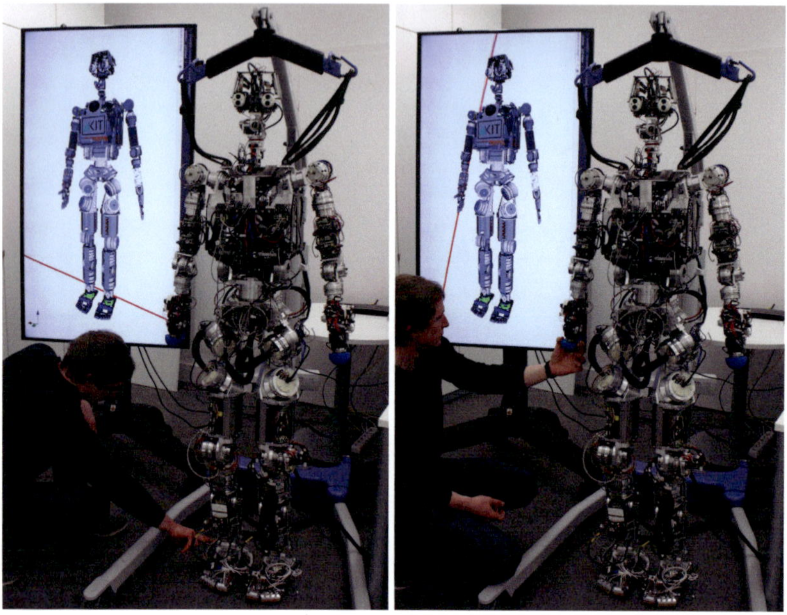

Figure 4.10: Validation experiment on the ARMAR-4, demonstrating online force line computation from ankle F/T sensors using Equation 4.6 for a push against the ankle (left) and a pull on the right arm (right).

The close correspondences of the computed line and the actual force application point in this experiment validate the method and show that, using the proposed computation, the line of force action of an external contact can be computed online from the measured foot contact wrenches in a dual contact configuration.

4.3 Dynamic Stability Estimation with Multiple IMUs

It was shown in Section 4.1 that a single body-worn inertial sensor can provide sufficient information for detecting a push, and serve as an indicator for whether a recovery step is necessary or not. This holds for a human subject initially standing still and was achieved by thresholding the estimated push intensity, adjusting the threshold according to the push direction.

The following section builds on these findings and is concerned with the exploration of novel methods for the case of a human or humanoid that is pushed while *in motion*. This problem, detecting dynamic instability from body mounted IMUs while executing *dynamic* motions, is significantly more involved due to the fact that the motion itself causes non-negligible IMU measurements that cannot be filtered out by direct thresholding.

While the work presented here is based on the hypothesis that a small number of inertial sensors can convey the information necessary to distinguish between dynamically stable and unstable states, it is neither assumed that one IMU is sufficient nor that thresholding on a one-dimensional feature will lead to satisfactory results. This work will therefore resort to supervised machine learning and will systematically investigate the number of sensors, their placement along the body and the type of classifier that leads to the best possible classification results. Trained on data acquired in human trials, the envisioned classifier predicts for every instant of the motion whether it is dynamically stable or unstable. Stable states in the training data of human motion recordings are the instants after which the human continues its motion normally, whereas dynamically unstable states are identified by subsequent active recovery actions such as side-stepping. A system like this, effectively representing the expert knowledge of humans with respect to the question whether a dedicated recovery action is necessary, will be useful for humanoid robots or assistive exoskeletons by helping to answer the same question. An overview over the envisioned system with the research questions to be answered is depicted in Figure 4.11. By limiting the system to a small number of easy to install sensors, applicability to a wide range of systems is facilitated.

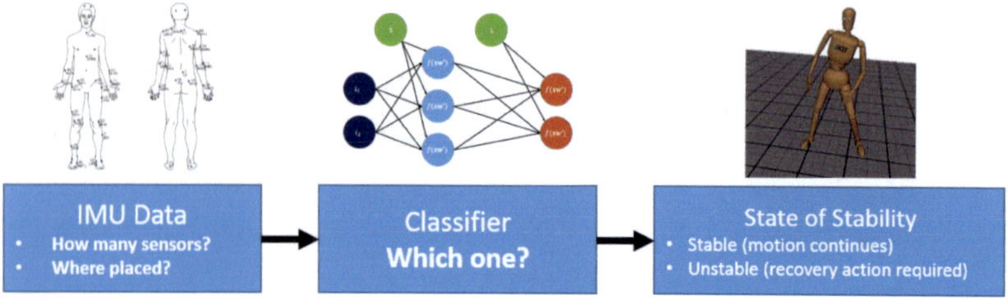

Figure 4.11: The aim is to find a classification system that maps data from a small number of body mounted IMUs to the binary state of dynamic stability. Such a system, trained on human expertise, can enable humanoid robots and wearable assistive devices to initiate balance recovery actions when necessary.

4.3.1 Methodology

For the training of different classifiers and comparison of their performance, suitable training data needs to be provided. Training the classification system on data that does not contain falls but only disturbed situations that the human subject could successfully recover from ensures that the resulting classifier is useful for *fall prevention*, and not a mere fall detector. Training on a dataset that includes recordings in which the disturbance occurred amidst dynamic locomotion assures that the classifiers learn to classify stability in diverse dynamic situations, and not implicitly learn to simply apply thresholding to the raw accelerations.

Data Preparation

The data used for training originates from the KIT Whole-Body Human Motion Database[5], a large collection of human motion data acquired using high-precision optical motion capture based on a set of 51 strategically placed reflective markers on the human body[6] [Mandery et al. 2016]. The motion data in this database is consistently represented in the *Master Motor Map* (MMM) data format[7] that represents motions as consecutive motion frames, sampled at 100 Hz. Each frame contains the 6 DoF pose (position and orientation) of the pelvis along with all individual joint angles.
The data in the database contains neither features in form of IMU measurements nor labels providing stability information, both of which are necessary for training IMU-based classifiers that can predict whether the state represented by a frame is unstable and thus necessitates active push recovery. These features and labels need to therefore be added by means of computational *data augmentation.*

Emulated IMUs Each IMU sensor mounted on the body provides a 9D signal, containing the 3D linear acceleration, 3D angular velocity and 3D orientation (obtained by means of sensor fusion)[8]. These sensor modalities need to be computationally emulated to augment the motion data and prepare it for the purpose of training the envisioned classification systems. From the infinite number of possible sensor locations along the human body, the 51 optical marker positions that constitute the MMM marker set were chosen. With the application of wearable assistive devices in mind, 17 sensor locations that were deemed impractical in daily activities because they would be difficult to integrate or to hide (such as on the head, the toes or

[5] `https://motion-database.humanoids.kit.edu/`
[6] `https://motion-database.humanoids.kit.edu/marker_set/`
[7] `https://mmm.humanoids.kit.edu/dataformat.html`
[8] Integrated IMU sensors typically provide 3-axis magnetometer signals in addition, which are not explicitly considered in this study.

the fingers) were excluded from the study, leaving 34 sensor locations for further investigation. Figure 4.12 shows all 51 optical marker positions, including the 34 positions of the emulated IMUs.

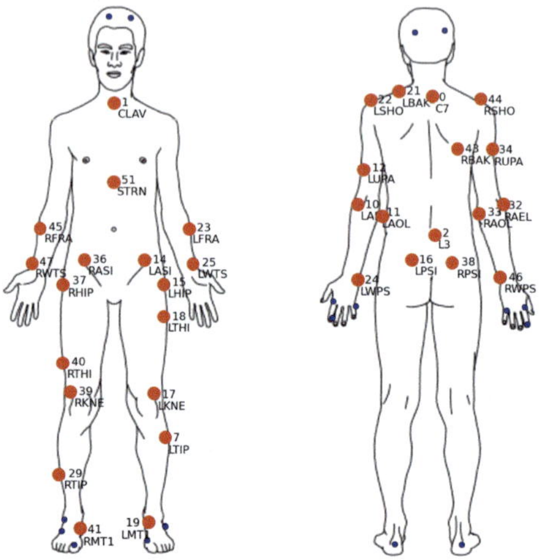

Figure 4.12: All 51 optical marker positions of the standard MMM marker set. Only these with a numerical label (highlighted in orange) were considered as locations for emulated IMUs (adapted from [Steffan et al. 2017], © 2017 IEEE).

The MMM motion files contain the pelvis (base) orientation and angular position of each joint. From this data and the kinematic description included in each MMM file, each link's orientation, as it would be measured by an actual IMU, can be computed with methods provided by the Simox toolbox [Vahrenkamp et al. 2013]. Obtaining the angular velocities and linear accelerations requires time differentiation and double time differentiation of the data, respectively. As numerical differentiation of the position-based data introduces significant noise, the derivatives are computed differently: To this end, the joint position data is represented by differentiable piece-wise cubic splines, and the local derivatives are computed analytically. This leads to significantly smoother rotational velocity and linear acceleration signals that were found to closely resemble those provided by real sensors. The computed emulated IMU-data is stored along the initial motion data and serves as the set of features associated with each motion frame for training the classifiers.

Labels Besides the features in form of emulated IMU data, training the different classifiers further requires labels associated with each motion frame. The binary label should represent a notion of stability, divided into two classes:

- **Dynamically Stable**: From the motion frame in question, the motion continues without noticeable changes to the initial intent, i. e. no dedicated push recovery effort is necessary.
- **Dynamically Unstable**: From the motion frame in question, the motion continues with a noticeable balance recovery effort, i. e. the current state necessitates dedicated measures of push recovery.

Different indicators of dynamic stability that can be derived from the body's kinematic and dynamic properties as well as from its base and joint velocities and accelerations were introduced in Chapter 2. The indicator that is most widely used is the ZMP, which can be calculated from data available in any original MMM motion file after computing the links' accelerations, using Equation 2.14 and Equation 2.15. As long as the ZMP is located within the support polygon (SP), the current state is guaranteed to be dynamically stable. This condition is commonly referred to as the *ZMP-criterion*. However, this geometric correlation only constitutes a sufficient criterion for dynamic stability, but not a necessary one. As such it is of great use for motion planning and control, but not for assessing highly adept motions of humans, which regularly violate this condition despite being dynamically stable. In fact, analyzing the motion recordings selected for training revealed that this strict criterion can be violated even during normal human walking.

To reliably assess the stability of highly dynamic whole-body motions, a novel ZMP-based criterion was devised that represents a relative measure of *how much* the ZMP criterion is violated. The underlying idea is that the violation, i. e. the distance between the current ZMP and the outer edge of the support polygon, must be viewed in relation to the size of the support polygon.

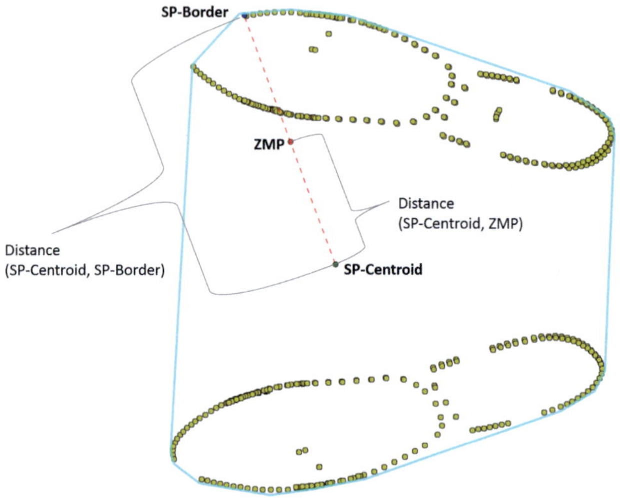

Figure 4.13: Exemplification of the ZMP-Ratio in a dynamically stable dual contact situation. Yellow dots mark contact points between the ground and the edges of the feet. The cyan line represents the outer boarder of the support polygon. The red dashed line is defined by the ZMP and the centroid of the support polygon. The ZMP-Ratio (Equation 4.10) in this case is smaller than one, indicating that the ZMP-criterion is fulfilled (adapted from [Steffan 2017]).

The size is expressed by the distance between the centroid of the support polygon and its edge, measured along the line that connects the centroid and the ZMP. This ratio, called the ZMP-Ratio, can be expressed as the fraction

$$\text{ZMP-Ratio} = \frac{\text{Distance(SP-Centoid, ZMP)}}{\text{Distance(SP-Centroid, SP-Border)}} \tag{4.10}$$

where SP stands for the support polygon and SP-Border for the intersection of the support polygon and the line between its centroid and the ZMP. Figure 4.13 visualizes the construction of the ZMP-Ratio.

A ZMP-Ratio that is smaller than 1 indicates that the ZMP lies inside the support polygon, in which case the ZMP-criterion is met and the sufficient condition for dynamic stability is fulfilled. A ZMP-Ratio greater than one indicates a violation of the ZMP-criterion and a potential dynamically unstable body configuration. The hypothesis that there exists a threshold value for the ZMP-Ratio that leads to the desired classification is the basis for the automated labeling process of each individual motion frame.

Algorithm 1 Automatic Labeling

Require:
F – MMM-file containing the frames f to be labeled
t_s – ZMP-Ratio stability threshold
addLabel() – Adds a label to a motion frame in F

```
function GENERATELABELS(F, t_s)
    for each f in F do
        compute ZMP                          ▷ Zero Moment Point
        compute SP-Centroid                  ▷ Support Polygon
        compute SP-Border
        compute ZMP-Ratio
        if ZMP-Ratio ≤ t_s then
            f.addLabel(stable)
        else
            f.addLabel(unstable)
        end if
    end for
    return F
end function
```

For each frame, the current support polygon is computed as the convex hull around the intersections of the feet and the ground plane based on the position data. Based on the velocity and acceleration data, the current ZMP is computed using Equation 2.14 and Equation 2.15. The resulting ZMP-Ratio is computed from these two intermediate results and translated into a binary label by comparing against a heuristically determined threshold value. This process is iteratively executed for all frames in each motion file, and the respective label is stored together with each frame. Algorithm 1 summarizes the labeling procedure.

Classification System

The design of the classification system that assigns a binary stability label to each motion instant consists of two parts, namely the sensor setup (number and locations) and the classifier.

Sensor Setup With respect to the optimal sensor setup, the two questions that need to be answered are

1. *How many* IMU sensors need to be placed along the body to collect sufficient data?
2. *Where* should these sensors be placed?

In the presented study the number of sensors n_s is constrained to

$$1 \leq n_s \leq 6, n_s \in \mathbb{N} \tag{4.11}$$

due to practicality considerations, accounting for cost, ease of use and system complexity in a later application of an actual system with real sensors. The possible sensor locations are the 34 selected positions (that coincide with a subset of the MMM optical marker set) depicted in Figure 4.12.
In order to identify the best sensor setup within this search space, an exhaustive search over all possible sensor setups is conducted by training the classifiers in question on the input data resulting from every setup. To this

end, one dataset for each possible combination of the number of sensors and the sensor locations is constructed, resulting in

$$\sum_{i=1}^{6} \binom{34}{i} = 1,676,115 \qquad (4.12)$$

individual sets of input data.

Classifiers With respect to the classifiers, the question to answer is which classification technique is best suited for the problem of predicting instability (i. e. the need for recovery action) from IMU data. Six common classifier types were investigated:

1. Naive Bayes (NB)
2. k-Nearest Neighbors (kNN)
3. Bagged k-Nearest Neighbors (Bagged-kNN)
4. Perceptron
5. Neural Network (NN)
6. Support Vector Machine (SVM)

The standard implementations of these classifiers from the *scikit-learn* library for Python [Pedregosa et al. 2011] were used. The essential hyperparameters of the classifiers are listed in Section F of the appendix.

4.3.2 Training and Evaluation on Human Motion Data

For the evaluation of different classifiers and sensor arrangements, 50 motion recordings consisting of nearly 30,000 motion frames were selected as training data. All these recordings contain push disturbances that provoke active push recovery. All motion files used for the evaluation are available in the KIT Whole-Body Human Motion Database and are listed in Section E of the appendix.

ZMP-Ratio Threshold Analysis of the motion data of these 50 motion trials revealed that the ZMP-Ratio indeed separates the human motions into the classes *Dynamically Stable* and *Dynamically Unstable* as defined above. In regular, visibly intended and undisturbed motions, the ZMP-Ratio remains generally smaller than 2.5. In contrast, in moments in which a significant disturbance (i. e. a push) occur and the subject has to change the initially planned motion to mitigate the disturbance, ZMP-Ratios (significantly) greater than 2.5 occur. Figure 4.14 visualizes these relations for every 10th frame of a motion in which the human subject walked forward, was pushed from the left and then continued to walk towards the intended goal.

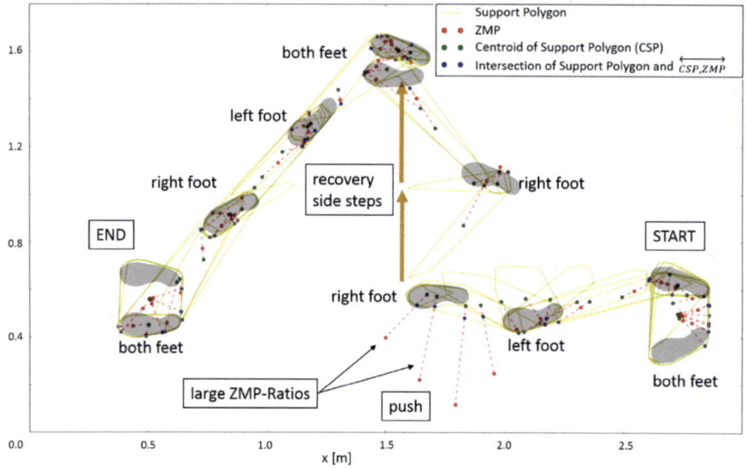

Figure 4.14: Top view of the support polygon (yellow), its centroid (green), the ZMP (red) and the intersection (blue) of the line (dashed red) defined by the ZMP and the centroid with the support polygon for every 10th frame of a motion in which the human subject walked forward, was pushed from the left and then continued to walk. Scale in meters (adapted from [Steffan et al. 2017], © 2017 IEEE).

Shown are the boundaries of the support polygon in yellow, its centroid as green dot, the current ZMP as red dot and the connection of the ZMP and the centroid as dashed red line. The intersection of this line and the boundary of the support polygon is marked with a blue dot. It is clearly visible that the ZMP leaves the support polygon and therefore the ZMP-Ratio becomes large during the time of the push, indicating that push recovery is necessary.

Classification System To find the best classification system consisting of the sensor arrangement (number of sensors and sensor locations) and the type of classifier, the performances of all possible combinations of the data from 1,676,115 different sensor arrangements and the six classifiers were compared. Evaluation of all systems was performed by means of stratified four-fold cross validation, a common evaluation metric in the related literature, as pointed out by [Jordao et al. 2018] in their survey on human activity recognition based on wearable sensor data. The reported results are the average results of the four validation sets.

Evaluation Metrics The annotated motion data has a strong bias towards the 'Stable' class, as the incidents of pushes and subsequent balance recovery only represent a small fraction of the recorded motion frames. This bias undermines the validity of the classification *accuracy* a (see Equation 4.13)[9] as a meaningful performance indicator, since a system that only predicts the label 'Stable' regardless of the input data achieves a high accuracy, despite its obvious flaw.

$$a = \frac{\#\text{CorrrectPredictions}}{\#\text{AllPredictions}} \tag{4.13}$$

A better suited performance indicator for binary classifiers on biased data is the F_1-*score* that takes precision and recall into account.

[9] Here and in the following, the symbol # is used as shorthand for 'number of'.

Precision p is the fraction of true positives (i. e. correctly identified instabilities) over all frames classified as positives, be it true or false. It thus indicates how trustworthy a positive classification is:

$$p = \frac{\#\text{TruePositives}}{\#\text{TruePositives} + \#\text{FalsePositives}} \tag{4.14}$$

Recall r is the fraction of true positives over all instabilities, detected or not (true positives and false negatives) that were correctly classified as such. It therefore indicates how reliable the classifier is.

$$r = \frac{\#\text{TruePositives}}{\#\text{TruePositives} + \#\text{FalseNegatives}} \tag{4.15}$$

The F_1-score finally is the harmonic mean of precision and recall, computed as

$$F_1 = 2\frac{p \cdot r}{p + r}. \tag{4.16}$$

An ideal binary classifier achieves an F_1 score of 100%, whereas the worst possible system achieves an F_1 score of 0%.

Results Table 4.3 presents the best obtained results for each of the six types of classifiers and each of the six investigated numbers of sensors in terms of the F_1-score, along with the underlying sensor placements. The last row gives the result for the respective classifier when trained on all 9 channels of all 34 emulated sensors, i. e. on 306 features.

Discussion The obtained results presented in Table 4.3, reveal a number of notable observations. Most interestingly, more sensors do no automatically lead to better classification results. In fact, the baseline result obtained by utilizing all 34 sensor locations is surpassed by the results obtained from a classifier operating on the single best sensor in the cases for the kNN, the Bagged-kNN and the Neural Net classifiers. The kNN-classifier for example reaches an F_1-score of 64% when trained on all 34 sensors, but reaches

# Sensors	Naive Bayes	k Nearest Neighbors	Nearest Neighbors Bagged	Perceptron	Neural Net	SVM
1	67% 40	68% 17	70% 32	63% 33	70% 38	55% 34
2	67% 14,40	75% 34,40	76% 0,36	70% 32,51	77% 24,36	67% 33,43
3	70% 39,40,43	76% 33,38,40	79% 10,16,44	73% 17,32,43	80% 1,40,47	73% 21,41,47
4	70% 1,2,41,46	75% 0,15,38,39	80% 29,34,37,44	76% 22,25,33,43	80% 0,39,40,46	74% 10,14,43,47
5	70% 14,32,40,41,51	78% 16,34,39,40,44	81% 0,43,36,37,39	76% 15,24,36,44,45	81% 23,38,39,46,51	76% 14,21,29,39,47
6	70% 15,33,39,40,41,51	77% 29,34,37,39,40,44	81% 29,33,34,36,38,43	73% 0,1,24,33,36,41	82% 1,2,23,41,46,47	76% 10,15,21,39,40,46
34 (all)	66%	64%	66%	61%	63%	66%

Table 4.3: Classification results (F_1-score in four-fold cross-validation) of the 36 classification systems as combinations of classification method (column) and number of used IMU sensors (row) that lead to the best F_1-scores among all possible systems with the same number of sensors. Each cell notes the sensor positions (see Figure 4.12 for reference) together with the achieved F_1-score. The result for each classification method operating on all 34 sensors is given in the last row as a baseline. Note that the numbers denote marker position indexes of the MMM reference marker set (that translate to emulated IMU positions) and thus can be higher than the number of 34 sensors. The red and green cells correspond to the red and green sensor positions depicted in Figure 4.15. Table adapted from [Steffan et al. 2017], © 2017 IEEE.

an even better result of 68% when trained on the single best sensor alone. Most of the classification systems show a relatively steep increase in performance when adding a second and a third sensor, exemplified by the SVM that improves from an F_1-score of 55% in the single sensor case to 73% when used with three sensors. For more than three sensors, performance often stagnates or even decreases, exemplified by the Bayes classifier that performs equally well at an F_1-score of 70% for 3, 4, 5 and 6 sensors. Only the Neural Net shows an improvement of one percentage point for the step from five to six sensors, with all other classifiers either stagnating or even degrading in performance during this step. An explanation for this observation could be what is commonly referred to as the *Curse of Dimensionality*. As the number of features increases the feature space exponentially expands, necessitating an ever larger amount of training data to appropriately fit high-dimensional models. The training data eventually becomes too sparse, and model performance decreases. This emphasizes the need for rigorous feature selection, as it was carried out in this study.

Another interesting observation is that the information about dynamic stability conveyed in the sensor signals is not cumulative, but a property of the specific combination of sensors used. That is to say that the optimal set of n sensors is in general not a subset of the optimal set of $n+m$ sensors. An example for this is the Bagged-kNN classifier, for which the best single sensor configuration consists of a sensor at position 32. However, this sensor position is not included in any of the other optimal configurations with 2, 3, 4, 5, or 6 sensors. This indicates that, while it is time consuming, an exhaustive search over all possible configurations must be performed in order to find the optimal system. Simply searching for the best sensor to add to an already evaluated setup is not likely to lead to the best performing system.

It is furthermore noteworthy that the questions of the absolute best (i. e. most informative) sensor location cannot be answered in isolation, only in conjunction with the classification algorithm being used. All of the six classifiers 'choose' a different sensor for the single sensor setup, even located on different body parts. While the Bayes and the kNN classifier choose a sensor on the leg, the neural network chooses one on the torso, and the remaining three choose a sensor on the arm.

4.3.3 Best Classification System

Of all the classification systems that were investigated, the neural network with access to six sensors at locations 1, 2, 23, 41, 46 and 47 performs the best with an F_1-score of 82%. Notably, and in congruence with the observations stated above, reducing the number of sensors down to three (replacing the four sensors at locations 2, 23, 41 and 46 by a single sensor at location 40) leads ot a performance drop of only two percentage points down to 80% (which is still the overall third best performance).

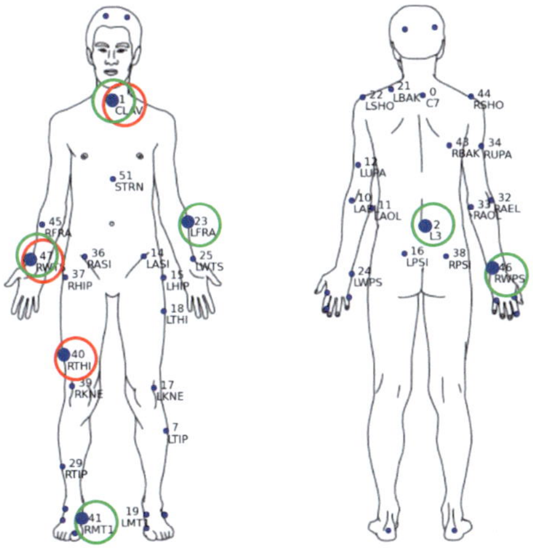

Figure 4.15: Sensor placements (large blue dots) for the best classification system based on a neural network classifier operating on the data of six sensors (green circles), and for the best setup with only three sensors (red circles), also based on a neural network (adapted from [Steffan et al. 2017], © 2017 IEEE).

This allows the conclusion that the neural network is the best suited classification algorithm for this task, and that even with as little as three sensors, results almost en par with the overall best system can be achieved. The sensor placements for both systems (six sensors and three sensors) are depicted in Figure 4.15.

With the reduced system, the dynamic stability can be assessed virtually instantly (at 100 Hz), well before a fall is inevitable. Inference of the neural network model with three sensors takes an average of 1.45 ms on an *Intel Core i7* CPU.

4.4 Summary and Review

This chapter introduced and validated the hypothesis that the first step in reacting to external disturbances, namely the perception of those disturbances and the resulting instable state, can be achieved with a small set of sensors. The proposed sensor setups are more specific than those commonly used for humanoid state estimation, and the proposed methods are fast. Viewing the human capabilities for balancing and push recovery as a remarkable and valuable source of information and inspiration for research of humanoid balance motivates the utilization of data captured in human push recovery trials.

First, it was shown that even a single, body-mounted inertial sensor (IMU) can be sufficient to sense the occurrence, the direction and the intensity of a push that an initially standing human is subjected to, and methods therefore were presented. It was shown that the perceived push intensity can indicate which strategy the human will choose to mitigate the push, i. e. either balancing in place or taking a recovery step. This insight can be leveraged for humanoid push recovery.

Secondly, a method was presented that enables a humanoid robot, equipped with F/T sensors in its ankle joints, to perceive the action line of a force that is exerted on arbitrary locations along its body. This extends the previously developed IMU-based capabilities to perceive the direction of the force, and hence can enable a robot to react more efficiently. The proposed method was validated on the ARMAR-4 humanoid robot. The IMU-based method and the F/T sensor-based method can be regarded as complementary: While a gravity-compensated acceleration signal can only be obtained in dynamic situations, the correct force line estimation relies on the assumption that dynamic effects are negligible. A combination of both methods is therefore a promising approach for detecting both, dynamic and static disturbances.

Lastly, building on the insights gained in the first part, a study on using supervised machine learning techniques for building a system that detects the necessity of push recovery actions from body worn inertial sensors even during dynamic locomotion was presented. This investigation was based on 50 recordings of human locomotion that were disturbed in a way that required significant recovery actions, but did not lead to falls. An exhaustive search to identify the ideal number of sensors, their ideal placement and the most suitable classification algorithm was conducted. The results indicate that a neural network with access to the data of only three inertial sensors on the human body can detect situations in which a human initiates active push recovery actions. A system like this, trained on human expert knowledge, together with disturbance estimation methods described earlier, can help humanoid robots and wearable assistive devices (such as robotic exoskeletons) to initiate successful push recovery actions when necessary, with minimal computational demands.

A notable feature of the presented classification method is the fact that it treats every frame individually. Future work could explore the possibility to operate on a window of a certain number of consecutive frames instead, potentially degrading the reaction time but increasing the overall F_1-score, as individual outliers could be detected and corrected.

5 Whole-Body Postural Balancing

Balancing in place by dynamically changing the body pose without taking a step, i. e. *Postural Balancing*, is the preferred human reaction to comparatively weak pushes. There are several advantages of postural balancing that motivates its priority over stepping. These advantages are valid for humans, for wearable assistive devices and for humanoid robot applications:

- Postural balancing takes place on footholds that are already known and proven to be stable, eliminating the risk of stepping on possibly unstable footholds (e. g. when traversing debris).
- Postural balancing can be performed in confined areas (e. g. close to a wall), where footholds required for stepping might not be available.
- The mechanical stress on the system (human or humanoid) associated with postural balancing is lower compared to the impact of a step.

This chapter therefore investigates the problem of robotic postural balancing and contributes to the ongoing research on how to devise an efficient (i. e. computationally light-weight) controller that can stabilize a humanoid robot after a push disturbance by generating whole-body motions. Many state-of-the-art methods address the postural balancing problem by generating joint torques for the humanoid robot by means of non-linear online optimization, formulated as a quadratic program (QP) that minimizes some notion of instability (see Section 3.3). While these methods are promising, their reliance on very accurate robot models and on the availability of powerful on-board computation hardware to solve a high-dimensional QP in real-time at high frequencies can be a significant hindrance to their application.

To alleviate the problematic need for powerful computational resources, attempts have been made to use *linear* optimal control theory for whole-body postural balancing, specifically linear quadratic regulators (LQR), notably in [Mason et al. 2014] and [Mason et al. 2016]. An LQR for whole-body balancing can be *optimized offline* and then executed on the robot in a real-time control loop. Since executing an LQR at runtime essentially only requires to perform a single matrix multiplication at each time step, the computation required is vastly smaller than in the aforementioned methods based on online optimization (see Section 2.3). This dramatic reduction in computational complexity is what makes this approach so interesting. However, applying linear control methods to whole-body postural balancing is not trivial, since the equations of motion of a humanoid robot are non-linear. When the robot is in ground contact its motion is unilaterally constrained (i. e. it can push but not pull on the ground), which is another fundamentally non-linear characteristic that needs to be reflected in the equations of motion. Horizontal stiction and friction forces in the ground contact also add to the overall non-linearity. While linearizing the unconstrained equations of motions around a nominal posture is straight-forward, finding a suitable linear model for the ground contact constraints that is sufficiently descriptive for the synthesis of capable linear balance controllers is still an open problem and has not been thoroughly addressed in the literature. The first main research question addressed in this chapter is therefore

1. Can a better *linear ground contact model* for the derivation of a whole-body balancing LQR improve its performance?

Once a linear model for the robot dynamics and ground contacts is formulated, the LQR method with weight matrices $\mathbf{Q}$ and $\mathbf{R}$ can be used to derive the state-feedback matrix $\mathbf{K}$ (see Equation 2.19 and Equation 2.20). This state-feedback controller with feedback gain $\mathbf{K}$ will be locally optimal for the linearized model, but not necessarily for the real, non-linear robot dynamics. To tune this controller in a way that makes it successfully applicable to the non-linear control problem one can systematically manipulate the entries of the design weight matrices **Q** and **R** in the design phase of the controller. This concept of weight-optimized LQR was described in the context of robotics by [Trimpe et al. 2014] and demonstrated on a low-dimensional robotic application (balancing a non-linear inverted pendulum) in [Marco et al. 2016]. In this thesis, it will be investigated whether this general approach can be used to optimize the design weights of a postural balancing LQR synthesized for a linear model that can then be applied to an accurately simulated, non-linear robot model. The second main research questions is therefore

2. Can the design matrices **Q** and **R** be systematically *optimized* to improve the performance of the resulting LQR postural balance controller for a non-linear simulated robot?

Eventually, both questions will be addressed in parallel by optimizing **Q** and **R** for different ground contact models. The final goal is to derive a linear balance controller that can stabilize the simulated ARMAR-4 robot by utilizing its entire body, i. e. the legs, the torso and the arms (see Figure 5.1). Table 5.1 summarizes the challenges of LQR balancing control. Dedicated contact modeling and weight optimization are envisioned to mitigate these challenges.

Benefits	**Challenges**
Highly efficient	• Only locally optimal due to linearization • No explicit constraint handling • No explicit consideration of the floating base

Table 5.1: The main benefit and the main challenges in applying linear balance control with the LQR method to the problem of whole-body balancing.

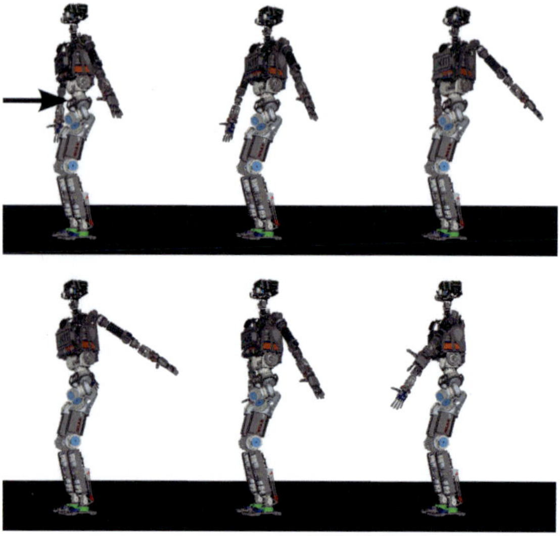

Figure 5.1: Preview of the intended result of the method presented in this chapter: The ARMAR-4 robot performing coordinated postural balancing motions with its legs, arms and torso to recover its balance after a frontal push (adapted from [Bäuerle et al. 2018], © 2018 IEEE).

The simulation-based evaluation embedded in the proposed optimization cycle requires a high number of trials in a physically consistent dynamics simulation. Due to small integration timesteps these simulations are very time-consuming, especially for robot models with a high number of DoFs (such as ARMAR-4 with 63 DoF in total). The proposed methods are therefore initially developed and evaluated using a simplified 2D humanoid model with only three DoFs (ankle, knee, hip) to make simulation and optimization more tractable (see Figure 5.8).

Based on the results obtained from the simplified model, the method is then generalized to 3D and a dual ground contact situation, and extended to take into account the possibility of swinging the arms. This extension is applied to the ARMAR-4 robot model and validated in simulated experiments. Parts of the Simulated Annealing based LQR weight optimization for whole-body balancing have been presented in [Bäuerle et al. 2018].

5.1 LQR for Whole-Body Balancing

Designing an LQR controller for a robot with m DoFs and n state variables (i. e. joint angles and velocities) requires three inputs:

1. A linear state space representation of the *open-loop system dynamics* in the form of the two matrices $\mathbf{A} \in \mathbb{R}^{n \times n}$ and $\mathbf{B} \in \mathbb{R}^{m \times m}$ (see Equation 2.17)

2. The *state cost matrix* $\mathbf{Q} \in \mathbb{R}^{n \times n}$ to penalize the deviation from the desired system state

3. The *control weight matrix* $\mathbf{R} \in \mathbb{R}^{m \times m}$ to penalize the control action

In the case of a humanoid robot as an underactuated system, the state vector $\mathbf{x} \in \mathbb{R}^{n \times 1}$ contains the positions and velocities of the k actuated DoFs of its joints and the v unactuated DoFs of the floating base.
For the here considered *simplified 2D model* with $m = 6$ DoFs ($k = 3$ actuated joints and $v = 3$, i. e. position and orientation of the floating base), the dimensionality n of the state vector $\mathbf{x}$ becomes

$$n = 2m = 12. \tag{5.1}$$

These relations are visualized in Figure 5.2. With $n = 12$ even in this simplified case, $\mathbf{Q}$ has 144 and $\mathbf{R}$ has 36 entries to be optimized. The quadratic growth of the number of entries of the weight matrices in the number of states lets optimizing the design weights of an LQR quickly become intractable. A common simplification is therefore to only take the *diagonal* entries of $\mathbf{Q}$ and $\mathbf{R}$ into account, the number of which is only linearly dependent on the number of states (see e. g. [Bryson and Ho 1975], [Lewis et al. 2012]). The off-diagonal elements remain zero in this case. Since this simplification significantly reduces flexibility in the controller design process, the next sections will introduce a method how physically meaningful (w. r. t. balancing) off-diagonal elements of **Q** can be constructed as *diagonal* elements in subspaces of **Q**.

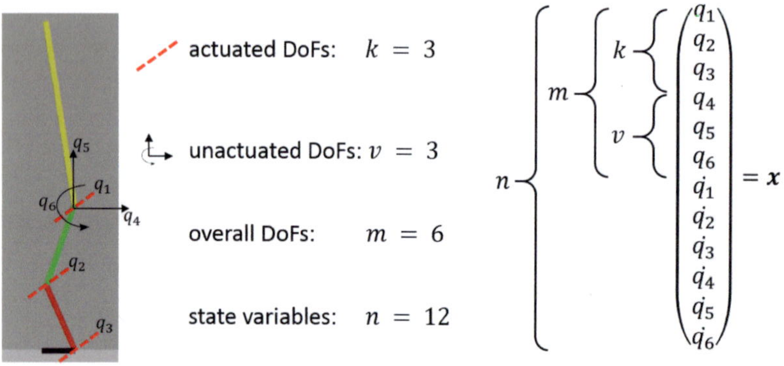

Figure 5.2: Composition of the state vector **x** of the simplified planar humanoid model with three actuated DoFs (hip, knee, ankle) and three unactuated DoFs of the floating base. Note that the hip is an actuated DOF, but the global orientation of the floating base that coincides with the hip is unactuated.

5.2 Cost Terms

The generic LQR cost with weight matrices **Q** and **R** is given in Equation 2.20. One of the underlying ideas of this chapter is that the gap between an LQ-controller and the physical, non-linear plant can be bridged by optimizing the entries of **Q** and **R**. This section will specify which entries are optimized and how they are chosen.

5.2.1 State Cost

The standard LQR-formulation with diagonal state cost matrix $\mathbf{Q}$ is generic in the sense that it directly penalizes the deviation from a desired system state $\mathbf{x}$, but no task-specific linear combinations of these deviations. For a mechanical system such as a balancing humanoid robot, the state $\mathbf{x}$ contains the joint positions $\mathbf{q}$ and velocities $\dot{\mathbf{q}} = 0$ of a nominal stable pose (see Figure 5.2).

However, penalizing the individual state-deviations does not directly incentivize the resulting controller to balance the robot, as long as no notion of stability is encoded in the structure of the state cost matrix (and hence in the objective of the controller). To reduce the dimensionality of the problem but still allow the optimization to find a capable balancing controller, a small number of additional, highly balancing-specific terms are added to $\mathbf{Q}$. These additional terms lead to a pre-structured cost matrix $\mathbf{Q}$ that is better suited to produce balancing controllers than a mere diagonal, but has less entries and can hence be optimized more efficiently than the complete $\mathbf{Q}$.

The idea behind creating such task-specific cost terms is that any quantity that can be represented as a linear combination of the state variables can be penalized by a task-specific *diagonal* cost matrix [Mason et al. 2014]. To this end, a transformation matrix $\mathbf{T} \in \mathbb{R}^{k \times n}$ transforms the system state into a more task specific quantity, which is penalized by a task-specific diagonal cost matrix $\mathbf{Q}_t \in \mathbb{R}^{k \times k}$ and transformed back into the space of $\mathbb{R}^{n \times n}$ of the state cost matrices by $\mathbf{T}^T$:

$$J = \int_0^\infty (\mathbf{x}(t)^T (\mathbf{T}^T \mathbf{Q}_t \mathbf{T}) \mathbf{x}(t) + \mathbf{u}(t)^T \mathbf{R} \mathbf{u}(t)) dt \qquad (5.2)$$

Using this method, task specific costs can be introduced by means of physically meaningful entries on the diagonals of the task-specific weight matrices $\mathbf{Q}_t$ rather than by means of off-diagonal entries in $\mathbf{Q}$ itself. As the resulting weight matrices are all elements of $\mathbb{R}^{n \times n}$ they can be summed to form a final overall cost matrix $\mathbf{Q}_f$, including a nominal cost matrix $\mathbf{Q}$ and an arbitrary number p of task-specific cost-terms $\mathbf{Q}_i$ such that

$$\mathbf{Q}_f = \mathbf{Q} + \mathbf{T}_1^T \mathbf{Q}_{t,1} \mathbf{T}_1 + ... + \mathbf{T}_p^T \mathbf{Q}_{t,p} \mathbf{T}_p \qquad p \in \mathbb{N} \tag{5.3}$$

In the work presented here, two such task-specific cost terms are added, namely on the deviation of the position of the CoM and on the overall angular momentum, following the suggestion of an *LQR-momentum controller* brought forward in [Mason et al. 2014]. The resulting final cost matrix $\mathbf{Q}_f$ thus incorporates the *pose cost* $\mathbf{Q}_0$, the *CoM cost* $\mathbf{Q}_1$ and the *angular momentum cost* $\mathbf{Q}_2$ matrices such that

$$\mathbf{Q}_f = \mathbf{Q}_0 + \mathbf{Q}_1 + \mathbf{Q}_2. \tag{5.4}$$

The following sections will elaborate on these three components of $\mathbf{Q}_f$.

Pose Cost

The diagonal elements of $\mathbf{Q}_0$ that penalize deviations from the nominal state ($\mathbf{q}$ and $\dot{\mathbf{q}}$) will be called the *pose cost.* A cost term exclusively associated with the joint velocities $\dot{\mathbf{q}}$ is already included in the angular momentum cost (see Equation 5.7). The velocity-related entries of the pose cost will therefore not be part of the optimization and remain at a constant value of 1. Only the pose cost entries associated with $\mathbf{q}$ will be part of the optimization, and $\mathbf{Q}_0$ is thus defined by the m entries of the diagonal pose weight matrix $\mathbf{Q}_P$ and structured as follows:

$$\mathbf{Q}_0 = \begin{pmatrix} \mathbf{Q}_P & \mathbf{0} \\ \mathbf{0} & diag(\mathbf{1}) \in \mathbb{R}^{m \times m} \end{pmatrix} \in \mathbb{R}^{n \times n} \tag{5.5}$$

CoM Cost

The position of the CoM is an important quantity in the context of humanoid balancing. If the robot is at rest, positioning the CoM over the support polygon ensures static stability. The CoM position is therefore added as an objective to the proposed controller in terms of a weight matrix that penalizes any horizontal deviation of the CoM from the center of the support polygon (or, in the 2D case, from the center of the foot). The initial state $\mathbf{x}_0$ of the robot is chosen such that the CoM of the resulting pose lies directly over the center of the support polygon, and the deviation from this positions is penalized. The position $\mathbf{r}_{CoM}$ of the CoM can be computed by multiplying the first m elements of the state vector $\mathbf{x}$ (the configuration vector $\mathbf{q}$) and the respective kinematic transformation matrix $\mathbf{T}_{CoM}(\mathbf{q})$ as

$$\mathbf{r}_{CoM} = \mathbf{T}_{CoM}(\mathbf{q})\mathbf{q}. \tag{5.6}$$

Since $\mathbf{T}_{CoM}(\mathbf{q})$ is in general non-linearly dependent on $\mathbf{q}$, the constant transformation matrix $\mathbf{T}_{CoM}(\mathbf{q}_0)$ formed at the pose of the nominal state $\mathbf{x}_0$ is used, making this transformation only locally correct. The position of the CoM can, once computed with Equation 5.6, be weighted in the cost function by the diagonal elements of the CoM weight matrix $\mathbf{Q}_{CoM}$ to form a weight matrix $\mathbf{Q}_1$ with

$$\mathbf{Q}_1 = \begin{pmatrix} \mathbf{T}_{CoM}^T(\mathbf{q}_0)\mathbf{Q}_{CoM}\mathbf{T}_{CoM}(\mathbf{q}_0) & \mathbf{0} \\ \mathbf{0} & \mathbf{0} \end{pmatrix} \in \mathbb{R}^{n \times n} \tag{5.7}$$

Angular Momentum Cost

Angular momentum, commonly denoted with the letter L, is a dynamic quantity of mechanical systems that can be intuitively understood as the product of the moment of inertia and the angular velocity of a rigid body (see Equation 2.4). Including the objective of minimizing the angular momentum

into balance control is motivated by the finding that the ground reaction forces exerted by humans during dynamic walking can largely be explained by a zero angular momentum hypothesis [Herr and Popovic 2008], implying that regulating the angular momentum to 0 is beneficial for human and humanoid balancing. This insight has already been applied to whole-body humanoid balancing, e. g. in [Lee and Goswami 2012].
In contrast to the CoM position, the angular momentum is dependent on the specific reference point it is computed for. In the case of a balancing system, a meaningful and commonly used reference point for the angular momentum is the system's overall CoM, in which case the angular momentum is referred to as the *centroidal momentum* and can be computed from the system state by multiplication with the centroidal momentum matrix $\mathbf{A}_G$:
„*The centroidal momentum of a humanoid robot is the sum of the individual link momenta, after projecting each to the robot's Center of Mass (CoM). Centroidal momentum is a linear function of the robot's generalized velocities and the Centroidal Momentum Matrix is the matrix form of this function.*"[Orin and Goswami 2008].
The vector $\dot{\mathbf{q}}$ of generalized velocities is the second half of the state vector $\mathbf{x}$, and with the relationship described in [Orin and Goswami 2008], the angular momentum can be computed as

$$\mathbf{L}_{CoM} = \mathbf{A}_G(\mathbf{q})\dot{\mathbf{q}}. \tag{5.8}$$

Analogously to $\mathbf{T}_{CoM}(\mathbf{q})$, the non-linear dependency of $\mathbf{A}_G$ on $\mathbf{q}$ is eliminated by using the constant centroidal momentum matrix $\mathbf{A}_G(\mathbf{q}_0)$ of the nominal pose $\mathbf{x}_0$, and the cost of non-zero angular momentum can be expressed by the diagonal elements of a dedicated weight matrix $\mathbf{Q}_L$. Under the above-mentioned linearization, the cost term $\mathbf{Q}_2$ in the overall LQR optimization criterion related to the angular momentum is independent of the joint positions and can consequently be expressed as

$$Q_2 = \begin{pmatrix} \mathbf{0} & \mathbf{0} \\ \mathbf{0} & \mathbf{A}_G^T(\mathbf{q}_0)\mathbf{Q}_L\mathbf{A}_G(\mathbf{q}_0) \end{pmatrix} \in \mathbb{R}^{n\times n} \tag{5.9}$$

5.2.2 Actuation Cost

The diagonal elements of **R** result in a direct penalization of the control effort exerted on the respective joint. For a system like the ARMAR-4 model where every joint is individually actuated and there is no actuation coupling, the off-diagonal elements of **R** can generally be left zero and only the diagonal elements that directly penalize the actuation need to be considered. Thus, the actuation weight matrix **R** becomes

$$\mathbf{R} = diag(r_i) \in \mathbb{R}^{m\times m}, \qquad i = 1...m \tag{5.10}$$

with r_i being subject to optimization.

Note on Floating-Base Systems It should be noted that the LQR design method is intended for fully actuated systems, and that the controller will produce control actions for the unactuated DoFs of the floating base (i. e. forces and torques), which the underactuated robot cannot exert. This, in addition to the non-linearity of the robot, is a structural mismatch between the controller and the real system that needs to be addressed by weight optimization. The diagonal of the matrix **R** contains elements that are in charge of appropriately penalizing these physically infeasible control actions.

Note on Constraints The LQR formalism, in contrast to control methods based on online optimization such as MPC or constrained QPs, is not able to directly take into account constraints on the state or the control. In the case of humanoid postural balancing, state constraints are the angle and velocity limits of the joints, and control limits are the maximum joint torques that can be provided by the robot's actuators. When designing the LQR, these constraints can only implicitly be taken into account by weighting the state deviation and control effort appropriately. During controller evaluation, the control action can be limited to the maximum admissible level, and it can be validated whether the state constraints are observed.

5.3 Linear Contact Models

The work presented in this chapter is based on the hypothesis that the deviation between the physical ground contact and any linearized representation thereof in the linear model of the robot dynamics (i. e. the equations of motion) significantly influences controller performance. This motivates a thorough investigation of different ground contact models and their influence on the resulting controller performance. To this end, two contact models that are novel in the context of linear balancing controllers are introduced, namely *Springs* and *High Inertia*, and compared to the established *Clamped* model of a rigid coupling between the robot and the ground (see Figure 5.3).

(a) Clamped (b) Springs (c) High Inertia

Figure 5.3: Three different ground contact modeling approaches: (a) clamped to the ground, (b) springs and (c) high foot inertia (adapted from [Bäuerle et al. 2018], © 2018 IEEE).

These models are used exclusively in the design phase of the balancing controller. All evaluation experiments are conducted in a simulated setup in which the ground contact is modeled in a non-linear manner, or, to put it in a more illustrative way: The controllers are designed in three different linear worlds, but evaluated in the same non-linear world.

5.3.1 Clamped

As the feet of the robot do not change their position during postural balancing, a common representation of the ground contact is a fixed connection to the ground, i. e. a strict pose constraint on each foot that does not allow it to move with respect to the world frame. This model will be referred to as the *clamped* contact model (see Figure 5.3(a)). While conceptually simple, this model has the significant disadvantage that the robot can exert arbitrarily large forces and moments on the ground that are not reflected in the state vector, and can thus not be prevented by any of the state cost terms. This incites the balancing controller to predominantly make use of the *ankle strategy*[1] (see Section 3.3), which is sufficient in the case of arbitrarily high possible moments between the feet and the ground, as opposed to whole-body motions including the legs, hips and arms to compensate the disturbance which are necessary in reality. This effect can be seen in Figure 3.5 taken from the work of [Mason et al. 2014], where the overall body-configuration remains largely the same during push recovery, while balancing is mainly achieved by relying on the ankle strategy.

5.3.2 Springs

Replacing the stiff coupling between the foot and the ground, i. e. the rigid pose constraint, by linear elastic elements (springs) can mitigate some of the problems resulting from the clamped contact model. A linear spring with a

[1] i. e. relying on the ankle joints and keeping the rest of the body stiff

given stiffness c_i is added between the world frame and the foot for every translational and rotational DoF, resulting in three springs for the planar 2D case (see Figure 5.3(b)) and six springs per foot for the 3D case. The springs simply add additional generalized forces $\mathbf{f}_i$ to the equations of motion by means of

$$\mathbf{f}_i = c_i \mathbf{A}_{t,i}(\mathbf{q}_0 - \mathbf{q}) \tag{5.11}$$

for the case of translational DoFs, where the matrices $\mathbf{A}_{t,i}$ transform deviations from generalized coordinates to foot coordinates and $\mathbf{q}_0$ are the coordinates of the nominal pose around which the dynamics are linearized. The springs thereby introduce a linear relationship between the forces and moments at the ground contact, which are *not* part of the robot state, and the generalized robot coordinates, which are part of the robot state. By penalizing the foot *rotation* (which does not exist in the clamped contact formulation) in the state costs, the ankle torque or the moment that the robot exerts on the ground can be penalized implicitly, and thus the controller can be incentivized to *limit this moment*. A similar consideration goes into the translational DoFs. By allowing the foot to *translate*, state cost terms can be found that penalize this translation and hence limit horizontal forces, which is crucial in the real-world to stay within *friction limits* and avoid slippage. Ultimately, the non-rigid contact formulation introduces some, albeit implicit, information about the contact forces and torques into the controller design process that can be exploited (in the optimization process described later) by finding state and actuation cost terms that result in a controller that will keep those forces and moments sufficiently small.

5.3.3 High Inertia

Alongside the hypothesized benefits of the linear spring-based contact model, there are two main disadvantages associated with it:

- Each spring is characterized by its stiffness c_i, adding three additional stiffness parameters to the model in the 2D case and six additional stiffness parameters per foot in the 3D case that enlarge the parameter space for the optimization described in Section 5.4.

- Modeling springs for the foot deviations as described in Equation 5.11 requires providing the linearized explicit matrices $\mathbf{A}_{t,i}$, which adds complexity to the equations of motion.

Another linear ground model is therefore proposed that, although being more abstract, has similar virtues as the spring model and is arguably more elegant and easier to implement. It only consists of an artificially inflated mass of the foot, schematically depicted in Figure 5.3(c). This method of representing the ground contact will be called the *High Inertia* model, as the increased mass results in high inertial forces and moments at and around the feet, which can be viewed as an emulation of the actual ground reaction forces and moments. In addition to providing emulated contact forces and moments, this formulation still allows the feet to rotate and translate in space (similar to the spring model), providing a relation between exerted forces and moments on the one hand and state deviations on the other. These deviations in the state vector can be penalized by the state cost term. This model only requires the adaptation of one scalar parameter in the equations of motion, namely the foot mass. Moreover, it is hypothesized that any sufficiently high mass (on the order of the overall nominal[2] robot mass) is an appropriate choice, and hence the mass parameter does not need to be included in the optimization.
In contrast to the spring model, the relationship between generalized forces and displacements however is not as intuitive, as deviations only occur over time caused by the force-induced accelerations.
Since the high inertia model is not able to reproduce any static forces that can act to compensate gravity, a constant vertical force $\mathbf{f}_g$ acting at the center of the foot and equating to the gravitational force caused by the overall robot

[2] *nominal* meaning without additional foot mass

mass m_r and the gravitational acceleration $\mathbf{g}$ is added to the equations of motion with

$$\mathbf{f}_g = m_r \mathbf{g}. \tag{5.12}$$

This contact emulation is simple and elegant, and can very easily be extended to multiple ground contacts by increasing the respective contact links' masses and distributing the gravity-compensating force f_g over those links.

5.4 Optimization of LQR Design Weights

The main hypothesis of the work presented in this chapter is that the performance of an LQR balance controller with the task-specific cost terms described in Section 5.2 can be improved by systematically optimizing the entries of these cost terms. The target for which parameters are optimized is the simulated robot's resilience against frontal pushes, expressed by the transmitted impulse p, measured in Ns. Since every optimization cycle requires the run of at least one evaluation experiment in a dynamics simulator, the optimization is very time consuming. The evaluation of the proposed methods is therefore carried out by making use of the planar 2D robot model with 3 actuated DoFs rather than using the much more complex 3D model of the ARMAR-4 robot, which will be used for later validation.

5.4.1 Optimization Cycle

Starting with a random initial distribution of the free parameters of the LQR weight matrices, a full state feedback LQR controller (i. e. a gain matrix $\mathbf{K}$) is synthesized by solving the discrete algebraic Ricatti equation (DARE), symbolized by the top box in Figure 5.4 ('LQR controller synthesis'). This process is *dependent* on the type of contact model used, as the contact model is reflected in the linearized robot model used for controller synthesis. In the next phase of the optimization cycle, the newly found controller is evaluated.

This is achieved through iterative simulated experiments, in which the simulated robot is pushed with increasing intensity until it falls over, depicted in the right box of Figure 5.4. This evaluation is *independent* of the contact model, i. e. the same, non-linear simulation is used to evaluate each controller independently of the contact model that underlies its synthesis. The maximum push intensity that the simulated robot is able to withstand is considered the *controller performance*. This performance measure, together with the weight parameters that define the controller, are then fed to the optimizer (left box in Figure 5.4), which generates a new set of *design weights*, i. e. entries of the cost matrices. This cycle repeats until the optimization converges or a pre-defined maximum number of iterations is executed.

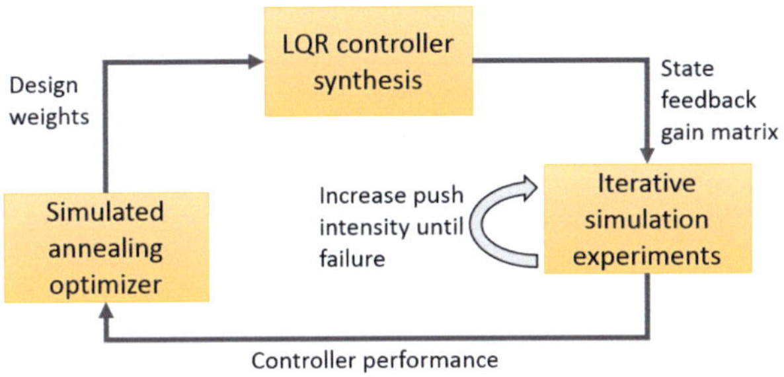

Figure 5.4: Iterative LQR weight parameter optimization through Simulated Annealing and simulation-based evaluation.

By far the most computation time within this cycle is needed for the iterative simulation-based evaluation experiments, which is why a simplified robot model that can be simulated faster significantly speeds up this optimization.

5.4.2 Simulated Annealing

The mapping from the weight parameters of the LQR synthesis to controller performance for which the optimization shall find the global optimum is unknown, and so is its gradient. This necessitates a gradient-free, sampling based optimization technique to generate new weight parameter candidates in the optimization cycle. The fact that evaluating these candidates in the dynamics simulation is expensive adds the requirement of sample-efficiency. A number of techniques to address this class of problems exists[3]. In this work, *Simulated Annealing* was chosen as it satisfies all aforementioned criteria.

Simulated Annealing is a meta-heuristic for the generation of new candidate solutions, given previous candidate solutions and their performance (or cost). Its functioning is inspired by the behavior of molecules in metallurgical heat-treatment processes (*annealing*), or more precisely during the cool-down phases of these processes. This behavior is governed by a decreasing temperature parameter. Simulated Annealing as an optimization procedure can be summarized by the following two steps:

1. For a given initial candidate solution W (a set of LQR weights in the presented case), the performance p (i. e. the maximum withstandable push) is sampled.

2. Repeat until termination with decreasing temperature T:

   a) A new solution candidate W_{new} in the *neighborhood* of the last candidate is chosen and evaluated.

   b) If the new candidate W_{new} results in better performance p_{new} than its predecessor W, W_{new} replaces W. If W_{new} also leads to the best performance seen so far, it is saved as W_{opt}. If it results in worse performance than W, it only replaces W with a certain probability $\varepsilon < 1$ that depends on its performance p_{new},

[3] e. g. Genetic Algorithms, Particle Swarm Optimization or Pattern Search, to name a few alternatives

the performance p of the previous candidate W and the current temperature T such that the acceptance probability ε is

$$\varepsilon = exp\left(\frac{p_{new} - p}{T}\right). \tag{5.13}$$

Pseudocode for the implementation of Simulated Annealing for LQR weight optimization is given in Algorithm A.4 in the appendix.

The essence of Simulated Annealing is captured in Equation 5.13. Note that ε_n is only computed when $p > p_{new}$ and hence the argument of the exponential function is always negative, confining the acceptance probability to the range $0 \leq \varepsilon \leq 1$. At an initially high temperature, ε is close to 1, and Simulated Annealing resembles a random walk, focusing on exploration of the solution space, virtually accepting every new solution candidate, be it better or worse than the previous one. This behavior ensures avoiding stagnation in local optima. As the temperature decreases so does ε, and the procedure becomes greedier, until it eventually resembles the hill-climbing meta-heuristic, only accepting candidate solutions that actually improve performance, ensuring convergence towards an optimum.

As with other gradient-free, stochastic optimization techniques, Simulated Annealing is not guaranteed to find the global optimum. However, starting from a high temperature and decreasing it slowly makes it less likely to prematurely end up in a local optimum (like purely greedy hill-climbing would).

5.4.3 Parameter Space of the 2D Model

The design weights of the balancing controller, which form the free parameters in the optimization, are the state cost **Q** described in Section 5.2.1 and the actuation cost **R** described in Section 5.2.2. The planar 2D model with $k = 3$ and $m = 6$ and an overall mass of 7.8 kg has three unactuated DoFs of the floating base and three actuated joints. This leads to six entries in the state vector that define the pose $\mathbf{q}$ and hence six entries along the diagonal of the pose cost $\mathbf{Q}_p$ (see also Figure 5.2 for clarification). The planar position of the CoM can be described by two spatial coordinates and hence the CoM cost $\mathbf{Q}_{CoM}$ has two entries on its diagonal. The angular momentum only exists around one axis, turning the angular momentum cost $\mathbf{Q}_L$ into a scalar parameter. The three actuated DoFs afford an actuation cost matrix $\mathbf{R}$ with three entries on the diagonal. Overall, the LQR design weight space consists of 15 parameters that will be optimized. The optimization will be carried out in the same manner for all three contact models described earlier. In addition, the stiffness parameters in the spring contact model are also parameters to be optimized, leading to an 18-dimensional space of free parameters in the case of the spring contact formulation. Table 5.2 lists all free parameters, their type and their dimensionality.

Type		**Name**	**#Parameters**
State cost	Posture	$\mathbf{Q}_p$	6
	CoM position	$\mathbf{Q}_{CoM}$	2
	Momentum	$\mathbf{Q}_L$	1
Actuation cost		$\mathbf{R}$	6
(Contact)		(c_i)	(3)
			15 (18)

Table 5.2: The 15 free parameters in the LQR optimization for the planar 2D model (see Section 5.2 for further explanations). The stiffness parameters are only part of the optimization when the spring contact model is considered, leading to 18 free parameters in this case.

5.4.4 Parameter Space of the 3D Model

Only accounting for the legs, the torso, the shoulder and the arms (i. e. the *major* joints), the ARMAR-4 robot with an overall mass of 73.9 kg has 30 actuated and six unactuted DoFs, as opposed to 3 actuated and 3 unactuated DoFs in the 2D planar model. Owing to the exponential increase of possible parameter combinations with the number of DoFs of the robot and the significant evaluation time due to more complex simulation, it is therefore necessary to reduce the size of the parameter space of the 3D model. This is to ensure that the optimization converges within a feasible timeframe (on the order of weeks on a standard *Intel Core i7* CPU). The necessary dimensionality reduction of the parameter space is achieved by applying the following four heuristics:

1. **Model reduction:** Only a subset of the 30 major DoFs of the robot is chosen to take part in the balancing motions. These are the six DoFs per leg, two DoFs of the torso, and two DoFs per shoulder that enable arm swing, totaling 18 actuated DoFs and the 6 unactuated DoFs of the floating base.
2. **Symmetry exploitation:** Taking advantage of the robot's symmetry about the sagittal plane, identical state and actuation weights are chosen for the left and right instances of a joint, e. g. both knees share the same weight parameters.
3. **Consolidation:** Several joints are grouped and share the same weight parameters based on their semantic similarity. Concretely, all three joints of a hip share the same state and actuation cost parameters, as do the six DoFs of the floating base.
4. **Cost Simplification:** Although the controller for the 2D model includes the angular momentum in the cost term, it is omitted in the cost formulation of the 3D model, eliminating three dimensions from the parameter space. This is partially motivated by [Mason et al. 2014], who found that controllers with and without taking the angular momentum into account show similar performance. The CoM position is only considered in the frontal and vertical direction. Furthermore,

only the high inertia contact model with constant feet masses is considered, eliminating the spring parameters from the parameter space.

Applying those heuristics leads to a 20-dimensional parameter space for the 3D model, the entries of which are detailed in Table 5.3.

Type		Name	#Parameters	#Free parameters
State cost	Posture	$\mathbf{Q}_p$	24	9
	CoM Position	$\mathbf{Q}_{CoM}$	2	2
Actuation cost		$\mathbf{R}$	24	9
				20

Table 5.3: The 20 free parameters in the controller optimization for the 3D ARMAR-4 model. The number of parameters is reduced by means of model reduction and simplification, and the number of resulting free parameters is further reduced by consolidating joints and exploiting the robot's symmetry.

5.4.5 Implementation

The entire optimization cycle depicted in Figure 5.4 was implemented in *MATLAB/Simulink*, with the dynamics simulation experiments being executed in the *SimMechanics* simulation environment. Once the equations of motion are set up and linearized around a stable initial pose, the state feedback balance control gain matrix $\mathbf{K}$ can be obtained by handing the parameter matrices $\mathbf{A}$ and $\mathbf{B}$ of the open loop dynamics together with the LQR weight matrices $\mathbf{Q}$ and $\mathbf{R}$ to the MATLAB *lqr()*-routine.
The evaluation of the controller with state feedback $\mathbf{K}$ is then carried out in the dynamics simulation, in which pushes are iteratively increased for each successive experiment until the simulated robot falls. The pushes are applied from the front at hip height, and implemented as a rectangular force profile with a force duration of 500 ms for the planar model and 250 ms for the 3D model. Figure 5.8 shows several snapshots of the simulation visualization of the planar robot. The strongest push the root could withstand is returned to

the Simulated Annealing procedure, implemented in MATLAB, to generate the next set of design weights to be evaluated.

Non-linear Contact Model for Evaluation The ground contact model in the Simulink simulation is implemented by means of unilateral springs ($10^5\,\frac{\mathrm{N}}{\mathrm{m}}$) and dampers ($10^4\,\frac{\mathrm{Ns}}{\mathrm{m}}$) in the vertical direction and viscous friction ($1.5 \cdot 10^3\,\frac{\mathrm{Ns}}{\mathrm{m}}$) in the horizontal direction. Springs and dampers are attached to the corners of the model's feet, resulting in two force application points on the 2D model and four application points per foot for the 3D model. The vertical damped springs are only active and exclusively pushing the robot up when the respective point on the foot is below the ground level, mimicking the stiffness of the floor and the robot's soles. The horizontal viscous damping is also only active when the respective point on the foot has ground contact (i. e. is below the floor surface), mimicking the actual contact friction. The parameters of the ground model are chosen such that a stiff contact behavior with no visible slip is achieved, and stable and reproducible simulation results can be obtained. Simulink automatically choses sufficiently small simulation timesteps well below 1 µs to ensure that the simulation is reproducible even in the presence of very stiff contacts.

5.5 Evaluation in Dynamics Simulation

The goal of the evaluation is to address the two initial main questions, i. e. to show whether the linear ground contact abstraction has an influence on the controller performance, and whether the proposed parameter optimization cycle can successfully improve balance performance. The quantitative evaluation is based on the planar 2D model, as it is a sufficient platform that captures the non-linear robot dynamics and the ground contact, while allowing for much faster data generation than the 3D model. A similar optimization process, over the parameter space described in Section 5.4.4, is subsequently carried out to validate the feasibility of the approach for the more complex 3D model of the ARMAR-4 robot and to assess the qualitative characteristics of the resulting balancing motions.

5.5.1 Contact Model

The first question to answer is whether the contact formulation incorporated in the linearized robot model affects the balance controller performance.

Setup To evaluate the effects of the contact model on the balancing performance in an isolated manner, the optimization cycle depicted in Figure 5.4 is modified to incorporate fully randomized design weight generation instead of the Simulated Annealing optimizer, essentially swapping the Simulated Annealing meta-heuristic for a Random Walk through the parameter space. The same set of randomized parameters is used to synthesize and evaluate a controller for each of the three contact models. The controller performance is not fed back to the parameter generator, but saved for later analysis. This process is schematically depicted in Figure 5.5.

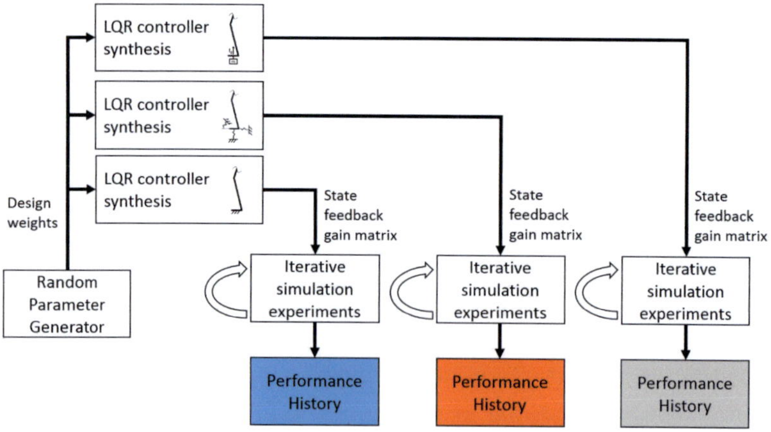

Figure 5.5: Automated data generation process for isolated contact model evaluation.

Results Overall, 10,000 random parameter sets for the 2D model were generated and the resulting controllers were evaluated, requiring 30,000 iterative simulated experiments. Figure 5.6 shows a histogram of the balancing performance for the obtained controllers resulting from the three contact model types (10,000 controllers per contact model), where only controllers that could withstand pushes of 3.5 Ns or more are taken into account. Shown are the numbers of controllers for each contact model that achieve a certain performance in terms of the maximum push they can withstand, where higher numbers for stronger pushes indicate a better contact model. Without active balance control, the model falls from a push of as little as 1 Ns.

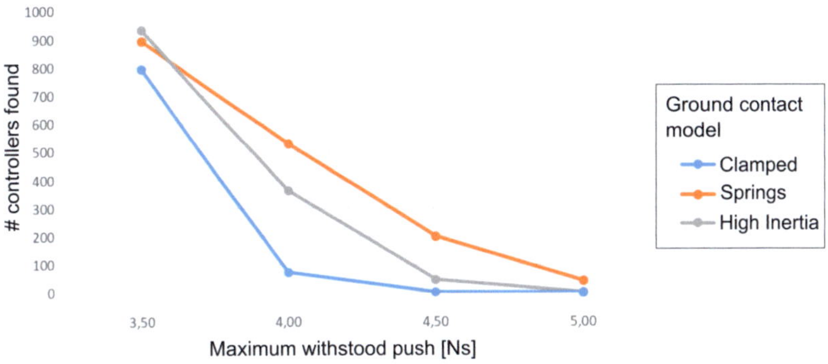

Figure 5.6: Results after 10,000 runs of the performance data generation process with random weight parameters depicted in Figure 5.5. Shown are the numbers of controllers with a certain performance (performance occurrences) for the three contact models clamped (blue), springs (orange) and high inertia (gray) (adapted from [Bäuerle 2018]).

The histogram shows distinct differences between the capability of the contact model types to produce good controllers. The spring contact model produces controllers that perform better in the non-linear simulation environment for stronger pushes than the other two contact models. For the strongest considered pushes of 5 Ns, spring model based controllers are in

fact the only ones that can stabilize the robot, with controllers based on the clamped model already entirely failing at pushes of 4.5 Ns.
From this analysis it can be concluded that the contact model considered in the linearized open loop dynamics has in fact an influence on the controller performance in the non-linear evaluation, and that other models than the clamped contact model used in the literature lead to better balancing controllers. This is true for both novel contact models considered here, where the spring contact model leads to the best results, followed by the high inertia contact model.

5.5.2 Optimization

The second main question to answer in this chapter is whether systematic optimization of the weight parameters, as opposed to choosing them randomly as in Section 5.5.1, can lead to improved controller performance. To answer this question, the optimization cycle with Simulated Annealing depicted in Figure 5.4 was run for 10,000 times, for each of the three contact models. The evolution of the current best performance values over the course of the optimization is shown in Figure 5.7 (note that the horizontal axis is scaled logarithmically).
It can be seen that for all three contact models, the performance of the current best controller improves continuously throughout the optimization process. The majority of the improvements are made early on in the optimization, with the steepest performance gain during the first 100 iterations, i. e. in the first 1% of the iterations. While the results continuously improve, the performance gain slows down significantly during the remainder of the optimization process.
The final performance after 10,000 iterations of Simulated Annealing is higher in all three contact model cases than after random parameter sampling by at least 10% (see Table 5.4).

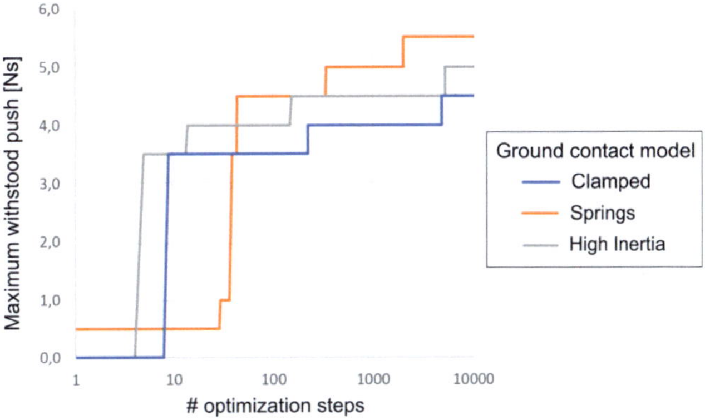

Figure 5.7: Current best performance (measured by the impulse in *Ns* of the applied push) of the balance controllers based on the three investigated contact models over the course of 10,000 steps of weight parameter optimization with Simulated Annealing (adapted from [Bäuerle 2018]; see also Figure 5.4).

Model	Random	Simulated Annealing	Improvement
Clamped	4.0	4.5	12.5%
Springs	5.0	5.5	10%
High Inertia	4.5	5.0	11.1%

Table 5.4: Maximum balance controller performance measured in *Ns* of the applied frontal push after 10,000 iterations of random parameter selection, and after 10,000 iterations of Simulated Annealing (SA) optimization for all three contact models. The rightmost column shows the improvement achieved with SA over random parameter selection.

This leads to the conclusion that the application of systematic parameter optimization with Simulated Annealing is in fact a successful method to improve the overall push recovery performance of LQR balance controllers, independent of the underlying linear contact model. These results are furthermore consistent with the results obtained from purely randomized parameter sampling, as both methods reveal the influence of the contact model on the overall performance, and show the same ascending order in performance from the clamped model to the spring model. Figure 5.8 shows a visualization of one of the simulated experiments with the four-link 2D model executed during simulated controller evaluation in the optimization cycle.

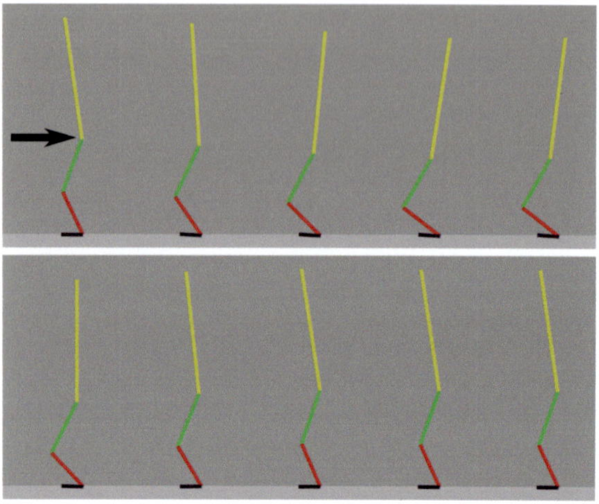

Figure 5.8: The planar 2D model reacting to a frontal push under whole-body LQR control. Depicted is a sequence of motion frames, temporally spaced 0.2 s apart. The robot bends its torso backward to compensate the induced angular momentum, and moves its hip forward to regulate the position of the CoM (taken from [Bäuerle et al. 2018], © 2018 IEEE).

5.5.3 Validation on the ARMAR-4 Humanoid Robot Model

The two main questions of this chapter, i. e. whether the performance of a whole-body LQR balance controller can be improved with novel linear contact models and by systematic optimization of the design weights, were already answered by evaluation on the planar robot model. Given the success of these methods, the modeling and parameter optimization procedure was additionally carried out to validate their applicability to the more complex 3D robot model of the ARMAR-4 robot. This allows for a qualitative assessment of the generated motion characteristics and also a more direct comparisons to related works in the literature. To achieve results in a reasonable time despite the much more demanding simulation, care was taken to reduce the number of free parameters of the optimization. Resulting from this objective, noteworthy differences between the optimization procedure for the 2D and the 3D model are the exclusion of the angular momentum from the cost term and the sole investigation of the high inertia contact model. The parameters that are optimized in this case are listed in Table 5.3. Similarly to the 2D case, 10,000 iterations of the Simulated Annealing based optimization cycle were run. The internal evaluation scheme was enhanced to use an adaptive step-width of the applied pushes, initially using a coarse step width of 2.5 Ns and a fine-grained iterative impulse reduction in steps of 0.5 Ns from the first failed attempt.

Despite the much longer optimization time for the simulation as compared to the 2D model (roughly three weeks on an *Intel Core i7* CPU), the process of finding a successful linear balance controller for the non-linear ARMAR-4 simulation model was successful. The resulting final balance controller can stabilize the ARMAR-4 model under the influence of push disturbances, utilizing all 18 joints specified in Section 5.4.4 (legs, torso, shoulders) and thus generating *whole-body* motions. Figure 5.9(a) shows a motion sequence of the ARMAR-4 simulation under the best controller, reacting to a frontal push. Similar to the 2D model, the robot initially bends its torso backwards and moves the hips forward. In addition, it quickly swings its arms backwards, generating an inertial force that pushes its body forward.

The employment of this whole-body strategy, rather than just relying on the ankle strategy to shift the CoP within the support polygon, is both a virtue of the employed contact model and the parameter optimization. The wholisticity of the generated motions sets this method apart from related works that use linear control for balancing (e. g. Figure 3.5). The maximum push impulse that the ARMAR-4 model can withstand using this controller amounts to 29 Ns, almost twice as much as the highest value for which successful tests in simulation of a full-body *Sarcos* humanoid are reported in [Mason et al. 2014] that use full-body LQR *without* weight optimization[4].

Lastly, the exact same controller used to create the balancing behavior shown in Figure 5.9(a) can be used to stabilize a squatting motion, in which the deviation from a time-varying state $x_{des}(t)$ rather than from the initial point of linearization x_0 (see Equation 2.19) is amplified by the gain matrix K to compute the joint torques. Even with the knees bent and therefore with the joint positions in the legs far from their initial point of linearization, the controller can successfully keep the robot balanced. Successive frames of this balance-controlled squatting motion are depicted in Figure 5.9(b).

(a) The simulated ARMAR-4 reacting to a frontal push under LQR whole-body control

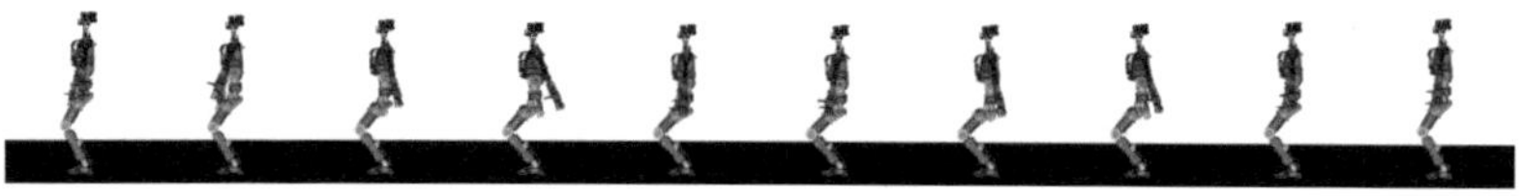

(b) The simulated ARMAR-4 performing a squatting motion under LQR whole-body control

Figure 5.9: Validation of the proposed weight-optimized LQR balance controller on the full ARMAR-4 model, performing balance recovery after a frontal push and a balanced squatting motion, despite deviating substantially from the initial state of linearization (taken from [Bäuerle et al. 2018], © 2018 IEEE).

5.6 Summary and Review

This chapter addressed the questions whether a linear and locally optimal postural balance controller that simultaneously takes into account multiple

[4] It should be noted that the two results were not acquired with the same simulation model (albeit both with models of full-size humanoids), and hence certain care must be taken when directly comparing the results merely based on the whithstood impulse.

major joints of the robot's body can be improved by alternative ways of formalizing the ground contact in the linearized robot dynamics, and by optimizing the weights in the cost term via an iterative process. Quantitative evaluation of the proposed methods was conducted on a simplified planar humanoid simulation model, and the feasibility of the found methods was validated by applying them to the ARMAR-4 robot model.

Contact Models Two novel ground contact abstractions for the synthesis of linear balance controllers were proposed, namely a spring model and a high inertia model. Both of them were evaluated against the standard, rigidly constrained contact model which they *outperformed*, leading to more capable balance controllers. In these evaluations, the spring model led to the overall best results.

Optimization Using simulated annealing in an iterative optimization process to find suitable weight parameters for balance controllers consistently led to *better performance* across all investigated contact formulations than an equal number of randomly chosen parameter samples. Simulated annealing found good weight parameters after as little as 100 iterations, and kept improving until the optimization was terminated after 10,000 cycles.

Validation on the ARMAR-4 Model Applying controller synthesis based on the high inertia method (chosen for its virtue of a lower number of free parameters) and weight optimization with simulated annealing, a linear whole-body balance controller could be derived for ARMAR-4 that shows better performance than previously published work from the literature while creating human-like balancing motions, most notably making use of arm-swing and torso bending.

6 Recovery Stepping

It was shown in Chapter 4 that different disturbances afford different reactions in humans to recover stability, and that these reactions can be grouped into the two classes of those that do not involve taking a step (see Chapter 5) and those that do require taking a step. This chapter is concerned with the latter class of reactions, i. e. *dynamic recovery stepping*. The method that will be presented is based on the execution of parametric step motion primitives and will be implemented on the velocity control level, as opposed to the balancing method described in Chapter 5 that was formulated on the torque control level.

The goal of the work presented in this chapter is the development of a method that lets the humanoid robot ARMAR-4 efficiently generate and execute a recovery step, bringing it back to a stable state after being pushed. This goal is pursued by addressing the following two questions:

1. How can recovery steps efficiently be generated, taking into account the kinematic complexity, capabilities and limitations of a humanoid robot?
2. How to find the right parameters for such a recovery step in order for it to be successful?

Figure 6.1 exemplifies the envisioned capabilities.

The motion generation is based on human motions that are recorded in a motion capture environment, following the hypothesis that leveraging the advanced stepping capabilities of humans for humanoid push recovery can

substantially alleviate the computational burden of motion generation, leading to motions that are grounded in the refined experience of human subjects. The motions will be encoded as joint-level dynamic movement primitives (DMPs) to enable flexible adaptation to different disturbances.
As the human subject and the robot have different kinematic and dynamic properties, some essential parameters of the recorded motions need to be adapted during execution for successful push recovery on the robot. Identifying these adaptations and appropriate, disturbance-specific parameterizations will be addressed by means of simulation-based learning. The final system will be evaluated in a dynamics simulation of the ARMAR-4 robot. Parts of the motion generation and learning based step parameter adaption have been presented in [Pankert et al. 2018].

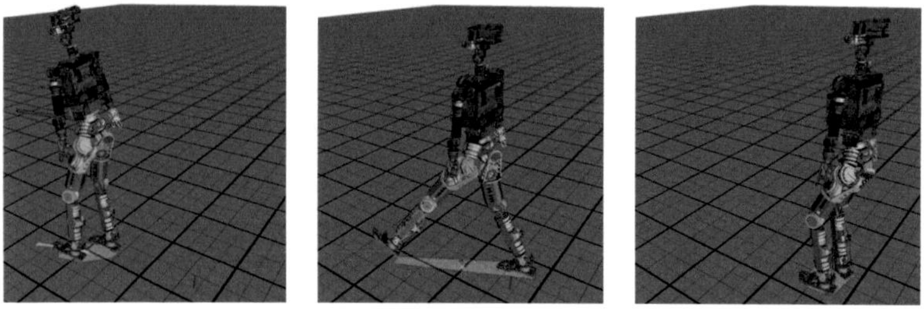

(a) Strong push while standing

(b) Capture step

(c) Stably standing after successful recovery

Figure 6.1: The goal of this chapter is to develop a method that lets the ARMAR-4 robot efficiently take a recovery step in order to regain balance after being pushed. The images exemplify such a push recovery stepping sequence. The red arrow indicates the push force. The support polygon is shown in light green.

6.1 Learning Stepping-DMPs from Human Demonstrations

Traditionally, the generation of end-effector motions for robots (such as a foot motion for stepping) is addressed in the task space, i. e. in the 6-dimensional space of end-effector poses. After defining the start and the end point of the motion, the entire trajectory is generated, e. g. by means of constrained path planning, or by adding additional via points for interpolation. Once the end-effector trajectory is generated in form of a list of 6D poses that encode the evolution of the end-effector's position and orientation, this list needs to be converted to a list of joint angles that can be commanded to the robot's control system. An example of this class of approaches, taking advantage of the possibility to directly incorporate task-space constraints into the motion plan, is presented in [Behnisch et al. 2010]. The downside of task space motion planning is that solving the inverse kinematic (IK) problem typically requires significant computational resources when the number of DoFs is high, kinematic redundancies need to be resolved and task-specific constraints need to be respected. All of these complicating elements are present in the problem of generating humanoid step trajectories: The kinematic chain that spans from the stance foot to the swing foot in the case of ARMAR-4 has a total of 12 DoFs (six per leg), presenting a significant kinematic redundancy that calls for a heuristic approach to choose among the infinite number of IK solutions. Task specific constraints such as keeping an upright upper-body posture also need to be fulfilled.

6.1.1 Methodology

In order to alleviate the computational burden that arises from solving the resulting IK-problem under real-time constraints, and to avoid the problem of redundancy resolution, this thesis proposes to learn parametric step trajectories from human motion data. If the demonstrated motions are learned

directly on the joint level, then the need to solve a series of IK-problems vanishes. Learning from human demonstrations has the advantage that the original motions are already compliant with task-space constraints such as the occurrence of self-collisions, and that there is thus no need to check for violations of these constraints prior to execution on the robot.
However, to be able to react to a wide variety of pushes, a wide variety of different stepping motions is necessary, and it is infeasible to have one demonstration for every possible step. It is therefore necessary to learn an *adaptive* representation of the steps that can be influenced with a small set of parameters, chosen according to the needs of the specific disturbance. The parameters that will be considered in the following are:

1. The final step position (2D)
2. The duration of the first half step, i. e. the time between breaking[1] and making contact of the first foot, exemplarily depicted in Figure 6.1(a) and Figure 6.1(b)
3. The duration of the second half step, i. e. the time between breaking and making contact of the second foot, exemplarily depicted in Figure 6.1(b) and Figure 6.1(c)

A method that lends itself to addressing these requirements is the representation of demonstrated motions as joint-level DMPs (see Section 2.4), with one set of synchronized DMPs for each half-step. A half-step denotes the motion from lifting up and putting down one foot, and a full step recovery consists of two half steps (see Figure 6.1). DMPs have an explicit timing parameter that can readily be used to adapt the duration of each of the half-steps. In contrast, the final step position cannot be directly manipulated when the motion is encoded in form of joint level DMPs. Computing the

[1] *Breaking* contact denotes the moment when the foot is lifted from the ground. *Making* contact denotes the moment when the foot comes into ground contact.

final goal for all joint-level DMPs thus still requires one solution of the IK problem that translates the final foot position from the 6D Cartesian space to the final joint positions. However, computing one IK-solution, scaling the DMPs and solving the canonical and transformation systems to generate joint trajectories is computationally cheaper than computing dozens or hundreds of IK solutions for the entire foot trajectory.

6.1.2 Human Motion Recordings

The human motion recordings that serve as the basis for recovery step learning were collected in the H^2T's motion capture environment following the standard procedure of the Master Motor Map (MMM) data collection process [Mandery et al. 2016][2]. The experimental setup was in large parts identical to the setup described in Section 4.1.1 and the trials were conducted in a similar fashion to the ones described in Section 4.1.2: During the experiments, a human subject wearing a motion tracking suit with reflective markers is initially standing still in a neutral pose, with the feet at shoulder width and the arms hanging down. It is then pushed at shoulder height by another human, at a level of intensity that requires the subject to take a step in order to mitigate the push and regain balance. In addition to the overall subject motion, the torso accelerations and the applied push force profile are measured with a torso mounted IMU on the subject and a force measuring push device (see Figure 4.1).

To allow the stepping motion primitives (DMPs) to generalize over the entire feasible space of push parameters, different stepping motions were collected, varying both in the length (denoting the distance between the subject's CoM before and after step recovery) and the direction of the step. These two parameters were varied according to a polar coordinate grid with angle increments of 30° and step lengths of 30 cm and 50 cm. Additionally,

[2] https://motion-database.humanoids.kit.edu/

steps with step lengths of 80 cm to the front and the back as reactions to very hard pushes, and 30 cm and 50 cm steps at angles of 45° and 135° were recorded. All parameter combinations for which stepping motions were recorded are listed in Table 6.1.

	0°	30°	45°	60°	90°	120°	135°	150°	180°
30 cm	X	X	X	X	X	X	X	X	X
50 cm	X	X	X	X	X	X	X	X	X
80 cm	X	-	-	-	-	-	-	-	X

Table 6.1: List of combinations of step directions (angles in degrees) and step lengths for which recovery steps were recorded in the human motion capture experiments. Since motions into the other half-plane can be generated computationally by mirroring at the subject's sagittal plane, motions in the parameter space from 180° to 360° were not recorded.

Provoking these steps requires the person that exerts the push to do this in the right direction and at the right level of intensity. To help guide the experiments, the above described grid was visibly marked on the laboratory floor, and the subject performing the step was positioned at its center at the beginning of each trial. To minimize the experimental effort, steps were only recorded into one half-plane of the grid, as the kinematics of the human body and of the ARMAR-4 robot are symmetric with respect to the sagittal plane, and thus motions can be mirrored at the sagittal plane to obtain stepping motions into the opposing half-plane. Figure 6.2 depicts an experiment in which the subject is pushed at a 90° angle and performs a step, after which its CoM comes to rest 30 cm from its initial position.
All motions that were recorded in these experiments (three trials for each parameter combination) are available from the KIT Whole-Body Human Motion Database under subject-ID #1721[3].

[3] https://motion-database.humanoids.kit.edu/list/motions/?subjects=1721

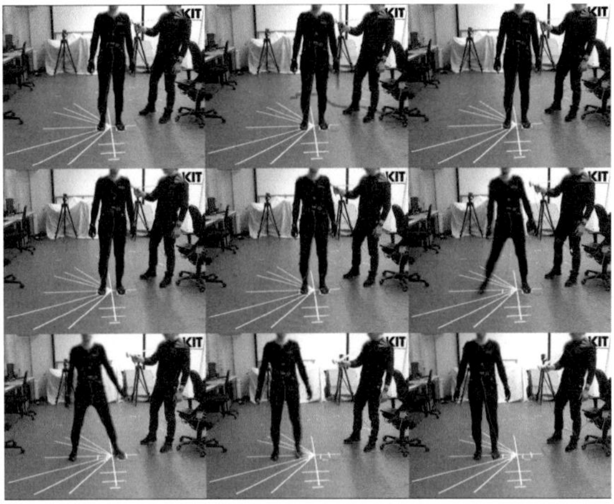

Figure 6.2: An example trial of the motion data collection process to learn robotic stepping motions from human demonstration. The human subject is pushed from the side (90 °) and takes a 30 cm step to recover its balance. The order of the images is from left to right and top to bottom. Temporal spacing is 200 ms (taken from [Pankert 2018]).

Motion Conversion

The collected human motion data needs to undergo two steps of further data processing before it can be used for step recovery learning: It needs to be converted to robot specific motions, taking into account the ARMAR-4's kinematics, and the converted motions need to be represented as joint-level DMPs.

The motion conversion is necessary since the kinematics of the human body and the ARMAR-4 are not identical. In the MMM data format, the recorded motions are stored as sequences of joint angles. However, due to kinematic differences, there exists no trivial mapping from human joint angle trajectories to a given robot. To address this problem, the MMM framework offers optimization-based, target-specific motion converters that can bridge the gap between different kinematic structures [Terlemez 2017]. The underlying idea of the conversion is that the overall appearance of the motion shall be preserved, and that the joint-angle trajectories of the target kinematic structure (ARMAR-4 in the here presented case) are generated from this criterion. Formally, this is achieved by optimizing the target joint angles such that semantically similar locations of the original (human) and target (robot) move in a similar way, i. e. have a minimal distance when overlaying the two structures. Figure 6.3 shows four frames of an exemplary stepping motion conversion (see also Figure A.1).

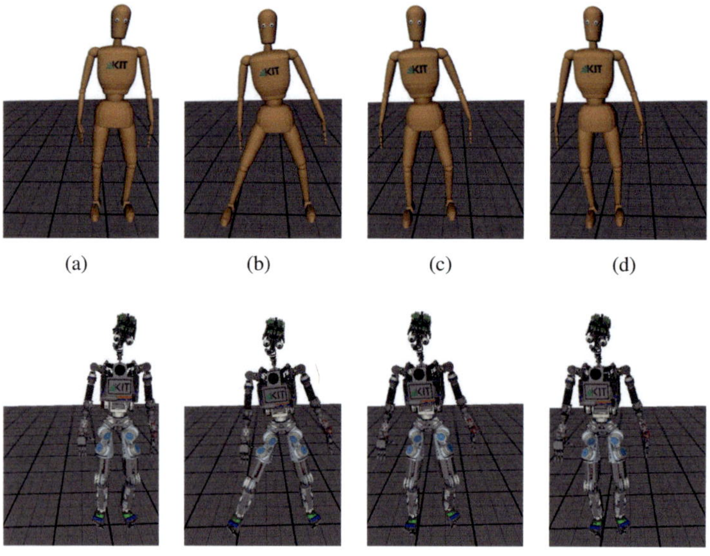

Figure 6.3: Example frames of the ARMAR-4 motion (e)-(h) that results from the kinematic human-to-robot conversion process of a recorded step to the right, represented on the normalized MMM reference model (a)-(d). Temporal order from left to right, with 330 ms temporal spacing (adapted from [Pankert 2018]).

These locations are created by equipping the motion target with 'virtual markers' that semantically correspond to the optical motion tracking markers attached to the human subject (e. g. a virtual marker on the knee of the robot model corresponds to an optical marker on the human knee), and each motion frame of the target is generated by finding joint angles that minimize the sum of squared distances between corresponding pairs of real and virtual markers. The converter that converts motions from the generic MMM reference model to the ARMAR-4 is part of the *MMMTools* package[4].

6.1.3 DMP Representation

The last step of data processing is to represent the converted motions as sets of joint level DMPs. It proved useful to split the stepping trajectories into two parts, the first and the second half step. The first half step will be called the *capture step*, in accordance with the use of this term in the related literature. The main reason for this split is the ability to individually scale the execution times of each half step. Another reason is to enable a simple ankle control for the stance and swing foot that benefit from this split, which is crucial for successful stepping (see paragraph 6.1.4). After the capture step, one of the robot's feet is still at its initial position while the other is placed at the *capture location* (see Figure 6.1(b)). While this configuration in itself could be statically stable and represent the end of the recovery action, this work aims at producing a motion that brings the robot back into its original configuration. A second half step therefore has to follow. Since this step recovers the initial configuration of the robot (i. e. standing with parallel feet, see Figure 6.1(c)), this motion will be called the *recovery step*.

For training appropriate DMPs, the two segments forming the capture step and the recovery step have to be identified within the motion recordings and isolated. In this work, the timestamps of the beginning of the capture step, the transition from capture to recovery step and the end of the recovery step are identified by manual inspection of the recordings. Joint

[4] https://gitlab.com/mastermotormap/mmmtools

level DMPs for each interval, with 100 Gaussian kernel functions per joint, are then trained separately with locally weighted Gaussian regression, using the DMP-library (see Section A of the appendix). Each set of joint angle DMPs for each interval contains a transformation system for each joint and a shared canonical system to ensure time synchronization between the individual joints. Note that only 14 robot joints were considered in the DMP representation of the stepping motions, namely the 12 DoFs of the two legs (excluding the toes) as well as the torso pitch and the torso yaw joint (see Figure A.3 of the appendix for reference). The remaining joints (essentially the arms and the neck) remain in their neutral positions during DMP-generated motion execution.

After this process, the DMPs can be used to produce parametric stepping motions by passing a list of sampling times (at intervals of 10 ms) to the canonical system, computing its respective list of outputs $\mathbf{x}$ and subsequent synchronous numerical integration of the transformation systems to produce joint angle trajectories. The required inputs for this process are the initial joint configuration, the intermediate capture configuration and the final joint configurations, as well as the two temporal scaling factors for the two parts of the motion.

6.1.4 Parametric Step Motion Generation

An efficient, self-contained, DMP-based parametric step trajectory generator was implemented with the building-blocks described previously. The developed trajectory generator takes a small set of six high-level step parameters and generates trajectories for each of the 14 joints that are involved in the stepping motion. The six input parameters belonging to the three light blue boxes on top of Figure 6.4 are:

- Step Target
  1. **Step Angle** ϕ_1: The direction in which the step should be performed. Straight ahead refers to 0°, with increasing angles in the clockwise direction
  2. **Step Length** d_1: The horizontal distance between the centroid of the support polygon in the initial configuration and in the final configuration
- Trajectory Selection
  3. **Selection Angle** ϕ_2: Direction parameter to select the original sets of DMPs
  4. **Selection Length** d_2: Step length parameter to select the original sets of DMPs
- Execution Times
  5. **Capture Step Duration** τ_1: The duration of the first half step (capture step) that represents the transition from the initial configuration to the capture configuration
  6. **Recovery Step Duration** τ_2: The duration of the second half step (recovery step) that represents the transition from the capture configuration to the final configuration

From the step target, the foot position of the capture configuration is computed. A single constrained IK-problem is subsequently solved that generates leg and torso joint angles that correspond to a robot configuration with the first foot at the initial location and the second foot at the desired capture configuration. A constraint is added to enforce an upright orientation of the upper body. The trajectory selection parameters serve to choose the original DMPs that are modified to produce the desired step, based on the corresponding parameters of their underlying motion recordings. Each initially recorded trajectory can be represented on a polar grid (see colored points in

Figure 6.5), occupying a cell on this grid (represented by the dashed black lines).

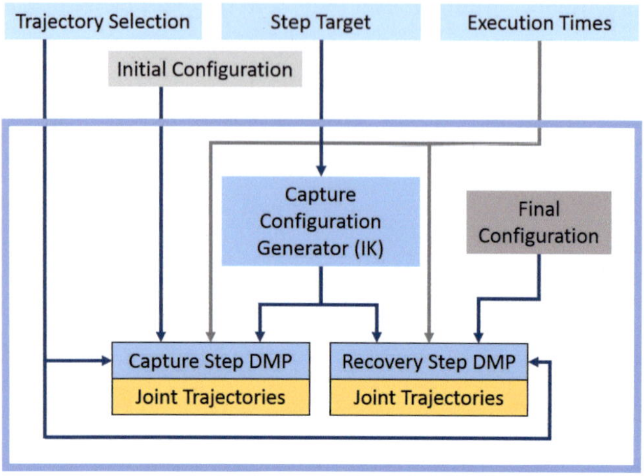

Figure 6.4: The DMP-based parametric step trajectory generator. Provided with parameters for trajectory selection, step target and execution speeds as well as the current robot configuration it efficiently generates stepping trajectories by rolling out DMPs for the captures and the recovery step that are based on recorded human motion data.

The trajectory selection parameters define a point on this grid that belongs to one of the cells, and the original trajectory in the same cell is chosen. Intuitively, the step target parameters could be used for the same purpose. However, this has proved to be problematic for the parameter learning process described later due to discontinuities at the cell boundaries. Allowing the learned policy to choose the underlying motion recording and step target individually avoids such problems, stabilizing the learning process. After the underlying motion recording is identified, the respective DMPs are selected and their start- and end-configurations are adapted as described above.
The execution time parameters are used to determine the temporal scaling of the DMPs, such that their execution times match the desired durations.

With this information, the two DMPs are rolled out and the joint trajectories are generated.

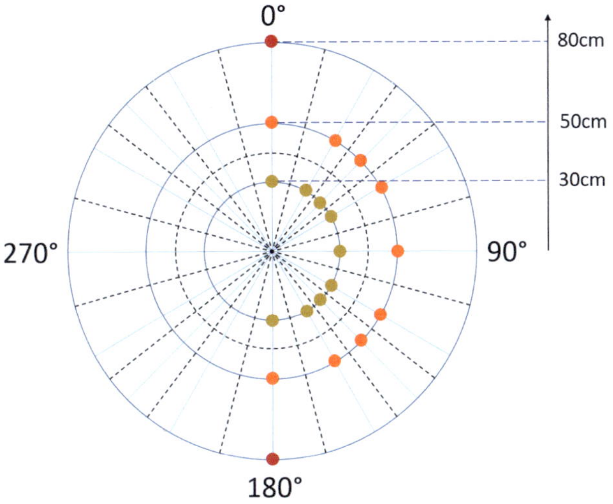

Figure 6.5: Top view of the polar grid containing the 20 step locations of all recorded human stepping motions (yellow, orange and red dots) and the decision boundaries for DMP selection based on the trajectory selection parameters (dashed black lines).

Initial, Intermediate and Final Configuration The *initial configuration* (light gray box in Figure 6.4) influences the scaling of the capture step DMP. It is not a selectable input parameter, instead it is always chosen as the current robot configuration to ensure a seamless transition from the current robot state to the stepping motion. In the simulation-based trials, the initial configuration is always the same and computed from the initial poses of all recorded human trials. To this end, the joint angles from all recorded initial configurations are averaged to obtain a reference initial configuration. To ensure a symmetric configuration with respect to the robot's sagittal plane,

the averaged joint angle configuration for the left leg is identically used for the right leg.
Due to imprecisions in the motion capture of the feet, the orientation of the feet in the converted motions is not parallel to the ground. As this is necessary for a stable stance, the feet orientations are corrected to align with the ground by computing corrective offsets to the ankle joints. Lastly, the initial configuration is required to be statically stable, as the (simulated) robot would otherwise tip over before a push has even occurred. This is achieved by adjusting the pitch angles of the ankle joints such that the robot's CoM lies above the center of the support polygon. This joint angle configuration is used both as initial configuration of he capture step and as the final configuration of the recovery step, since both share the same set of requirements.
The *intermediate (capture) configuration* is much more specific to each stepping motion and depends on the step length and the direction of the step. It therefore remains largely unchanged from the recorded configuration, with the exception of the ankle joints being aligned in parallel with the ground.
The *final configuration* is the same symmetric, statically stable average of the recorded initial configuration that also forms the initial configuration. It is not an input parameter, but a fixed component of the generator itself.

Ankle Joint Control To prevent the robot from rolling over one edge of its capture foot after this foot touches the floor, the orientation of the capture foot is set to be parallel to the ground in the capture configuration, and the target angles for the ankle joints are computed accordingly. The orientations of both, the swing foot and the stance foot, need to be controlled during the entire stepping process, as the foot orientations from the motion recordings are potentially infeasible. If not taken into account, this can result in undesired ground contact of the swing foot during step motion execution. To this end, a simple controller was devised and integrated into the motion generator and constantly aligns the current swing foot with the ground, ensuring sufficient clearance between the ground and each part of the foot. The stance foot is separately driven such that its orientation changes linearly over time from the initial to the target orientation. These specific controllers for the ankle joints of the swing and stance feet override the joint controller that aims at tracking the DMP trajectory.

6.2 Learning Viable Step Parameters

The previously described parametric motion generator is one of the two building blocks for fast, human-inspired recovery stepping, and constitutes the proposed answer to the question of how to efficiently generate stepping motions for a humanoid robot.

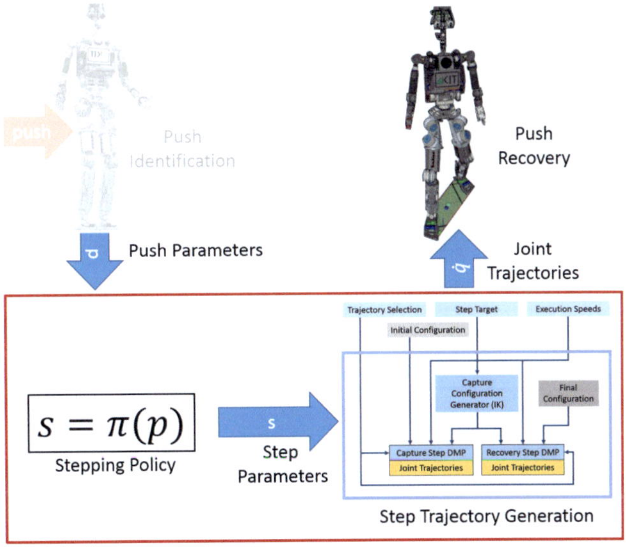

Figure 6.6: Context of the individual components presented in this chapter, namely the *Stepping Policy* and the *Step Trajectory Generator* in the red box. *Push Identification* is the subject of Chapter 4, and *Push Recovery* is the ultimate goal (adapted from [Pankert et al. 2018], © 2018 IEEE).

The second question stated at the beginning of this chapter is how to find the appropriate stepping parameters for a given push disturbance. As already stated in Chapter 4, the appropriate reaction to a push is strongly correlated to its direction and intensity (as it can be observed in humans). Further it was shown that these parameters can be inferred from body worn sensors or from the robot's internal sensors. Therefore, a link needs to be established between those measurable *push parameters* and the *step parameters* that, when fed to the step trajectory generator, produce a stepping motion that leads to successful push recovery. This link can be regarded as a mapping from push parameters $\mathbf{p}$ to step parameters $\mathbf{s}$. The remainder of this section will develop a solution to the problem of finding this mapping by framing it as a reinforcement learning problem, and learning the policy $\mathbf{s} = \pi(\mathbf{p})$. The entire pipeline, from estimating the push parameters as investigated in Chapter 4 to successful recovery stepping, via step parameter computation by the policy π and trajectory generation via the DMP-based motion generator, is depicted in Figure 6.6.

6.2.1 Parameter Spaces and Policy Structure

Input Parameters Motivated by the results presented in Chapter 4, a 2 D vector of push parameters $\mathbf{p}$ is chosen to capture the necessary information about he push that the robot needs to react to, and thus as input to the policy that produces the adequate step parameters. These parameters are the direction of the push (*push angle*) and the intensity of the push (*push impulse*).

The push angle captures the horizontal direction of the applied force, as it is depicted in Figure 6.5. It is assumed that the push force does not have any significant vertical component that needs to be taken into account.

The second defining parameter of the push disturbance is the push intensity. No standardized methodology has yet been established in the related literature to reproducibly specify the push intensity applied in push recovery experiments. Common approaches are to report on the force profile or the overall transmitted impulse to a (simulated) robot, i. e. the time integral of the applied force $\int_t f(t)dt$. Push recovery is significantly more challenging for a very light robot subjected to the same transmitted impulse than for a much heavier one, since the resulting acceleration a from a push with impulse p is directly dependent on the robot's mass m with $a = p/m$. To foster comparability amongst different robots, push intensities are defined in this chapter by means of the *specific impulse* p_n, i. e. the transmitted total impulse p_t normalized by the robot's mass m:

$$p_n = \frac{p_t}{m} \tag{6.1}$$

The unit of the specific impulse is $\frac{Ns}{kg}$ which can be simplified to $\frac{m}{s}$. However, to enhance clarity, the more intuitive notation of $\frac{Ns}{kg}$ will be used for the unit of the specific impulse. If in the remainder of this chapter a push impulse p without index is used for brevity it refers to the specific impulse p_n. The input vector to the stepping policy thus becomes

$$\mathbf{p} = \begin{pmatrix} \text{push angle } \theta \\ \text{push intensity } p_n \end{pmatrix} \in \mathbb{R}^2 \tag{6.2}$$

Output Parameters The output parameters of the policy $\pi(\mathbf{p})$ are the input parameters $\mathbf{s}$ of the step trajectory generator, and hence a 6-dimensional vector containing the step angle, the step length, the selection angle, the selection length, and the the durations of the two half steps. The output vector **s** is therefore

$$\mathbf{s} = \begin{pmatrix} \text{step angle } \phi_1 \\ \text{step length } d_1 \\ \text{selection angle } \phi_2 \\ \text{selection length } d_2 \\ \text{capture step duration } \tau_1 \\ \text{recovery step duration } \tau_2 \end{pmatrix} \in \mathbb{R}^6 \tag{6.3}$$

Policy Structure Mapping from the push parameters $\mathbf{p} \in \mathbb{R}^2$ to the step parameters $\mathbf{s} \in \mathbb{R}^6$ requires a policy of the form

$$\mathbf{s} = \pi(\mathbf{p}) \in \mathbb{R}^2 \to \mathbb{R}^6.$$

Since this mapping will later be learned in an iterative process, the policy representation needs to be parametric. While there exist a number of possible candidates for such parametric representations, artificial neural networks have recently been shown to be a very promising general purpose template for highly non-linear relationships. Inspired by these successes a neural network will be used in the presented work. The problem at hand is comparatively low-dimensional, thanks to the trajectory generator requiring only a small set of parameters. This motivates the use of a small neural network that can be efficiently trained on a small amount of training examples, in contrast to a deep neural network with millions of free parameters that are common in other contemporary research on data-driven motion generation (e. g. [Peng et al. 2017]), typically requiring vast amounts of simulated training data.

Here, a neural network with a single hidden layer and ten hidden units will be used. Note that although the output is 6-dimensional, the output layer has only five activation functions, as it was found feasible to keep a constant capture step duration scaling of 1, thus always choosing τ_1 of the original trajectory. Figure 6.7 shows a visualization of the network structure, produced by MATLAB's Neural Network toolbox in which the network was implemented.

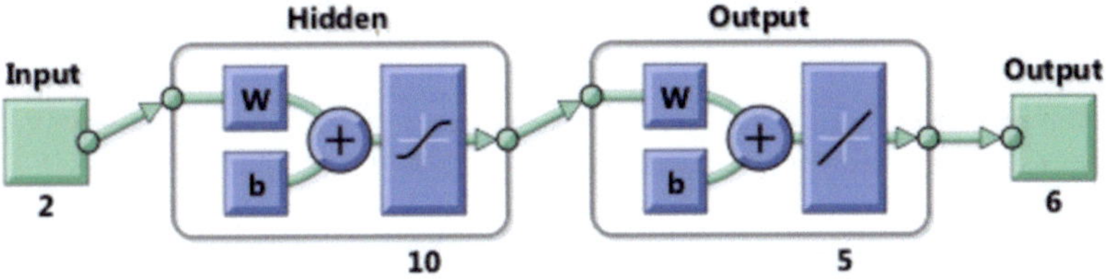

Figure 6.7: Schematic depiction of the policy $\pi(\mathbf{p})$ implemented as neural network with one hidden layer and 10 hidden units. Numbers denote dimensions. W symbolizes the weights and b stands for the biases. Graphs symbolize the activation functions (adapted from [Pankert 2018]).

6.2.2 Training Procedure

Training the above described policy is performed entirely in simulation, since dynamic stepping experiments are very costly on actual robotic hardware as they involve a high risk of damage to the robot. The training is framed as a reinforcement learning problem: The simulated ARMAR-4 robot acts as the *agent*, which has access to the parameters of the push that it is subjected to. These parameters are made readily available in the simulated setup and constitute the *state*[5]. The agent *acts* by choosing step parameters according to the push parameters, following the learned policy

[5] On the real robot, push parameter estimation, e. g. with internal IMUs or ankle F/T sensors, based on the methods described in Chapter 4, would be required.

that was pre-trained on a small initial set of successful parameter combinations provided (either found manually or originating from the demonstration experiments). The step trajectory generator turns these step parameters into a stepping motion (capture step and recovery step) which are then executed. The success of the stepping action is evaluated, and parameter combinations **p** and **s** that lead to successful push recovery are added to a list of all *positive examples* L and their success indicators R. After a certain number of experiments (*episodes*) are performed, the policy is updated by training on the current list of positive examples.

Algorithm 2 Learning a policy that maps push parameters to step parameters (adapted from [Pankert et al. 2018], © 2018 IEEE).

Require:

L_0 – Initial set of training examples
N – Number of training iterations
TRAIN(L,R) – Optimize the policy on training data
EXPLORE(L,successRate) – Generate new pushes for testing
PUSHRECOVERYTESTING(L) – Policy roll-out

function LEARNSTEPPARAMETERS(L_0)
  $R_0 \leftarrow$ PUSHRECOVERYTESTING(L_0)
  $successRate \leftarrow 1$
  for $i \leftarrow 1 \ldots N$ **do**
    $\pi_i \leftarrow$ TRAIN(L_{i-1}, R_{i-1})
    $\{\tilde{p}_1, \ldots, \tilde{p}_{10}\} \leftarrow$ EXPLORE($L_{i-1}, successRate$) ▷ Algorithm 3
    $\tilde{L} \leftarrow \{(\tilde{p}_1, \pi_i(\tilde{p}_1)), (\tilde{p}_2, \pi_i(\tilde{p}_2)), \ldots, (\tilde{p}_{10}, \pi_i(\tilde{p}_{10}))\}$
    $\tilde{R} \leftarrow$ PUSHRECOVERYTESTING($\tilde{L}$) ▷ Evaluation
    $successRate \leftarrow$ MEAN($\tilde{R}.success$)
    $L^+ \leftarrow \tilde{L}$ where ($\tilde{R}.success = true$)
    $R^+ \leftarrow \tilde{R}$ where ($\tilde{R}.success = true$)
    $L_i \leftarrow \{L_{i-1}, L^+\}$
    $R_i \leftarrow \{R_{i-1}, R^+\}$
  end for
  $\pi_{final} \leftarrow$ TRAIN(L_N, R_N)
  return π_{final}
end function

Throughout this process, outlined in Algorithm 2, the policy is expected to improve as more and more positive examples are found via rolling out the improving policy, which in turn can be improved by training on this growing list of positive examples. Critical aspects of this procedure are how to find the initial set of parameters to train on, how to select a set of new push parameters for the next iteration of policy evaluation episodes, and how to evaluate the outcome of these policy roll-outs. These aspects will be detailed in the following paragraphs.

Initial Parameter Set The 8-dimensional space that includes the combinations of push and step parameters is so large that it is very tedious to manually find feasible parameter combinations leading to successful push recovery steps. Suitable parameter sets were therefore primarily inferred from the human motion recordings of successful stepping motions. However, it became evident that choosing the same push and step parameters that could be observed in the human experiments do not lead to successful trials in the ARMAR-4 dynamic simulation. The generated steps were too short, and the robot tipped over in all cases. The reason for this discrepancy might be that humans employ the entire range of push recovery actions, including ankle and hip strategies prior to and during stepping, whereas the simulated robot exclusively resorts to stepping and therefore needs to take longer steps. Successful parameter sets were obtained by reducing the push impulse from the impulse measured in the experiments by factors ranging from 0.25 to 0.8, depending on the push direction. Two sets of initial positive example parameter sets derived from the human experiments by reducing the push impulse are listed in Table 6.2.
Initial examples of hard pushes which require very large steps were found entirely manually by means of trial and error, since no suitable parameter examples were available from the human motion capture trials.

p		**s**					
θ [°]	p [Ns/kg]	ϕ_1 [°]	d_1 [mm]	ϕ_2 [°]	d_2 [mm]	τ_1 [ms]	τ_2 [ms]
90	0.125	75	619	90	510	450	450
180	0.124	152	392	180	300	600	400

Table 6.2: Two example parameter sets for pre-training the stepping policy, based on the human motion recordings and reduced push impulse.

Experiment Selection An important part in the learning process is to efficiently generate a large number of positive training examples that cover a wide range of the input space of the policy, i. e. the 2-dimensional space spanned by the push parameters **p**. This space will be called the p-space, for short. Prior to every iteration of experimental data generation, a list of **p**-values is generated that define the applied pushes in these experiments, and thereby the experiments in their entirety (since the motion generation is deterministically dependent on the push parameters). These parameters thus need to be chosen in a way that balances both the goal of creating positive examples of successful push recovery trials, and the goal of exploring new areas of the p-space. These goals are inherently contradictory, as successful experiments are more likely to result from parameter sets for which the policy has already been trained (i. e. for which the knowledge of the policy can be *exploited*) than for new areas of the p-space that still have to be *explored*. To address this challenge, a method was devised that adaptively adjusts the trade-off between exploitation and exploration depending on the success rate of the experiments in the last iteration. The underlying idea is that exploration should be emphasized if the previous success rate was high, indicating that the policy is well adapted to the already known areas of the p-space. If the previous success rate was low, more training in the already known area of the p-space is necessary, and thus exploration should be inhibited. To realize this, the sample generation algorithm initially creates n new random parameter pairs (points) in the p-space. For each new point, the distance (in normalized dimensions) to its nearest neighbor of already existing positive samples is computed. Only the new point with the largest distance is added to the final list of new samples, and all others are discarded. This process is repeated until the desired number of new samples was generated and added to the list. Depending on n, which ranges from

$$0 < n < N, n \in \mathbb{N}, \tag{6.4}$$

(where N denotes the number of already existing samples) this process is more exploitative or more exploratory. If $n = 1$, the newly generated random sample is definitely added to the final list, resulting in a purely random list of new parameters. These points are likely to lie at least partially in already explored parts of the p-space, resulting in exploitative behavior (see Figure 6.8(a)).

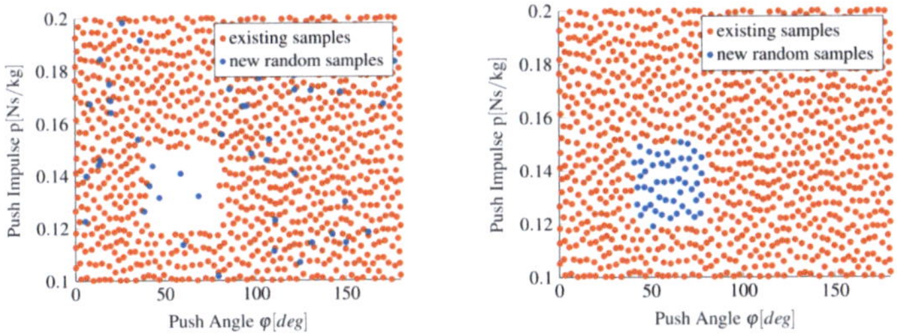

(a) Exploitation

(b) Exploration

Figure 6.8: Generation of new training parameters (blue) in a section of the p-space populated with already explored points (red). Shown are random sampling (a) and specifically targeting of unexplored areas (b) (adapted from [Pankert 2018]).

If $n > 1$, the chosen sample with the highest nearest neighbor distance is likely to be relatively distant from all existing samples. A large n will therefore generate samples generally far from the already existing ones, resulting in exploration (see Figure 6.8(b)). To control n, it is linearly scaled within its limits by the success rate of the last iteration's experiments. The experiment selection algorithm (*Explore*) is outlined in Algorithm 3. The two edge cases for maximum exploitation (previous success rate was 0) and maximum exploration (previous success rate was 1) are exemplified on synthetic data in Figure 6.8. A list of 10 push parameters with the generated step parameters for one instantiation of the policy is shown in Table 6.3.

$\mathbf{p}$		$\mathbf{s} = \pi_i(\mathbf{p})$					
θ [°]	p [Ns/kg]	ϕ_1 [°]	d_1 [mm]	ϕ_2 [°]	d_2 [mm]	τ_1 [ms]	τ_2 [ms]
66.665	0.14338	54.693	547.07	642.08	76.193	506.44	447.36
132.160	0.12123	112.47	109.47	538.22	88.134	469.04	596.21
31.834	0.15287	33.001	540.92	647.40	29.792	477.5	784.96
47.758	0.15018	46.992	494.77	642.41	38.227	494.53	626.35
40.279	0.10506	20.207	403.61	586.69	28.001	574.54	611.09
15.750	0.12689	31.142	322.36	596.25	10.137	521.25	721.54
32.511	0.07816	30.729	397.16	546.39	48.126	587.68	622.71
130.170	0.10292	107.78	148.79	549.65	86.428	470.16	579.50
118.91	0.10590	87.156	338.96	599.50	77.974	477.14	515.20
112.920	0.07624	80.77	395.78	613.03	76.945	481.36	493.62

Table 6.3: Ten exemplary sets of generated push parameters and the respective step parameters, generated with a specific instance π_i of the mapping policy.

This list is provided to the simulation based policy evaluation that will be described in more detail later.

The devised method represents an on-policy learning scheme, since the step parameters for newly generated push parameters are chosen by following the current, deterministic policy. On-policy schemes are less effective at extrapolating from the initial examples, but typically more sample-efficient at interpolating than off-policy schemes.

Evaluation After a single experimental trial (i. e. an episode) with a given set of push parameters operating under the current policy is finished, the result needs to be evaluated in order to generate new training data. The evaluation assigns two attributes to the tested set of parameters $(\mathbf{p}, \mathbf{s})$: A *binary* label indicating the general success of the trial, and a *continuous* error that is used to weigh the resulting positive samples in the learning process.

Algorithm 3 Generation of push parameters for next policy roll-out experiments (adapted from [Pankert 2018]).

Require:
L – List of successful push parameters and their success
numSamples – Required number of samples to produce
succRate – Success rate of last policy roll-out
NNDIST(*sample*, *L*) – Distance from sample to nearest neighbor in L

```
function EXPLORE(L, numSamples, succRate)
    N ← SIZE(L)
    numRandomSamples ← ROUND(succRate · N)
    r ← RANGE(L)
    s ← RANDOM(numRandomSamples)
    randomSamples ← SCALE2RANGE(s, r)
    for sample in randomSamples do
        distances(sample) ← NNDIST(sample, L)
    end for
    newSample ← sample with MAX(distances)
    if numSamples = 1 then
        return newSample
    else
        e ← EXPLORE({L, newSample}, numSamples − 1, succRate)
        return {newSample, e}
    end if
end function
```

The general success is determined 3 s of simulated time after the push was applied, by the angle between the robot's vertical axis and the global vertical axis. If this angle exceeds 60 °, the robot is considered fallen and the trial a failure, and the underlying parameter combination is discarded. In any

other case the trial is considered successful and the parameter combination is added to the list of positive examples for policy optimization.
The MATLAB implementation of the neural network accepts individual weights to the training examples to influence their effect on the trained model, where a higher weight increases the sample's effect on the final policy. Two weighting terms are used to increase the weights of those positive training samples that (1) lead to better push recovery performance and that (2) lie in relatively unexplored regions of the p-space. Push recovery performance is measured 3 s after the application of the push by means of a slight variation of the *Stopping Energy* $E_{stopping}$, a dimensionless quantity for the assessment of push recovery experiments initially introduced in [Rebula et al. 2007]. It is defined over the CoM velocity v_{CoM} and the horizontal distance $|\vec{x}|$ between the CoM and the centroid of the support polygon as

$$E_{stopping} := \frac{1}{2} v_{CoM}^2 + \frac{1}{2} \frac{g}{l} |\vec{x}|^2 \tag{6.5}$$

and increases for higher distances $|\vec{x}|$ and higher velocities v_{CoM}. It becomes 0 when the CoM is located exactly over the centroid of the support polygon and the CoM is at rest, in which case the robot is also statically stable. It is positive in all other cases. From this quantity, a sample weight $W_s(\mathbf{p}, \mathbf{s})$ is computed by applying the negated logarithmic function and MinMax-scaling.

$$W_s(\mathbf{p}, \mathbf{s}) = \text{MinMax}(-log(E_{stopping}(\mathbf{p}, \mathbf{s}))). \tag{6.6}$$

The negated logarithm ensures that large Stopping Energies result in small weights, and vice versa. MinMax-scaling normalizes its input $x, x_{min} \leq x \leq x_{max}$ to the range from 0 to 1 by applying

$$MinMax(x) = \frac{x - x_{min}}{x_{max} - x_{min}}.$$

The second weighting term is designed to improve policy generalization over the p-space. If the positive examples are distributed unevenly over the p-space, with areas of high and areas of low density, the policy is likely to overfit to the areas with higher sample density, and perform poorly in that of lower density. Samples from lower density areas are therefore endowed with a larger weight to prevent this overfitting and foster generalization. The inverse density is approximated by the Euclidean distance d_{nn} of a parameter to its nearest neighbor in the p-space, and turned into a training weight $W_d(\mathbf{b})$ by MinMax-scaling:

$$W_d(\mathbf{p}) = MinMax(d_{nn}(\mathbf{p})) \tag{6.7}$$

The sum of these two error terms forms the total sample weight W_t for a positive training example, which is used to scale the influence of this example on the trained model:

$$W_t(\mathbf{p},\mathbf{s}) = W_s(\mathbf{p},\mathbf{s}) + W_d(\mathbf{p}) \tag{6.8}$$

6.2.3 Implementation

The implementation of the entire system needed for learning a valid stepping policy, schematically depicted in Figure 6.6, was realized partially in the ArmarX software framework (see Section C of the appendix), and partially in MATLAB. While the parametric motion generator, the push provider and the dynamic robot simulator are part of ArmarX (see Figure 6.10), the policy itself as well as the generation of push parameters for the next experiments described in paragraph 6.2.2 and the learning process were realized in MATLAB. A fully automated loop for running successive experiments and policy updates was implemented by letting the two parts (ArmarX and MATLAB) communicate via the file system. This implementation was previously described in [Pankert 2018].

Simulator The underlying engine of the ArmarX dynamic simulator is the Bullet physics engine [bulletphysics 2018]. Bullet is primarily a gaming engine, and with its default parametrization prioritizes real-time computation over physical accuracy and reproducibility, e. g. simulation step-sizes are dynamically increased when the computational load of the host machine is high. In contrast to gaming applications, the presented research relies on reproducible behavior in order for the learning method to be grounded in sensible simulation results. Physical accuracy is further required to make the results obtained in simulation a meaningful basis for future applications on real robotic hardware. The simulation time step was therefore reduced and fixed at 0.5 ms, which is sufficiently small to generate reproducible simulations even in the presence of stiff ground contacts, which are one of the major sources of simulator instabilities (see [Chung and Pollard 2016]). The simulator publishes the current status of the simulation and accepts motor commands every 10 ms, i. e. after running 20 internal simulation steps. This outer interval was chosen since the original human motions are recorded at a frame rate of 100 Hz, and the motions computed by the DMP-based motion generator are of the same temporal resolution[6]. It is therefore not necessary to interact with the simulator at higher frequencies.
Running the simulator at such small time steps on the deployed simulation machine (*Intel Core-i7* CPU with four cores and 32 GB of RAM) slowed the simulation down to below real time. All other ArmarX components that interact with the simulator were therefore required to run synchronously to the simulated time rather than taking the system clock for time reference.

Push Provider The push provider applies the required push in the specified direction and with the specified impulse to the pelvis of the simulated

[6] This is implementation-specific. In principle, DMPs can provide arbitrary temporal resolution.

robot. Since the push impulse alone does not specify the force profile, a specific force profile (i. e. shape and duration) needs to be selected. To find a feasible shape and duration, the force profiles recorded during the human push recovery trials were analyzed. These force recordings revealed the approximate shape of isosceles triangles and had similar durations on the order of 500 ms, independent of their intensity (see Figure 6.9).

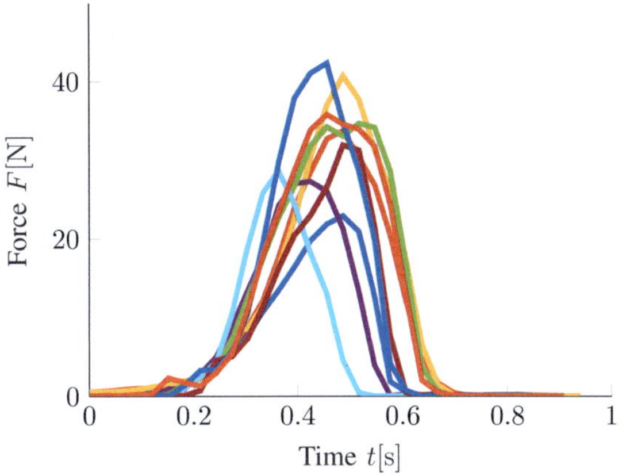

Figure 6.9: Multiple exemplary force profiles of pushes of different intensities, recorded during human push recovery trials. They are approximated in simulation by isosceles triangular profiles with a 500 ms base width and variable height (taken from [Pankert et al. 2018], © 2018 IEEE).

The force profile generated by the push provider is therefore implemented in the shape of an isosceles triangle, with a push duration $d_p = 500\,\text{ms}$ and a variable height F_{max} that depends on the required normalized impulse p_n and the robot mass m_r such that

$$F_{max} = \frac{2p_n m_r}{d_p}. \tag{6.9}$$

Evaluation Unit The Evaluation Unit is an ArmarX component that determines the result of a simulated recovery stepping trial by means of the binary criterion of standing upright, and by the continuous Stopping Energy, as detailed in Section 6.2.2. Evaluation results of successive trials are written to a result file that is passed to the optimizer which trains the stepping policy based on all available data.

Automated Training Cycle An ArmarX scenario was created that, in conjunction with a MATLAB script, automatically generates experience data and trains the stepping policy. This is an iterative process with iteration index i.

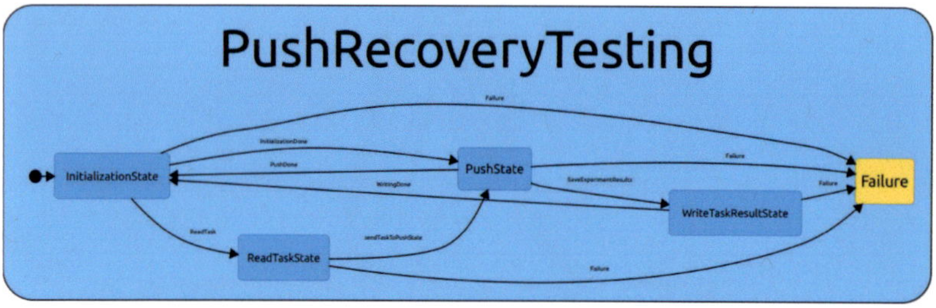

Figure 6.10: The *PushRecoveryTesting* ArmarX statechart used for automatic simulation-based experience data generation. A MATLAB script invokes the statechart which then performs all the simulation trials described in the task file and writes the results to a result file which is used for policy optimization.

- The MATLAB script initially generates a set of push parameters $\mathbf{p}_i$ and executes the current policy π_i for each of these parameters to obtain the associated step parameters $\mathbf{s}_i$. The list of push and step parameters is written to a file. Since every combination of $\mathbf{p}$ and $\mathbf{s}$ defines a simulated experiment and hence a task for the simulator, these files are called *task files*. Table 6.3 shows the content of such a task file. The script then starts the ArmarX scenario via the respective system call. The functionalities of the scenario are implemented as a statechart and form an inner loop, depicted in Figure 6.10.

  - The statechart starts in the *InitializationState*, in which the simulated robot is spawned in its initial, statically stable pose. After 2 s of simulated time for the robot to settle into a static state, the transition into the *ReadTaskState* is triggered.
  - *ReadTaskState* reads the previously generated task file, parses the first line and passes the push and step parameters to the *PushState*.
  - *PushState* applies the specified push to the robot and queries the motion generator to produce the capture and recovery steps, which are executed by the simulated robot. The transition to the *WriteTaskResultState* is then triggered and invokes the Evaluation Unit 3 s of simulated time after the push was applied.
  - *WriteTaskResultState* computes the results and appends them to a *result file*. The statechart then transitions back to the *InitilizationState* and this inner loop repeats until all experiments encoded in the task file are conducted.

- Once all experiments are conducted and evaluated, the MATLAB script terminates the ArmarX scenario and updates the policy by training (optimizing) the neural network on all generated results, including the latest ones, using backpropagation and Levenberg-Marquardt optimization.

The cycle then repeats with the incremented index $i+1$.

6.3 Evaluation in Dynamics Simulation

For evaluating the effectiveness of the above described training cycle it was executed 500 times, generating 500 iteratively improved mappings from push parameters to step parameters π_1 to π_{500}. To accommodate the on-policy nature of the proposed learning process, the space of push parameters that were chosen for future experiments was confined to the minimal rectangular area of the p-space that contains the initial training examples. This results in the policy being trained to interpolate between the initial positive samples. After 500 training iterations with 10 experiments each, i. e. after 5,000 simulated push recovery experiments[7], the final policy π_{500} was evaluated on a 10×10 grid spanned over the investigated subset of the p-space. For each of these 100 points in the p-space the step parameters were computed with π_{500} and the resulting experiments were conducted in the simulator. The success rate of all 100 evaluation experiments is computed from the resulting binary success indicator described in paragraph 6.2.2 and used as the evaluation metric for the policy. Figure 6.11 shows various successful evaluation experiments for pushes from various directions and of various intensities.

[7] As the simulation is running slower than real-time (see paragraph 6.2.3), each push experiments takes around 15 s to run, equating to proximately 21 h of simulation time for 5000 trials.

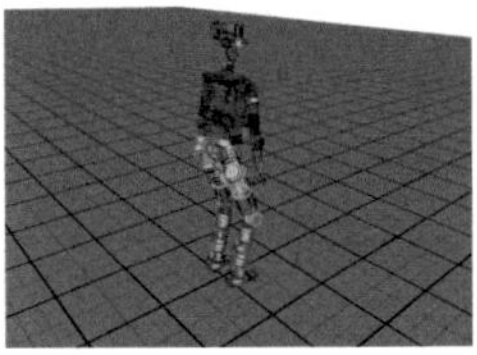

(a) Initial pose

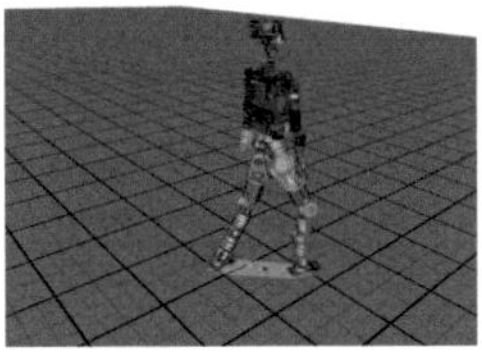

(b) Capture step towards front right

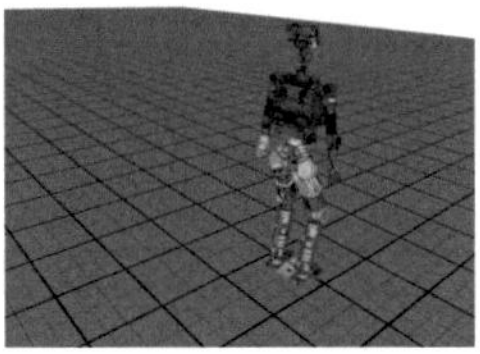

(c) Final stable pose

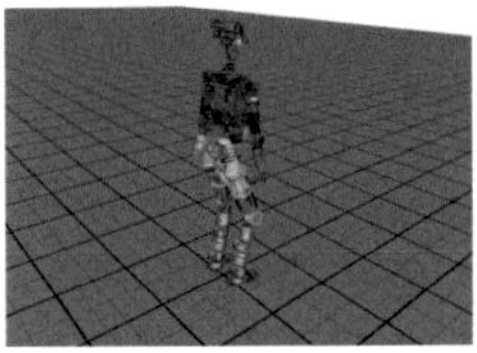

(d) Initial pose

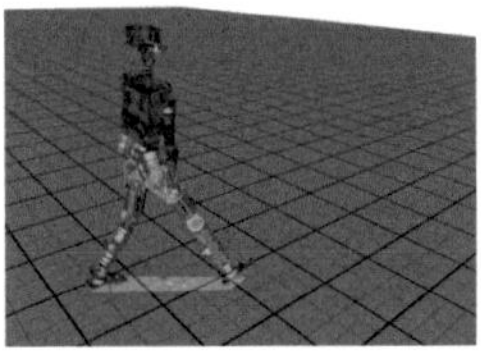

(e) Capture step towards back left

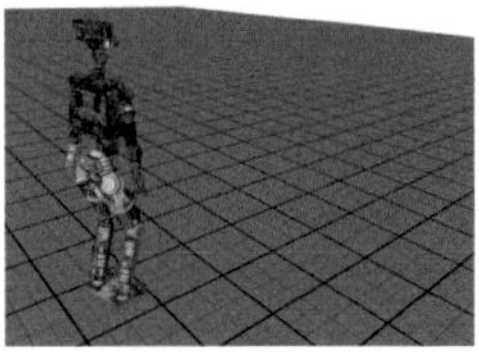

(f) Final stable pose

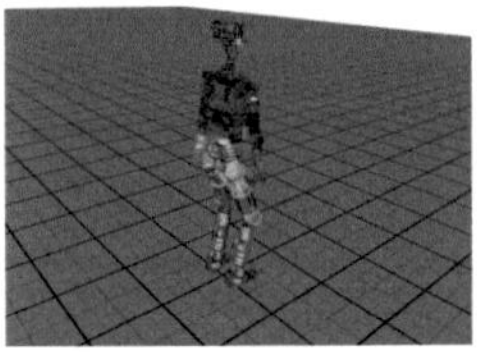

(g) Initial pose

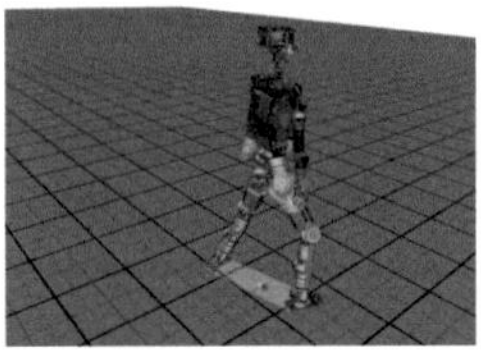

(h) Capture step towards the right

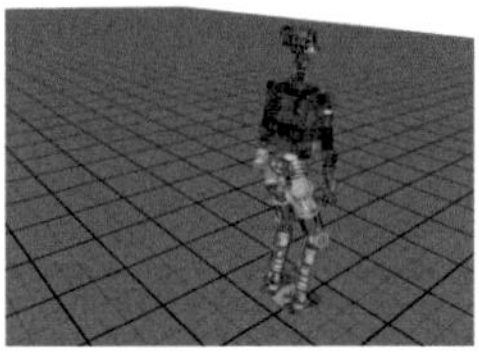

(i) Final stable pose

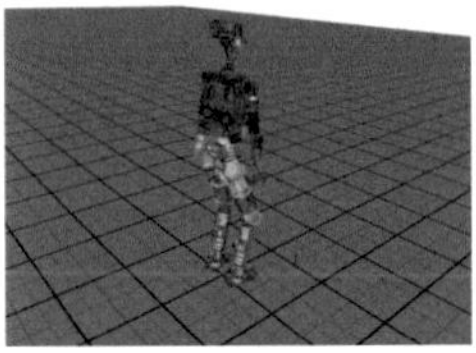

(j) Initial pose

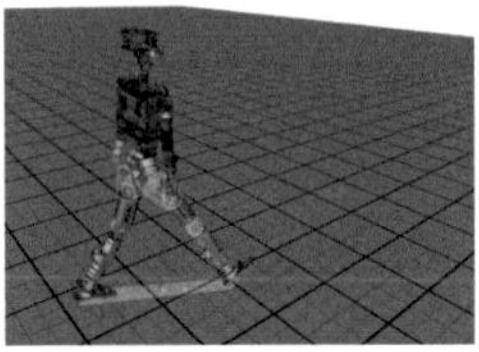

(k) Capture step towards the back

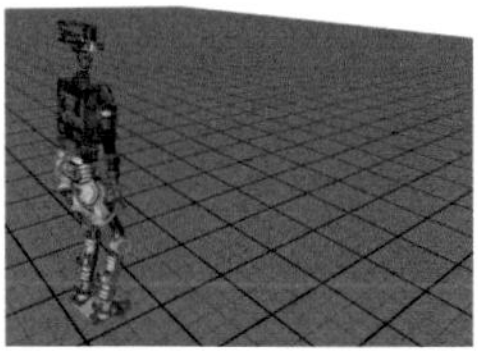

(l) Final stable pose

Figure 6.11: Multiple successful evaluation experiments for pushes from different directions and of different intensities. Pictures show the initial pose before the push is applied (left), the robot pose after the capture step in reaction to the push (middle) and after the recovery step that restores the initial pose (right). The green area is the current support polygon.

This evaluation method is conducted for two different sets of initial data, each defining a different p-area for the evaluation: The first initial dataset is derived from the human experiments and covers a range of comparatively weak pushes. Purely synthetic combinations for push and step parameters with stronger pushes similar to the pushes measured in the human experiments form the second initial dataset, for which the training procedure is independently evaluated.

6.3.1 Weak Pushes

The first set of initial training data consists of 18 combinations of push and step parameters derived from the human experiments. Only nine of these combinations resulted in successful push recovery. The other nine did not lead to successful recovery (i. e. the binary criterion was not fulfilled), but the Stopping Energy was low and the robot was able to perform both capture and recovery steps before falling, indicating that they were comparatively good, albeit failed, attempts. These parameter combinations were therefore included in the initial dataset to boost the early training but erased from the list of positive examples after 50 training iterations to not deteriorate the final result. The ranges of the push parameters (push angle and impulse) in this dataset were

$$\theta \in [0^\circ, 180^\circ] \tag{6.10}$$

$$p \in [0.075Ns/kg, 0.15Ns/kg] \tag{6.11}$$

which define the rectangular area of the p-space for which the policy was trained. These pushes are weak in comparison to the pushes applied during human motion trials. Note that the training for pushes in the range of $[0^\circ, 180^\circ]$ is sufficient for omni-directional push recovery, as the method is taking advantage of the robot's symmetry (e. g. once it 'knows' how to mitigate a push from the right, it can mitigate the same push from the left).

Over the course of 500 training iterations, the p-space was sampled 5,000 times with different policies for creating the respective step parameters. In Figure 6.12, all 5,000 samples are depicted. Each of these samples is associated with a set of 6-dimensional step parameters generated by the respective policy, which are not shown in the figure.

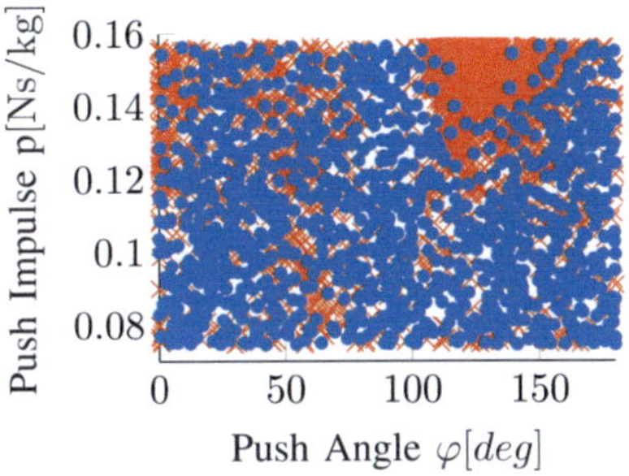

Figure 6.12: 5,000 evaluated samples in the p-space after 500 training iterations. Blue circles denote successful trials, red crosses denote unsuccessful trials (adapted from [Pankert et al. 2018], © 2018 IEEE).

The final policy $\pi_{500,weak}$ was trained on all the successful datapoints, i. e. the blue dots in Figure 6.12 and their associated step parameters. It was evaluated on 100 points evenly spread in the investigated portion of the p-space by generating step parameters for those 100 push parameters, generating stepping motions and performing the resulting experiments in the dynamics simulator. These tests resulted in an overall success rate of 75 %. Figure 6.13 shows the evaluation grid with the successful and failed evaluation experiments.

A disproportionately large number of failed trials are located in the upper right corner with relatively large push impulses and push angles, visible both in Figure 6.12 and in Figure 6.13. This shows that the data generation procedure was not able to generate positive training examples for these pushes, and hence the final policy could not learn how to successfully react to them.

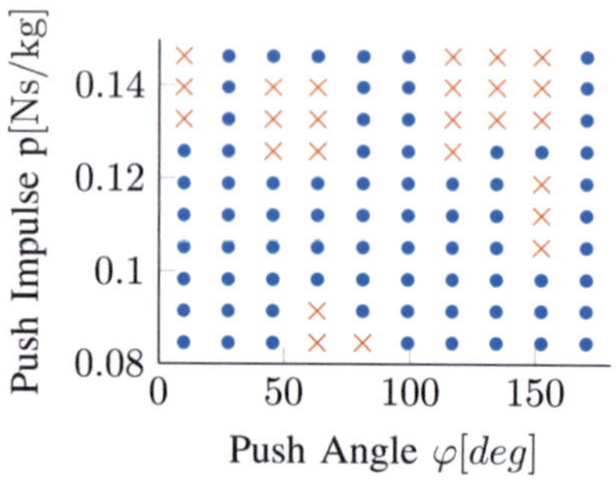

Figure 6.13: Grid-based evaluation of push recovery for comparatively weak pushes after 500 iterations of simulation-based policy improvement. Blue dots denote pushes for which $\pi_{500,weak}$ generates step parameters that lead to successful push recovery. Red crosses denote pushes for which the generated steps fail to recover the robot (adapted from [Pankert et al. 2018], © 2018 IEEE).

6.3.2 Strong Pushes

The second set of initial training examples consists of only five purely synthetic pairs of push and step parameters, for which successful push recovery was achieved in simulation. These parameters are confined to an area of the p-space with high push intensities and large push angles, characteristics for which the final policy evaluated in Section 6.3.1 was the least successful. This setup aims at investigating whether a higher density of training examples helps the learning process find a policy that can interpolate better in this seemingly difficult area. The parameter ranges of this dataset are

$$\theta \in [130°, 180°] \tag{6.12}$$

$$p \in [0.2Ns/kg, 0.3Ns/kg]. \tag{6.13}$$

The push impulse range of $[0.2Ns/kg, 0.3Ns/kg]$ was chosen to resemble the pushes recorded in the human push experiments, where the mean of of push impulses was $0.277Ns/kg$.
The grid-based evaluation was performed twice, once after 200 and once after 500 training iterations to evaluate the progress of the learning procedure. After 200 iterations, $\pi_{200,strong}$ was evaluated and led to an overall success rate of 69%. After 500 training iterations, $\pi_{500,strong}$ achieves successful push recovery on 89% of the same evaluation grid (see Figure 6.14). This indicates that the procedure is able to learn push recovery stepping for arbitrary areas of the space of push-parameters, provided sufficient initial examples, and also shows that the procedure improves the policy with increased number of training iterations, as expected.

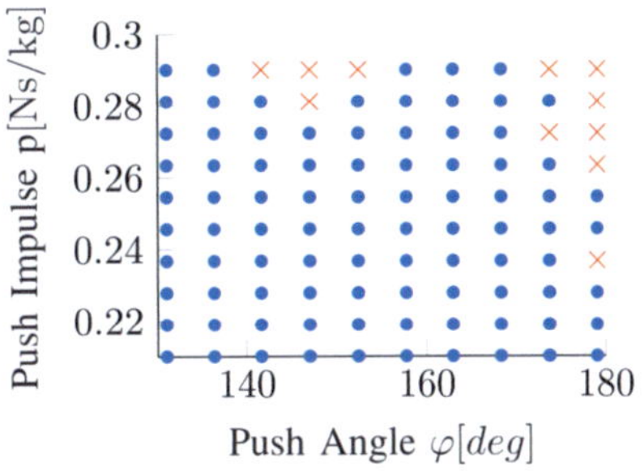

Figure 6.14: Grid-based evaluation of push recovery for strong pushes after 500 iterations of simulation-based policy improvement. Blue dots denote pushes for which $\pi_{500,strong}$ generates step parameters that lead to successful push recovery. Red crosses denote pushes for which the generated steps fail to recover the robot (adapted from [Pankert et al. 2018], © 2018 IEEE).

6.3.3 Computational Efficiency

One of the reasons for using coupled joint-level DMPs rather than traditional task-space motion generation and calculating successive solutions of the inverse kinematic (IK) problem were the hypothesized lower computational demands of the DMP-based approach. To validate this hypothesis, the computation times of both approaches were directly compared.

DMP For each time step of the DMP joint trajectories, the canonical system must be integrated by one time step to acquire the next value of the phase variable x, and subsequently all 14 transformation systems need to be integrated to this new value of x. Both is done by means of forward-integrating with the explicit Euler method (Euler 1-Step).

Constrained IK Advancing the joint trajectories with the IK-based approach once a new position and orientation of the swing foot is required necessitates the solution of a constrained, 14-dimensional IK problem. The constraints apply to the fixed pose of the stance foot and to the upright orientation of the torso. The IK-solver is initialized with the whole-body pose from the previous time step.

Results

Ten randomly picked successive steps were chosen from 12 different stepping trajectories both for the DMP-based and the IK-based method. The mean execution times of these ten successive steps are presented as t in Table 6.4. The overall mean of these t-values $\bar{t}$ as well as their standard deviation σ_t are presented as evaluation metrics.
The measurements reveal an, on average, more than ten times faster computation time of the DMP-based method. The standard deviation time is also significantly smaller. Both properties (low execution time, small standard deviation) are favorable in real-time applications such as reactive push recovery.

$T_{\text{ConstrainedIK}}$ [μs]			$T_{\text{Euler 1-Step}}$ [μs]		
t	$\bar{t}$	σ_t	t	$\bar{t}$	σ_t
1198			185		
6244			185		
314			186		
5300			189		
532			184		
738	**2507**	**2590**	189	**195**	**27**
1259			191		
6376			279		
329			191		
5960			189		
577			187		
1260			188		

Table 6.4: Computation times of 12 example constrained IK-solutions compared to 12 steps of forward integration of the canonical and all transformation systems of a stepping DMP. Also listed are their means $\bar{t}$ and their standard deviations σ.

6.4 Summary and Review

This chapter introduced a novel method to efficiently generate omni-directional steps for a humanoid robot to recover from pushes of different intensities, applied from arbitrary horizontal directions. The two pillars of the method are a parametric stepping motion generator and a learnable policy that generates suitable step parameters from measured push parameters.

Motion Generation The motion generator leverages human demonstrations that were captured during push recovery experiments in a motion capture laboratory, converted to motions for the ARMAR-4 robot, and encoded as joint-level motion primitives (DMPs). Leveraging human motion examples alleviates the need for self-collision checking or redundancy resolution. Each step motion consists of two parts, the *capture step* in which the first foot is placed on the step location, and the *recovery step* in which the second foot is moved to restore the initial pose (at a new location). The motion generator computes stepping motions from a small set of input parameters, most notably the step location and the execution durations of the capture and the recovery step. It was implemented as an encapsulated component of the ArmarX software framework. Thanks to the incorporation of human stepping demonstrations in the form of joint-level DMPs, the overall human motion characteristic is retained and motion generation is achieved in a highly efficient manner. Ankle motions proved to be difficult to learn from motion capture data and were instead generated with simple heuristics. Comparative evaluations of this method against task-space motion planning with subsequently solving the IK-problem revealed a ten-fold speedup and significantly lower standard deviation of the computation time, making the proposed method favorable for real-time applications.

Stepping Policy The step parameters that are fed to the motion generator must be estimated from push parameters that can be measured by the robot with on-board sensors (see Chapter 4). This mapping from push parameters $\mathbf{p}$ to step parameters $\mathbf{s}$ is formalized as a learnable policy $\mathbf{s} = \pi(\mathbf{p})$ and implemented as an artificial neural network. This network is trained on data (experience) generated in dynamics simulations of the ARMAR-4 robot performing push recovery steps. To make this data generation efficient and goal-directed, a dedicated method was introduced that explores new areas in the space of push parameters (the p-space) once the policy is sufficiently well trained in previously explored regions.

Evaluations of training in different regions of the p-space show that this process can generate suitable stepping motions for a wide variety of pushes from very few initial training data. The fact that successful push recovery can be achieved without any additional balance control in the final state highlights the quality of the learned stepping motions, and suggests that the addition of balance control could make the proposed method applicable to an even wider range of pushes.

Results The overall result is an efficient method to generate successful stepping motions from very few initial training samples and with comparatively little training, enabling the simulated ARMAR-4 robot to recover from a wide variety of pushes from different directions and of different intensities (see Figure 6.11). Experimental evaluation shows that a small neural network with one hidden layer is able to learn a suitable stepping policy after 500 policy roll-outs with ten episodes each. As an an on-policy method, the learning process trains the policy to interpolate the stepping parameters in the area of the p-space defined by the initial examples.

7 Conclusion

The goal of the work presented in this thesis was to find novel ways for answering the following question:

What does a bipedal humanoid robot need to perceive and to do in order to regain its balance after a forceful push?

Addressing this question was subdivided into three aspects, namely (1) classification of the current stability and the estimation of external perturbations, (2) push recovery by whole-body postural balancing in place, and (3) regaining balance by stepping. These three aspects are thematically coherent, yet they represent individual building blocks for a balance system that plays a fundamental role in enabling humanoid robots to find meaningful applications beyond research labs. A self-imposed constraint on possible answers to this question was the requirement for computational efficiency to ensure future applicability of the developed methods on real humanoid robots with limited resources. To allow the newly developed methods for push recovery specific state estimation to be deployed on a variety of humanoids and wearable assistive devices, one of the goals was to minimize the amount of sensors needed.

7.1 Scientific Contribution

The scientific contribution of this thesis can be summarized as follows.

Disturbance Estimation and Stability Classification Disturbance estimation with a small sensor setup was addressed by analyzing acceleration data from a single body-worn inertial measurement unit mounted on a human subject during push recovery trials. It was shown that even this minimalistic sensing equipment can indicate the direction and the intensity of pushes to the upper body, and that these quantities are related to the type of push recovery action (i. e. *stepping* or *no stepping*) chosen by the human. This methodology, with human-derived strategy decision boundaries, can be transferred to wearable assistive devices or humanoids where torso mounted IMUs are either readily available or can easily be retrofitted.
Furthermore, disturbance estimation specifically for humanoid robots with F/T sensors in the ankles was addressed. A method was presented that enables calculating the 3D action line of a push force applied at arbitrary locations on the humanoid's body based on measurements of the contact wrenches at the feet. This was achieved by projecting the individually measured contact wrenches into a common frame and pseudo-inverting the linear relation between the force application point and the force and torque values, represented as a skew-symmetric matrix. The presented method was implemented and validated on the ARMAR-4 robot.
Building on the premise and previously shown success of minimal sensor setups, a study based on a large collection of augmented human motion data was conducted to investigate whether body-mounted IMUs directly allow the estimation of the current necessity of push recovery in dynamic situations, without the explicit estimation of the disturbance. To this end, an exhaustive search for a classification system, consisting of a sensor setup (number and location of sensors on the body) and a classification technique that can map instantaneous IMU measurements to a binary assessment of

the current stability, was conducted. It was shown that the realization of such a classification system is possible with as little as three body mounted IMUs, using an artificial neural network as classifier.
A crucial component for automatically labeling the training data for this classification system was the development of a new indicator of dynamic stability, the *ZMP-Ratio*. It allows to quantitatively assess the violation of the ZMP-criterion, which on its own is too restrictive to judge the stability of dynamic human motions.

Whole-Body Postural Balancing The presented work on postural balancing is focused on computational efficiency. It was investigated whether inherently efficient linear LQR whole-body balance controllers can be enhanced by better methods of linearizing the ground contact, and by optimizing the weights in the LQR cost function. It was shown that less constrained (with respect to related approaches) linear formulations of the ground contact result in controllers with higher balancing performance, and that optimizing the weight parameters using iterative Simulated Annealing in a reduced parameter space can further increase the controller's capability. Evaluations were carried out in dynamics simulations of a planar robot model, and with the 3D full dynamics model of the ARMAR-4 robot. With the introduced improvements to linear postural balance control, the 3D robot model showed resilience against significantly stronger pushes than a similar approach in related work, based on a rigid ground contact model and not utilizing LQR weight optimization.

Recovery Stepping Aiming at computational efficiency, recovery stepping was realized by mimicking recorded human stepping motions and finding successful adaptations through simulation-based reinforcement learning. Recorded human stepping motions were transferred to the kinematics of ARMAR-4 and encoded as motion primitives on the joint level, allowing fast step parameter adaptation and motion generation without the need for more than one solution of the inverse kinematics (IK) problem per step segment. An efficient scheme for directed experience generation in simulation was devised, which allowed to train a stepping policy that maps the parameters of the push to parameters of the recovery step. This policy was represented as an artificial neural network. The resulting system enables the simulated ARMAR-4 robot to successfully react to pushes from a wide range of directions and intensities, and achieve static stability after taking an appropriate step, without requiring additional measures of balance control. Motion generation with the proposed motion primitive based method is an order of magnitude faster than a method based on task space motion generation and joint angle trajectory computation via iteratively solving the IK problem.

7.2 Discussion and Future Work

This thesis has led to novel approaches and promising results in all three areas that were investigated.

Disturbance Estimation and Stability Classification The unprecedentedly exhaustive search for an optimal classification system for dynamic stability described in Chapter 4, consisting of a small number of body-mounted IMU sensors and a suitable classification technique, has produced interesting results, suggesting that only three sensors and a neural network are a viable option to detect instantaneous instability and hence the need for active push recovery. Future work in this area could aim at further improving the performance of the proposed system by integrating several consecutive frames into the prediction, rather than making predictions based on a single motion frame alone. This measure might enhance robustness and overall performance of the system, especially when moving from emulated sensor data to data collected with actual sensors during human locomotion.

Another promising future line of research is the application of the newly developed ZMP-Ratio to humanoid walking. Many methods for the generation of dynamic walking motions are based on the premise that the ZMP-criterion needs to be fulfilled at all times – despite the fact that humans significantly violate it during dynamic motions. The ZMP-Ratio provides a quantitative measure for this violation that might be considered in novel motion generation methods to create humanoid walking that mimics the dynamic and highly efficient ways humans walk more closely than current methods.

Whole-Body Postural Balancing Both aspects of the optimization method for linear whole-body postural balancing controllers, i. e. less constrained ground contact models and weight optimization, proved successful at enhancing balancing performance. Since reacting to pushes in the sagittal plane (i. e. from the front and back) was identified in to be more challenging, the optimization was focused on these pushes rather than on pushes in the frontal plane (i. e. from left and right). Future work in this area could extend the presented optimization to cover the full range of push directions and investigate unified controllers that adeptly react to the entirety of feasible pushes. While the success of weight optimization was shown using Simulated Annealing, other optimization methods could be investigated and might lead to better results, or result in a faster optimization.

Recovery Stepping The developed step motion generator has proven to be efficient at producing viable, coordinated and effective stepping motions. Learning appropriate step parameters for given push parameters with a policy-gradient reinforcement learning approach was effective for different areas of the push parameter space, both for comparatively weak and strong pushes (in relation to the human experiments). Future work could apply this method to different humanoid robot models and leverage initial training data from different human subjects to assess the ability to generalize, as well as finding policies that generalizes over the entire feasible range of push parameters. Another interesting aspect of future work is to validate the stepping capability on an actual humanoid robot. The method developed in this work was evaluated purely in simulation. Transferring the obtained results to real robotic hardware, i. e. *Sim-to-Real* transfer, is an active research topic in its own right due to the inevitable and multifaceted differences between the simulation and the real world. Those differences originate, among others, from inaccuracies in the underlying simulation model, simplifications of the actual physics in the dynamics simulation for the sake of computational tractability, and from changing contact conditions. A promising method to address this problem is *Domain Randomization*, where a sufficiently expressive policy is trained and tested in a large number of slightly different simulated domains in terms of dynamics models, friction, and other relevant parameters. The obtained policy is expected to successfully generalize to the real world, which is then only another domain with yet slightly different parameters.

Appendix

A DMP Library

The DMP Library[1] is a C++ software library developed at the H^2T to facilitate working with Dynamical Movement Primitives (see Section 2.4). It provides the functionality to learn DMPs from example trajectories using locally weighted regression for single-DoF and multi-DoF setups with a shared canonical system. The number of Gaussian kernel functions can be chosen and varied for experimental purposes. When reproducing a DMP-encoded trajectory using the DMP library, the start-point, the end-point and the temporal scaling factor can be varied to differ from the example trajectory.

B MMM Framework

Recordings of human motions can be an invaluable resource for motion generation for humanoid robots. Human motion data can come from various sources, e. g. from marker-based and markerless optical motion capture, or motion capture with body-worn sensors. To make human motion data accessible for further research, a unified representation of this data, organization in a structured database and programmatic accessibility via an API are required. A large-scale system that fulfills those requirements has been developed at the H^2T [Mandery et al. 2016] and is used throughout this thesis.

[1] https://gitlab.com/h2t/DynamicMovementPrimitive

This system uses the MMM framework and its reference model of the human body for data representation and conversion [Terlemez et al. 2014].

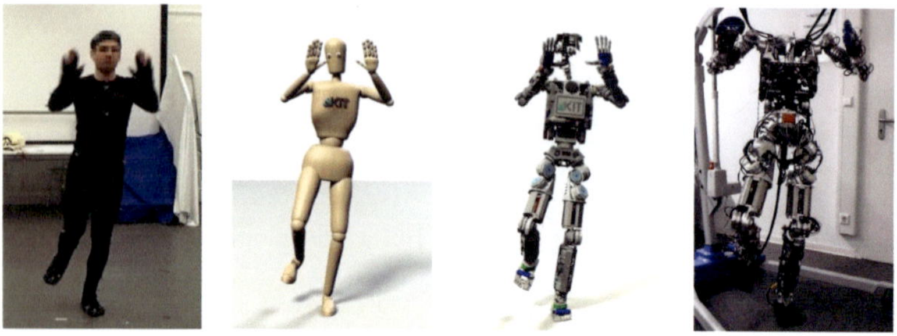

(a) (b) (c) (d)

Figure A.1: Snapshot of a motion that was converted from the human demonstration (a) via the MMM reference model of the human body (b) and the kinematic model of the ARMAR-4 robot (c) to a motion executed on the real robot (d).

Human motion data is acquired on a regular basis at the H^{2}T's Motion Capture Laboratory, which is equipped with a state-of-the-art marker-based optical motion capturing system. The data is organized and stored in the KIT Whole-Body Human Motion Database[2] that provides, among others, the entire motion converted to the MMM reference model in the MMM data format. The MMM framework provides automated converters that allow to adapt the human motions to other kinematic entities, such as the humanoid robot ARMAR-4. This automatic conversion greatly facilitates the generation of robot motions from recorded human motion data. An example of such a conversion is shown in Figure A.1.

[2] `https://motion-database.humanoids.kit.edu/`

C ArmarX

ArmarX[3] is the robot software development environment developed at the H^2T to control and program the robots of the ARMAR robot family[4]. It provides the functionalities and tools to efficiently develop software that can be executed on robots, accessing sensory information and commanding the robot's actuators. Development with ArmarX is facilitated by the use of statecharts that can be edited through a graphical interface and provide easy-to-use building blocks for high-level functionalities. An example statechart is shown in Figure A.2.

„*ArmarX is organized in three layers. The Middleware Layer provides all core facilities to implement distributed applications as well as basic building blocks for robot software architectures. Based on these building blocks, the Robot Framework Layer provides a robot API implementing more complex functionality like kinematics, memory, and perception. Robot specific APIs can be implemented by extending the provided generic robot API modules. Robot programs are realized in the Application Layer. [...] Specialized components can interact with the ArmarX Simulator or the robot hardware via ArmarX RT.*“ [Vahrenkamp et al. 2015]

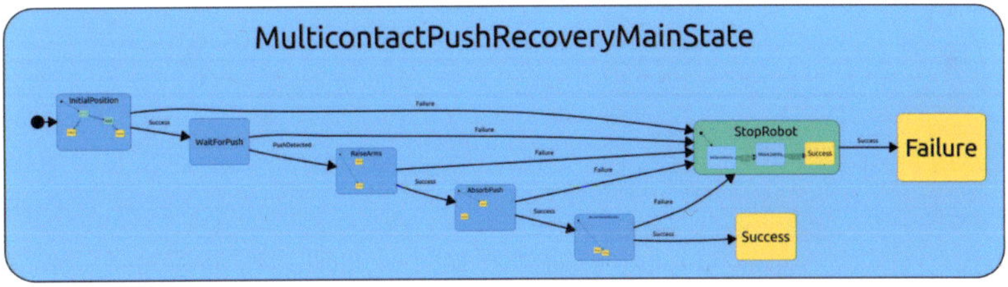

Figure A.2: Example of a robot program represented as an ArmarX statechart. High-level robot skills and behaviors can be built from lower-level building blocks.

[3] `https://armarx.humanoids.kit.edu/`

[4] `http://h2t.anthropomatik.kit.edu/english/397.php`

ArmarX is designed to be robot-agnostic. This means that a real robot can easily be exchanged with a simulation (and vice versa), allowing fast and low-risk development in simulation and later deployment on the real robot without the need of adapting components above the robot-specific real-time layer.

D ARMAR-4

ARMAR-4 [Asfour et al. 2013] is a full-body bipedal humanoid robot with torque-control capabilities in all of its 30 major joints, as well as a large set of proprioceptive sensors.

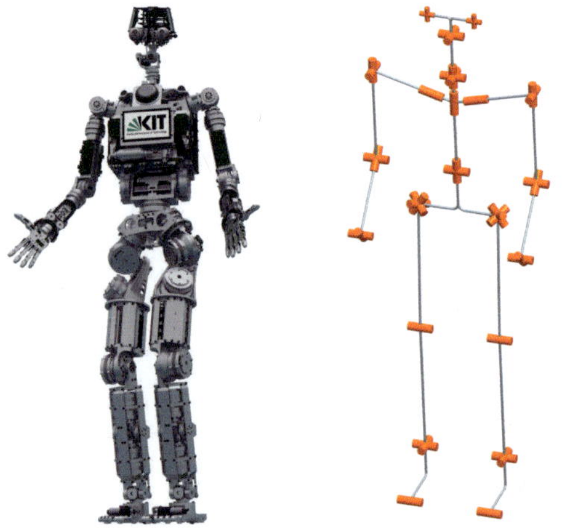

(a) The ARMAR-4 humanoid robot (rendered view)

(b) Kinematic structure of the ARMAR-4 humanoid robot

Figure A.3: Rendering of the ARMAR-4 humanoid robot (a) and the kinematic structure of the robot, excluding the joints of the hands (b). (Both images taken from [Asfour et al. 2013], © 2013 IEEE).

Kinematics and System Architecture The major joints of the robot include six joints per leg (three per hip, one per knee and two per ankle), eight joints per arm (four per shoulder including an inner shoulder joint, two per elbow including forearm rotation and two per wrist) and two for the torso (upper body pitch and rotation). All of these joints are based on similar integrated actuation units that include, amongst other components, an electric brushless DC motor, a *Harmonic Drive* reduction gear, position encoders and a torque sensor. The actuation units that drive the leg joints offer a maximum torque of 157 Nm and a maximum rotational speed of 336 deg/s. The eleven joints that move the neck, the eyes and the toes are based on brushed DC motors and do not feature torque sensors. The eleven joints of each hand are powered by pneumatic actuators. A central PC is responsible for real-time motion control and interfaces all actuators via six CAN-buses. Figure A.3 shows the robot and its kinematic structure.

Proprioceptive Sensing ARMAR-4 includes a large suite of proprioceptive sensors. The three most important sensor types in the context of this thesis are the joint torque sensors, the body-mounted IMU and the Force/-Torque sensors in the ankles. The joint torque sensors make ARMAR-4 a suitable target for torque-based control methods such as LQR whole-body balancing. The joints can also be operated in velocity control mode, enabling the robot to directly execute pre-computed motions such as DMP-based recovery stepping. The IMU mounted on the torso of ARMAR-4 provides the linear acceleration, rotational velocity and absolute orientation of the robot, which are important inputs for methods of state and disturbance estimation. The Force/Torque sensors mounted between the feet and the ankle joints of the robot provide a precise measurement of all forces and torques (i. e. the contact wrench) between the robot and the ground. This information can be used to obtain the Center of Pressure (CoP) and also to reconstruct forces acting on the robot at locations different from the feet.

E Motion Recordings

List of the motion recordings used for the study presented in Section 4.3. All of these 50 files are available from the KIT Whole-Body Human Motion Database[5].

1. push_recovery_right01.xml
2. push_recovery_right02.xml
3. push_recovery_right03.xml
4. push_recovery_right04.xml
5. push_recovery_right05.xml
6. push_recovery_right06.xml
7. push_recovery_right07.xml
8. push_recovery_right08.xml
9. push_recovery_right09.xml
10. push_recovery_right10.xml
11. push_recovery_right11.xml
12. push_recovery_stand_back01.xml
13. push_recovery_stand_back02.xml
14. push_recovery_stand_back03.xml
15. push_recovery_stand_back04.xml
16. push_recovery_stand_back05.xml
17. push_recovery_stand_back06.xml
18. push_recovery_stand_back07.xml
19. push_recovery_stand_back08.xml

[5] https://motion-database.humanoids.kit.edu/

20. push_recovery_stand_back09.xml
21. push_recovery_back02.xml
22. push_recovery_back04.xml
23. push_recovery_back05.xml
24. push_recovery_back06.xml
25. push_recovery_back07.xml
26. push_recovery_back08.xml
27. push_recovery_back10.xml
28. push_recovery_left01.xml
29. push_recovery_left02.xml
30. push_recovery_left03.xml
31. push_recovery_left05.xml
32. push_recovery_left06.xml
33. push_recovery_left07.xml
34. push_recovery_left08.xml
35. push_recovery_left09.xml
36. push_recovery_left10.xml
37. push_recovery_front04.xml,
38. push_recovery_front05.xml
39. push_recovery_front06.xml
40. push_recovery_front07.xml
41. push_recovery_front09.xml
42. push_from_behind08.xml
43. push_from_behind11.xml
44. push_from_behind12.xml

45. push_from_the_left_side10.xml
46. push_from_the_left_side11.xml
47. push_from_the_left_side12.xml
48. push_from_the_front09.xml
49. push_front_hard03.xml
50. push_recovery_stand_right11.xml

F Classifier Hyperparameters

The classifiers investigated in Section 4.3 of Chapter 4 were all implemented using their respective standard implementation from the *scikit-learn* Python library[6]. The essential hyperparameters are listed in Table A.1. Parameters that are not listed were set to their default values. Parameters that differed from the default values in scikit-learn are highlighted.

Classifier	Hyperparameter	Value
Naive Bayes	Distribution Type	Gaussian
k-Nearest Neighbors	k	10
Bagged-kNN	k	10
	# base classifiers	10
	# samples for base classifiers	0.5 #overall Samples
	# features for base classifiers	0.5 #overall Features
Perceptron	regularization type	L1
	regularization coefficient α	0.001
Neural Network	activation function	Hyperbolic Tangent
	# hidden layers	1
	# hidden units	100
Support Vector Machine	kernel type	Linear
	penalty coefficient C	1

Table A.1: Essential hyperparameters for the classifiers used in Section 4.3 of Chapter 4. Parameters that differ from the default values in scikit-learn are highlighted.

[6] https://scikit-learn.org/stable/

G Simulated Annealing

The Simulated Annealing algorithm for optimizing LQR weights W in the setting of Chapter 5, where the balancing performance p is evaluated in dynamics simulation.

Algorithm A.4 Simulated Annealing

Require:

T_0 – Initial temperature
α – Cooling coefficient $0 < \alpha < 1$
n_{max} – Number of iterations
evaluatePerformance(W) – Objective function (dynamics simulation)

function SIMULATEDANNEALING(T_0, α, n_{max})
  $W \leftarrow$ random ▷ Initialize current weights
  $W_{opt} \leftarrow W$ ▷ Initialize Current best weights
  $p \leftarrow$ evaluatePerformance(W) ▷ Performance from simulation
  $p_{opt} \leftarrow p$ ▷ Initialize current best performance
  $T \leftarrow T_0$ ▷ Initialize temperature
  for $n \leftarrow 1 \ldots n_{max}$ **do**
    $W_{new} \leftarrow$ randomFromGaussian ▷ Gaussian distr. around W
    p_{new} = evaluatePerformance(W_{new}) ▷ Dynamics Simulation
    if $p_{new} \geq p$ **then** ▷ New weights are better than current
      $W \leftarrow W_{new}$ ▷ Update current weights
      $p \leftarrow p_{new}$ ▷ Update current performance
      if $p_{new} > p_{opt}$ **then** ▷ New performance is current best
        $W_{opt} \leftarrow W_{new}$ ▷ Update current best weights
        $p_{opt} \leftarrow p_{new}$ ▷ Update current best performance
      end if
    else ▷ New weights are worse than current
      $(W \leftarrow W_{new}, p \leftarrow p_{new})$ with probability $exp\left(\frac{p(W_{new})-p(W)}{T}\right)$
    end if
    $T \leftarrow \alpha T$ ▷ Cooling
  end for
  return W_{opt}
end function

List of Figures

List of Tables

List of Algorithms

Acronyms

ADC Analog to Digital Converter

ANN Artificial Neural Network

CAN Controller Area Network

CoM Center of Mass

CoP Center of Pressure

DARPA Defense Advanced Research Project Agency

DCM Divergent Component of Motion

DDP Differential Dynamic Programming

DLR Deutsches Zentrum für Luft- und Raumfahrt

DMP Dynamic Movement Primitive

DNN Deep Neural Network

DoF Degree of Freedom

F/T sensor 6-DoF Force/Torque Sensor

FZMP Fictitious Zero Moment Point

H^2T High Performance Humanoid Technologies

HMM Hidden Markov Model

HRP Japanese Humanoid Robotics Project

ICP Instantaneous Capture Point

IK Inverse Kinematics

IMU Inertial Measurement Unit

KIT Karlsruhe Institute of Technology
kNN k-Nearest Neighbors

LIPM Linear Inverted Pendulum Model
LQR Linear Quadratic Regulator

MMM Master Motor Map
MPC Model Predictive Control

NASA National Aeronautics and Space Administration
NB Naive Bayes
NN Neural Network

PD Proportional Derivative

QP Quadratic Program

ReLU Rectified Linear Unit
RL Reinforcement Learning

SA Simulated Annealing
SP Support Polygon
SQP Sequential Quadratic Program
SVM Support Vector Machine

ZMP Zero Moment Point

Bibliography

Z. Aftab, T. Robert, and P.-B. Wieber. Ankle, hip and stepping strategies for humanoid balance recovery with a single model predictive control scheme. In *Humanoid Robots (Humanoids), 2012 12th IEEE-RAS International Conference on*, pages 159–164. IEEE, 2012. 68

C. E. Agüero, N. Koenig, I. Chen, H. Boyer, S. Peters, J. Hsu, B. Gerkey, S. Paepcke, J. L. Rivero, J. Manzo, et al. Inside the virtual robotics challenge: Simulating real-time robotic disaster response. *IEEE Transactions on Automation Science and Engineering*, 12(2):494–506, 2015. 55

B. D. Anderson and J. B. Moore. *Optimal control: linear quadratic methods*. Courier Corporation, 2007. 24

M. Andrychowicz, B. Baker, M. Chociej, R. Jozefowicz, B. McGrew, J. Pachocki, A. Petron, M. Plappert, G. Powell, A. Ray, J. Schneider, S. Sidor, J. Tobin, P. Welinder, L. Weng, and W. Zaremba. Learning dexterous in-hand manipulation. *ArXiv, arXiv:1808.00177*, 2018. 36

T. Asfour, J. Schill, H. Peters, C. Klas, J. Bucker, C. Sander, S. Schulz, A. Kargov, T. Werner, and V. Bartenbach. ARMAR-4: A 63 DOF Torque Controlled Humanoid Robot. In *2013 13th IEEE-RAS International Conference on Humanoid Robots (Humanoids)*, pages 390–396, Oct. 2013. 16, 198

S. Bäuerle. Entwurf und Implementierung eines LQ-Reglers zum Balancieren humanoider Roboter. Master thesis, Karlsruhe Institute of Technology (KIT), May 2018. 139, 141

S. Bäuerle, L. Kaul, and T. Asfour. Linear contact modeling and stochastic parameter optimization for LQR-based whole-body push recovery. In *IEEE/RAS International Conference on Humanoid Robots (Humanoids)*, pages 224–231, 2018. 118, 119, 126, 142, 144

M. Behnisch, R. Haschke, and M. Gienger. Task space motion planning using reactive control. In *Intelligent Robots and Systems (IROS), 2010 IEEE/RSJ International Conference on*, pages 5934–5940. IEEE, 2010. 149

A. Ben-Israel and T. N. Greville. *Generalized inverses: theory and applications*, volume 15. Springer Science & Business Media, 2003. 91

J. S. Bergstra, R. Bardenet, Y. Bengio, and B. Kégl. Algorithms for hyper-parameter optimization. In *Advances in neural information processing systems*, pages 2546–2554, 2011. 31

J. Borras and T. Asfour. A whole-body pose taxonomy for loco-manipulation tasks. In *Intelligent Robots and Systems (IROS), 2015 IEEE/RSJ International Conference on*, pages 1578–1585. IEEE, 2015. 14

Boston Dynamics. Atlas - the world's most dynamic humanoid. `https://www.bostondynamics.com/atlas`, 2018. Accessed: 2018-07-23. 16

K. Bouyarmane and A. Kheddar. On the dynamics modeling of free-floating-base articulated mechanisms and applications to humanoid whole-body dynamics and control. In *Humanoid Robots (Humanoids), 2012 12th IEEE-RAS International Conference on*, pages 36–42. IEEE, 2012. 14, 15

S. Boyd and C. Barratt. Linear controller design: limits of performance. Technical report, Stanford University Stanford United States, 1991. 24

A. Bryson. Time-varying linear-quadratic control. *Journal of optimization theory and applications*, 100(3):515–525, 1999. 60

A. Bryson and Y. Ho. Applied optimal control. *New York: Hemisphere*, 1975. 119

bulletphysics. Bullet physics engine. `http://bulletphysics.org/`, 2018. Accessed: 2018-08-20. 39, 174

G. Cannata, M. Maggiali, G. Metta, and G. Sandini. An embedded artificial skin for humanoid robots. In *Multisensor Fusion and Integration for Intelligent Systems, 2008. MFI 2008. IEEE International Conference on*, pages 434–438. IEEE, 2008. 45

S.-J. Chung and N. Pollard. Predictable behavior during contact simulation: a comparison of selected physics engines. *Computer Animation and Virtual Worlds*, 27(3-4):262–270, 2016. 39, 174

A. De Luca and R. Mattone. Actuator failure detection and isolation using generalized momenta. In *Robotics and Automation, 2003. Proceedings. ICRA'03. IEEE International Conference on*, volume 1, pages 634–639. IEEE, 2003. 47

A. De Luca and R. Mattone. Sensorless robot collision detection and hybrid force/motion control. In *Robotics and Automation, 2005. ICRA 2005. Proceedings of the 2005 IEEE International Conference on*, pages 999–1004. IEEE, 2005. 47

G. De Maria, C. Natale, and S. Pirozzi. Force/tactile sensor for robotic applications. *Sensors and Actuators A: Physical*, 175:60–72, 2012. 46

H. Diedam, D. Dimitrov, P.-B. Wieber, K. Mombaur, and M. Diehl. Online walking gait generation with adaptive foot positioning through linear model predictive control. In *IROS 2008-IEEE-RSJ International Conference on Intelligent Robots & Systems*, pages 1121–1126. IEEE, 2008. 66

M. Diehl and K. Mombaur. *Fast motions in biomechanics and robotics*. Springer, 2006. 21

W. Ding, X. Chen, Z. Yu, L. Meng, M. Ceccarelli, and Q. Huang. Fall protection of humanoids inspired by human fall motion. In *IEEE/RAS International Conference on Humanoid Robots (Humanoids)*, pages 827–833, 2018. 42

K. Doughty, R. Lewis, and A. McIntosh. The design of a practical and reliable fall detector for community and institutional telecare. *Journal of Telemedicine and Telecare*, 6(1_suppl):150–154, 2000. 44

J. Englsberger, C. Ott, M. A. Roa, A. Albu-Schäffer, and G. Hirzinger. Bipedal walking control based on capture point dynamics. In *Intelligent Robots and Systems (IROS), 2011 IEEE/RSJ International Conference on*, pages 4420–4427. IEEE, 2011. 63, 66

J. Englsberger, T. Koolen, S. Bertrand, J. Pratt, C. Ott, and A. Albu-Schäffer. Trajectory generation for continuous leg forces during double support and heel-to-toe shift based on divergent component of motion. In *Intelligent Robots and Systems (IROS 2014), 2014 IEEE/RSJ International Conference on*, pages 4022–4029. IEEE, 2014a. 66

J. Englsberger, A. Werner, C. Ott, B. Henze, M. A. Roa, G. Garofalo, R. Burger, A. Beyer, O. Eiberger, K. Schmid, et al. Overview of the torque-controlled humanoid robot TORO. In *Humanoid Robots (Humanoids), 2014 14th IEEE-RAS International Conference on*, pages 916–923. IEEE, 2014b. 16

J. Englsberger, C. Ott, and A. Albu-Schäffer. Three-dimensional bipedal walking control based on divergent component of motion. *IEEE Transactions on Robotics*, 31(2):355–368, 2015. 63, 66

S. Z. Erdogan, T. T. Bilgin, and J. Cho. Fall detection by using K-nearest neighbor algorithm on WSN data. In *GLOBECOM Workshops (GC Wkshps), 2010 IEEE*, pages 2054–2058. IEEE, 2010. 44

T. Erez, Y. Tassa, and E. Todorov. Simulation tools for model-based robotics: Comparison of Bullet, Havok, MuJoCo, ODE and PhysX. In *Robotics and Automation (ICRA), 2015 IEEE International Conference on*, pages 4397–4404. IEEE, 2015. 39

J. Ernesti, L. Righetti, M. Do, T. Asfour, and S. Schaal. Encoding of periodic and their transient motions by a single dynamic movement primitive. In *Humanoid Robots (Humanoids), 2012 IEEE-RAS International Conference on*, pages 57–64, 2012. 25

R. Featherstone. *Rigid body dynamics algorithms*. Springer, New York, 2008. ISBN 978-0-387-74314-1. 12, 13, 91

S. Feng, X. Xinjilefu, W. Huang, and C. G. Atkeson. 3D walking based on online optimization. In *Humanoid Robots (Humanoids), 2013 13th IEEE-RAS International Conference on*, pages 21–27. IEEE, 2013. 50, 51, 55

F. Flacco, A. Paolillo, and A. Kheddar. Residual-based contacts estimation for humanoid robots. In *Humanoid Robots (Humanoids), 2016 IEEE-RAS 16th International Conference on*, pages 409–415. IEEE, 2016. 48

T. Flash and N. Hogan. The coordination of arm movements: an experimentally confirmed mathematical model. *Journal of neuroscience*, 5(7): 1688–1703, 1985. 28

M. Fumagalli, M. Randazzo, F. Nori, L. Natale, G. Metta, and G. Sandini. Exploiting proximal F/T measurements for the iCub active compliance. In *Intelligent Robots and Systems (IROS), 2010 IEEE/RSJ International Conference on*, pages 1870–1876. IEEE, 2010. 47

S. F. Giszter, F. A. Mussa-Ivaldi, and E. Bizzi. Convergent force fields organized in the frog's spinal cord. *Journal of neuroscience*, 13(2):467–491, 1993. 25

I. Goodfellow, Y. Bengio, and A. Courville. *Deep Learning*. MIT Press, 2016. `http://www.deeplearningbook.org`. 32

R. J. Griffin and A. Leonessa. Model predictive control for dynamic footstep adjustment using the divergent component of motion. In *Robotics and Automation (ICRA), 2016 IEEE International Conference on*, pages 1763–1768. IEEE, 2016. 15, 66

R. J. Griffin, G. Wiedebach, S. Bertrand, A. Leonessa, and J. Pratt. Walking stabilization using step timing and location adjustment on the humanoid robot, Atlas. *Intelligent Robots and Systems (IROS), 2017 IEEE/RSJ International Conference on*, 2017. 67

S. Haddadin, A. De Luca, and A. Albu-Schäffer. Robot collisions: A survey on detection, isolation, and identification. *IEEE Transactions on Robotics*, 33(6):1292–1312, 2017. 46

T. Hastie, R. Tibshirani, and J. Friedman. Unsupervised learning. In *The elements of statistical learning*, pages 485–585. Springer, 2009. 32

B. Henze, M. A. Roa, and C. Ott. Passivity-based whole-body balancing for torque-controlled humanoid robots in multi-contact scenarios. *The International Journal of Robotics Research*, 35(12):1522–1543, 2016. 49

A. Herdt, H. Diedam, P.-B. Wieber, D. Dimitrov, K. Mombaur, and M. Diehl. Online walking motion generation with automatic footstep placement. *Advanced Robotics*, 24(5-6):719–737, 2010. 66, 68

H. Herr and M. Popovic. Angular momentum in human walking. *Journal of Experimental Biology*, 211(4):467–481, 2008. 124

G. Hettich, L. Assländer, A. Gollhofer, and T. Mergner. Human hip–ankle coordination emerging from multisensory feedback control. *Human movement science*, 37:123–146, 2014. 48

H. Hirukawa, F. Kanehiro, K. Kaneko, S. Kajita, K. Fujiwara, Y. Kawai, F. Tomita, S. Hirai, K. Tanie, T. Isozumi, et al. Humanoid robotics platforms developed in HRP. *Robotics and Autonomous Systems*, 48(4):165–175, 2004. 16

A. Hof, M. Gazendam, and W. Sinke. The condition for dynamic stability. *Journal of biomechanics*, 38(1):1–8, 2005. 63

A. L. Hof. The 'extrapolated center of mass' concept suggests a simple control of balance in walking. *Human movement science*, 27(1):112–125, 2008. 63

F. B. Horak and L. M. Nashner. Central programming of postural movements: adaptation to altered support-surface configurations. *Journal of neurophysiology*, 55(6):1369–1381, 1986. 48

Q. Huang, K. Yokoi, S. Kajita, K. Kaneko, H. Arai, N. Koyachi, and K. Tanie. Planning walking patterns for a biped robot. *IEEE Transactions on robotics and automation*, 17(3):280–289, 2001. 21

S.-H. Hyon. Compliant terrain adaptation for biped humanoids without measuring ground surface and contact forces. *IEEE Transactions on Robotics*, 25(1):171–178, 2009. 56

S.-H. Hyon, J. G. Hale, G. Cheng, et al. Full-body compliant human-humanoid interaction: Balancing in the presence of unknown external forces. *IEEE Trans. Robotics*, 23(5):884–898, 2007. 45

S.-H. Hyon, R. Osu, and Y. Otaka. Integration of multi-level postural balancing on humanoid robots. In *Robotics and Automation, 2009. ICRA'09. IEEE International Conference on*, pages 1549–1556. IEEE, 2009. 48, 49

A. J. Ijspeert, J. Nakanishi, and S. Schaal. Movement imitation with nonlinear dynamical systems in humanoid robots. In *Robotics and Automation, 2002. Proceedings. ICRA'02. IEEE International Conference on*, volume 2, pages 1398–1403. IEEE, 2002. 26

A. J. Ijspeert, J. Nakanishi, and S. Schaal. Learning attractor landscapes for learning motor primitives. In *Advances in neural information processing systems*, pages 1547–1554, 2003. 26

A. J. Ijspeert, J. Nakanishi, H. Hoffmann, P. Pastor, and S. Schaal. Dynamical Movement Primitives: learning attractor models for motor behaviors. *Neural computation*, 25(2):328–373, 2013. 26, 29

K. Ishihara and J. Morimoto. Real-time model predictive control with two-step optimization based on singularly perturbed system. In *Humanoid Robots (Humanoids), 2015 IEEE-RAS 15th International Conference on*, pages 173–180. IEEE, 2015. 15

S. Ivaldi, M. Fumagalli, M. Randazzo, F. Nori, G. Metta, and G. Sandini. Computing robot internal/external wrenches by means of inertial, tactile and F/T sensors: Theory and implementation on the iCub. In *Humanoid Robots (Humanoids), 2011 IEEE-RAS International Conference on*, pages 521–528, 2011. 47

D. H. Jacobson and D. Q. Mayne. *Differential dynamic programming*. American Elsevier Publishing Company New York, New York, 1970. 55

M. Johnson, B. Shrewsbury, S. Bertrand, T. Wu, D. Duran, M. Floyd, P. Abeles, D. Stephen, N. Mertins, A. Lesman, et al. Team IHMC's lessons learned from the DARPA robotics challenge trials. *Journal of Field Robotics*, 32(2):192–208, 2015. 55, 75

A. Jordao, A. C. Nazare Jr, J. Sena, and W. R. Schwartz. Human activity recognition based on wearable sensor data: A standardization of the state-of-the-art. *arXiv preprint arXiv:1806.05226*, 2018. 107

S. Kajita and K. Tani. Study of dynamic biped locomotion on rugged terrain-derivation and application of the linear inverted pendulum mode. In *Robotics and Automation, 1991. Proceedings., 1991 IEEE International Conference on*, pages 1405–1411. IEEE, 1991. 19

S. Kajita, F. Kanehiro, K. Kaneko, K. Yokoi, and H. Hirukawa. The 3D linear inverted pendulum mode: A simple modeling for a biped walking pattern generation. In *Intelligent Robots and Systems, 2001. Proceedings. 2001 IEEE/RSJ International Conference on*, volume 1, pages 239–246. IEEE, 2001. 19

S. Kajita, F. Kanehiro, K. Kaneko, K. Fujiwara, K. Harada, K. Yokoi, and H. Hirukawa. Biped walking pattern generation by using preview control of zero-moment point. In *Robotics and Automation, 2003. Proceedings. ICRA'03. IEEE International Conference on*, volume 2, pages 1620–1626. IEEE, 2003. 19, 22, 58, 66

S. Kajita, M. Morisawa, K. Harada, K. Kaneko, F. Kanehiro, K. Fujiwara, and H. Hirukawa. Biped walking pattern generator allowing auxiliary ZMP control. In *Intelligent Robots and Systems, 2006 IEEE/RSJ International Conference on*, pages 2993–2999. IEEE, 2006. 22

S. Kajita, M. Morisawa, K. Miura, S. Nakaoka, K. Harada, K. Kaneko, F. Kanehiro, and K. Yokoi. Biped walking stabilization based on linear inverted pendulum tracking. In *Intelligent Robots and Systems (IROS),*

2010 IEEE/RSJ International Conference on, pages 4489–4496. IEEE, 2010. 17, 21, 56, 57

S. Kalyanakrishnan and A. Goswami. Predicting falls of a humanoid robot through machine learning. In *Proceedings of the Twenty-second IAAI Conference on Artificial Intelligence*, pages 1793–1798. Association for the Advancement of Artificial Intelligence (AAAI), 2010. 42, 43, 44

K. Kaneko, F. Kanehiro, S. Kajita, H. Hirukawa, T. Kawasaki, M. Hirata, K. Akachi, and T. Isozumi. Humanoid robot HRP-2. In *Robotics and Automation, 2004. Proceedings. ICRA '04. 2004 IEEE International Conference on*, volume 2, pages 1083–1090 Vol.2, April 2004. doi: 10.1109/ROBOT.2004.1307969. 16

K. Kaneko, F. Kanehiro, M. Morisawa, K. Akachi, G. Miyamori, A. Hayashi, and N. Kanehira. Humanoid robot HRP-4-humanoid robotics platform with lightweight and slim body. In *Intelligent Robots and Systems (IROS), 2011 IEEE/RSJ International Conference on*, pages 4400–4407. IEEE, 2011. 16

O. Kanoun, F. Lamiraux, P.-B. Wieber, F. Kanehiro, E. Yoshida, and J.-P. Laumond. Prioritizing linear equality and inequality systems: application to local motion planning for redundant robots. In *ICRA 2009-IEEE International Conference on Robotics & Automation*, pages 2939–2944. IEEE, 2009. 52

D. M. Karantonis, M. R. Narayanan, M. Mathie, N. H. Lovell, and B. G. Celler. Implementation of a real-time human movement classifier using a triaxial accelerometer for ambulatory monitoring. *IEEE transactions on information technology in biomedicine*, 10(1):156–167, 2006. 44

G. Karer and I. Škrjanc. *Predictive approaches to control of complex systems*, volume 454. Springer, 2012. 14

N. Kashiri, J. Malzahn, and N. G. Tsagarakis. On the sensor design of torque controlled actuators: A comparison study of strain gauge and encoder-based principles. *IEEE Robotics and Automation Letters*, 2(2): 1186–1194, 2017. 15

L. Kaul and T. Asfour. Human push-recovery: Strategy selection based on push intensity estimation. In *ISR 2016: 47th International Symposium on Robotics; Proceedings of*, pages 547–554. VDE VERLAG, Berlin, Offenbach, 2016. 76, 78, 81, 84, 85, 88

M. Khadiv, A. Herzog, S. A. A. Moosavian, and L. Righetti. Step timing adjustment: A step toward generating robust gaits. In *Humanoid Robots (Humanoids), 2016 IEEE-RAS 16th International Conference on*, pages 35–42. IEEE, 2016. 68

J. Kober, J. A. Bagnell, and J. Peters. Reinforcement learning in robotics: A survey. *The International Journal of Robotics Research*, 32(11):1238–1274, 2013. 32, 36

A. Kolker, M. Jokesch, and U. Thomas. An optical tactile sensor for measuring force values and directions for several soft and rigid contacts. In *ISR 2016: 47st International Symposium on Robotics; Proceedings of*, pages 1–6. VDE, 2016. 46

T. Koolen, T. De Boer, J. Rebula, A. Goswami, and J. Pratt. Capturability-based analysis and control of legged locomotion, part 1: Theory and application to three simple gait models. *The International Journal of Robotics Research*, 31(9):1094–1113, 2012. 63, 66

T. Koolen, S. Bertrand, G. Thomas, T. De Boer, T. Wu, J. Smith, J. Englsberger, and J. Pratt. Design of a momentum-based control framework and application to the humanoid robot Atlas. *International Journal of Humanoid Robotics*, 13(01):1650007, 2016. 55

P. Kryczka, P. Kormushev, N. G. Tsagarakis, and D. G. Caldwell. Online regeneration of bipedal walking gait pattern optimizing footstep placement and timing. In *Intelligent Robots and Systems (IROS), 2015 IEEE/RSJ International Conference on*, pages 3352–3357. IEEE, 2015. 68

S. Kudoh, T. Komura, and K. Ikeuchi. The dynamic postural adjustment with the quadratic programming method. In *Intelligent Robots and Systems, 2002. IEEE/RSJ International Conference on*, volume 3, pages 2563–2568. IEEE, 2002. 54

S. Kuindersma, F. Permenter, and R. Tedrake. An efficiently solvable quadratic program for stabilizing dynamic locomotion. In *Robotics and Automation (ICRA), 2014 IEEE International Conference on*, pages 2589–2594. IEEE, 2014. 12, 13, 53, 55, 58

S. Kuindersma, R. Deits, M. Fallon, A. Valenzuela, H. Dai, F. Permenter, T. Koolen, P. Marion, and R. Tedrake. Optimization-based locomotion planning, estimation, and control design for the Atlas humanoid robot. *Autonomous Robots*, 40(3):429–455, 2016. 50, 51

S.-H. Lee and A. Goswami. A momentum-based balance controller for humanoid robots on non-level and non-stationary ground. *Autonomous Robots*, 33(4):399–414, 2012. 124

S. Levine and V. Koltun. Learning complex neural network policies with trajectory optimization. In *ICML '14: Proceedings of the 31st International Conference on Machine Learning*, 2014. 69

F. L. Lewis, D. Vrabie, and V. L. Syrmos. *Optimal control*. John Wiley & Sons, 2012. 119

W. Li and E. Todorov. Iterative linear quadratic regulator design for nonlinear biological movement systems. In *ICINCO (1)*, pages 222–229, 2004. 60

D. Luo, X. Han, Y. Ding, Y. Ma, Z. Liu, and X. Wu. Learning push recovery for a bipedal humanoid robot with dynamical movement primitives. In *Humanoid Robots (Humanoids), 2015 IEEE-RAS 15th International Conference on*, pages 1013–1019. IEEE, 2015. 70, 71

E. Magrini, F. Flacco, and A. De Luca. Estimation of contact forces using a virtual force sensor. In *Intelligent Robots and Systems (IROS 2014), 2014 IEEE/RSJ International Conference on*, pages 2126–2133. IEEE, 2014. 47

C. Mandery, Ö. Terlemez, M. Do, N. Vahrenkamp, and T. Asfour. Unifying representations and large-scale whole-body motion databases for studying human motion. *IEEE Transactions on Robotics*, 32(4):796–809, 2016. 99, 151, 195

L. Manuelli and R. Tedrake. Localizing external contact using proprioceptive sensors: The contact particle filter. In *Intelligent Robots and Systems (IROS), 2016 IEEE/RSJ International Conference on*, pages 5062–5069. IEEE, 2016. 46

A. Marco, P. Hennig, J. Bohg, S. Schaal, and S. Trimpe. Automatic LQR tuning based on gaussian process global optimization. In *Robotics and Automation (ICRA), 2016 IEEE International Conference on*, pages 270–277. IEEE, 2016. 61, 117

S. Mason, L. Righetti, and S. Schaal. Full dynamics LQR control of a humanoid robot: An experimental study on balancing and squatting. In *Humanoid Robots (Humanoids), 2014 14th IEEE-RAS International Conference on*, pages 374–379. IEEE, 2014. 25, 58, 59, 60, 116, 121, 122, 127, 135, 144

S. Mason, N. Rotella, S. Schaal, and L. Righetti. Balancing and walking using full dynamics LQR control with contact constraints. In *Humanoid*

Robots (Humanoids), 2016 IEEE-RAS 16th International Conference on, pages 63–68. IEEE, 2016. 25, 59, 60, 116

MathWorks. Simscape multibody. `https://de.mathworks.com/products/simmechanics.html`, 2018. Accessed: 2018-08-20. 40

T. Matsubara, S.-H. Hyon, and J. Morimoto. Learning parametric dynamic movement primitives from multiple demonstrations. *Neural networks*, 24 (5):493–500, 2011. 29

R. B. McGhee and G. I. Iswandhi. Adaptive locomotion of a multilegged robot over rough terrain. *IEEE transactions on systems, man, and cybernetics*, 9(4):176–182, 1979. 19

M. Mistry, J. Buchli, and S. Schaal. Inverse dynamics control of floating base systems using orthogonal decomposition. In *Robotics and Automation (ICRA), 2010 IEEE International Conference on*, pages 3406–3412. Citeseer, 2010. 13

P. Mittendorfer and G. Cheng. Humanoid multimodal tactile-sensing modules. *IEEE Transactions on robotics*, 27(3):401–410, 2011. 45

V. Mnih, K. Kavukcuoglu, D. Silver, A. A. Rusu, J. Veness, M. G. Bellemare, A. Graves, M. Riedmiller, A. K. Fidjeland, G. Ostrovski, et al. Human-level control through deep reinforcement learning. *Nature*, 518 (7540):529, 2015. 36

K. Mombaur. Using optimization to create self-stable human-like running. *Robotica*, 27(3):321–330, 2009. 50

J. Moya, J. Ruiz-del Solar, M. Orchard, and I. Parra-Tsunekawa. Fall detection and damage reduction in biped humanoid robots. *International Journal of Humanoid Robotics*, 12(01):1550001, 2015. 44

F. A. Mussa-Ivaldi. Nonlinear force fields: a distributed system of control primitives for representing and learning movements. In *Computational Intelligence in Robotics and Automation, 1997. CIRA'97., Proceedings., 1997 IEEE International Symposium on*, pages 84–90. IEEE, 1997. 25

V. Nair and G. E. Hinton. Rectified linear units improve restricted boltzmann machines. In *Proceedings of the 27th international conference on machine learning (ICML-10)*, pages 807–814, 2010. 34

O. Ojetola, E. I. Gaura, and J. Brusey. Fall detection with wearable sensors – SAFE (SmArt Fall dEtection). In *2011 Seventh International Conference on Intelligent Environments*, pages 318–321. IEEE, 2011. 44

D. E. Orin and A. Goswami. Centroidal momentum matrix of a humanoid robot: Structure and properties. *dynamics*, 4:6, 2008. 124

C. Ott and Y. Nakamura. Admittance control using a base force/torque sensor. *IFAC Proceedings Volumes*, 42(16):467–472, 2009. 48

J. Pankert. Human-inspired capture-stepping for push-recovery of humanoid robots. Master thesis, Karlsruhe Institute of Technology (KIT), June 2018. 153, 154, 165, 169, 171, 173

J. Pankert, L. Kaul, and T. Asfour. Learning efficient omni-directional capture stepping for humanoid robots from human motion and simulation data. In *IEEE/RAS International Conference on Humanoid Robots (Humanoids)*, pages 503–509, 2018. 148, 161, 166, 175, 181, 182, 183

F. Pedregosa, G. Varoquaux, A. Gramfort, V. Michel, B. Thirion, O. Grisel, M. Blondel, P. Prettenhofer, R. Weiss, V. Dubourg, J. Vanderplas, A. Passos, D. Cournapeau, M. Brucher, M. Perrot, and E. Duchesnay. Scikit-learn: Machine learning in Python. *Journal of Machine Learning Research*, 12:2825–2830, 2011. 105

X. B. Peng, G. Berseth, K. Yin, and M. Van De Panne. Deeploco: Dynamic locomotion skills using hierarchical deep reinforcement learning. *ACM Transactions on Graphics (TOG)*, 36(4):41, 2017. 70, 164

X. B. Peng, P. Abbeel, S. Levine, and M. van de Panne. Deepmimic: Example-guided deep reinforcement learning of physics-based character skills. *arXiv preprint arXiv:1804.02717*, 2018. 70

M. B. Popovic, A. Goswami, and H. Herr. Ground reference points in legged locomotion: Definitions, biological trajectories and control implications. *The International Journal of Robotics Research*, 24(12):1013–1032, 2005. 21

M. Posa, C. Cantu, and R. Tedrake. A direct method for trajectory optimization of rigid bodies through contact. *The International Journal of Robotics Research*, 33(1):69–81, 2014. 50

G. Pratt and J. Manzo. The DARPA robotics challenge [competitions]. *IEEE Robotics & Automation Magazine*, 20(2):10–12, 2013. 51

J. Pratt, J. Carff, S. Drakunov, and A. Goswami. Capture point: A step toward humanoid push recovery. In *Humanoid Robots, 2006 6th IEEE-RAS International Conference on*, pages 200–207. IEEE, 2006. 19, 62, 63, 64

J. Pratt, T. Koolen, T. De Boer, J. Rebula, S. Cotton, J. Carff, M. Johnson, and P. Neuhaus. Capturability-based analysis and control of legged locomotion, part 2: Application to M2V2, a lower-body humanoid. *The International Journal of Robotics Research*, 31(10):1117–1133, 2012. 65, 66

N. A. Radford, P. Strawser, K. Hambuchen, J. S. Mehling, W. K. Verdeyen, A. S. Donnan, J. Holley, J. Sanchez, V. Nguyen, L. Bridgwater, et al. Valkyrie: NASA's first bipedal humanoid robot. *Journal of Field Robotics*, 32(3):397–419, 2015. 16

J. Rebula, F. Canas, J. Pratt, and A. Goswami. Learning capture points for humanoid push recovery. In *Humanoid Robots, 2007 7th IEEE-RAS International Conference on*, pages 65–72. IEEE, 2007. 65, 172

R. Renner and S. Behnke. Instability detection and fall avoidance for a humanoid using attitude sensors and reflexes. In *Intelligent robots and systems, 2006 IEEE/RSJ international conference on*, pages 2967–2973. IEEE, 2006. 45

A. Roncone, M. Hoffmann, U. Pattacini, and G. Metta. Learning peripersonal space representation through artificial skin for avoidance and reaching with whole body surface. In *Intelligent Robots and Systems (IROS), 2015 IEEE/RSJ International Conference on*, pages 3366–3373. IEEE, 2015. 46

N. Rotella, M. Bloesch, L. Righetti, and S. Schaal. State estimation for a humanoid robot. In *Intelligent Robots and Systems (IROS 2014), 2014 IEEE/RSJ International Conference on*, pages 952–958. IEEE, 2014. 75

N. Rotella, S. Mason, S. Schaal, and L. Righetti. Inertial sensor-based humanoid joint state estimation. In *Robotics and Automation (ICRA), 2016 IEEE International Conference on*, pages 1825–1831. IEEE, 2016. 75

L. Saab, O. E. Ramos, F. Keith, N. Mansard, P. Soueres, and J.-Y. Fourquet. Dynamic whole-body motion generation under rigid contacts and other unilateral constraints. *IEEE Transactions on Robotics*, 29(2):346–362, 2013. 51

S. Schaal. Dynamic movement primitives – a framework for motor control in humans and humanoid robotics. In *Adaptive motion of animals and machines*, pages 261–280. Springer, 2006. 26

T. B. Sheridan. Three models of preview control. *IEEE Transactions on Human Factors in Electronics*, HFE-7(2):91–102, June 1966. 58

D. Silver, A. Huang, C. J. Maddison, A. Guez, L. Sifre, G. Van Den Driessche, J. Schrittwieser, I. Antonoglou, V. Panneershelvam, M. Lanctot, et al. Mastering the game of Go with deep neural networks and tree search. *nature*, 529(7587):484, 2016. 36

L. Steffan. Using data from inertial measurement units for stability prediction in humans and humanoids. Master thesis, Karlsruhe Institute of Technology (KIT), April 2017. 102

L. Steffan, L. Kaul, and T. Asfour. Online stability estimation based on inertial sensor data for human and humanoid fall prevention. In *IEEE/RAS International Conference on Humanoid Robots (Humanoids)*, pages 171–177, 2017. 76, 100, 106, 109, 111

B. Stephens. Humanoid push recovery. In *Humanoid Robots, 2007 7th IEEE-RAS International Conference on*, pages 589–595. IEEE, 2007. 48

E. E. Stone and M. Skubic. Fall detection in homes of older adults using the Microsoft Kinect. *IEEE J. Biomedical and Health Informatics*, 19(1): 290–301, 2015. 43

K. Suita, Y. Yamada, N. Tsuchida, K. Imai, H. Ikeda, and N. Sugimoto. A failure-to-safety "Kyozon" system with simple contact detection and stop capabilities for safe human-autonomous robot coexistence. In *Robotics and Automation, 1995. Proceedings., 1995 IEEE International Conference on*, volume 3, pages 3089–3096. IEEE, 1995. 47

N. Sünderhauf, O. Brock, W. Scheirer, R. Hadsell, D. Fox, J. Leitner, B. Upcroft, P. Abbeel, W. Burgard, M. Milford, et al. The limits and potentials of deep learning for robotics. *The International Journal of Robotics Research*, 37(4-5):405–420, 2018. 35

R. S. Sutton and A. G. Barto. *Reinforcement Learning: An Introduction*, volume 135. MIT press Cambridge, 1998. 35

T. Takenaka, T. Matsumoto, and T. Yoshiike. Real time motion generation and control for biped robot -1st report: Walking gait pattern generation-. In *Intelligent Robots and Systems, 2009. IROS 2009. IEEE/RSJ International Conference on*, pages 1084–1091. IEEE, 2009. 63

Y. Tassa, N. Mansard, and E. Todorov. Control-limited differential dynamic programming. In *Robotics and Automation (ICRA), 2014 IEEE International Conference on*, pages 1168–1175. IEEE, 2014. 60

Ö. Terlemez. *Referenzmodell des menschlichen Körpers zur Generierung und zum Transfer menschlicher Bewegungen auf humanoide Roboter*. PhD thesis, Karlsruher Institut für Technologie (KIT), 2017. 153

Ö. Terlemez, S. Ulbrich, C. Mandery, M. Do, N. Vahrenkamp, and T. Asfour. Master Motor Map (MMM) - framework and toolkit for capturing, representing, and reproducing human motion on humanoid robots. In *IEEE/RAS International Conference on Humanoid Robots (Humanoids)*, pages 894–901, 2014. 196

E. Todorov. MuJoCo. `http://mujoco.org/`, 2018. Accessed: 2018-08-20. 39

M. Tokic and G. Palm. Value-difference based exploration: adaptive control between epsilon-greedy and softmax. In *Annual Conference on Artificial Intelligence*, pages 335–346. Springer, 2011. 37

T. P. Tomo, W. K. Wong, A. Schmitz, H. Kristanto, A. Sarazin, L. Jamone, S. Somlor, and S. Sugano. A modular, distributed, soft, 3-axis sensor system for robot hands. In *Humanoid Robots (Humanoids), 2016 IEEE-RAS 16th International Conference on*, pages 454–460. IEEE, 2016. 46

L. Tong, Q. Song, Y. Ge, and M. Liu. HMM-based human fall detection and prediction method using tri-axial accelerometer. *IEEE Sensors Journal*, 13(5):1849–1856, 2013. 44

S. Trimpe, A. Millane, S. Doessegger, and R. D'Andrea. A self-tuning LQR approach demonstrated on an inverted pendulum. *IFAC Proceedings Volumes*, 47(3):11281–11287, 2014. 61, 117

N. G. Tsagarakis, S. Morfey, G. M. Cerda, L. Zhibin, and D. G. Caldwell. Compliant humanoid COMAN: Optimal joint stiffness tuning for modal frequency control. In *Robotics and Automation (ICRA), 2013 IEEE International Conference on*, pages 673–678. IEEE, 2013. 68

N. Vahrenkamp, M. Kröhnert, S. Ulbrich, T. Asfour, G. Metta, R. Dillmann, and G. Sandini. Simox: A robotics toolbox for simulation, motion and grasp planning. In *Intelligent Autonomous Systems 12*, pages 585–594. Springer, 2013. 100

N. Vahrenkamp, M. Wächter, M. Kröhnert, K. Welke, and T. Asfour. The robot software framework ArmarX. *it-Information Technology*, 57(2): 99–111, 2015. 197

J. Vorndamme, M. Schappler, and S. Haddadin. Collision detection, isolation and identification for humanoids. In *Robotics and Automation (ICRA), 2017 IEEE International Conference on*, pages 4754–4761. IEEE, 2017. 47

M. Vukobratović and B. Borovac. Zero-Moment Point — Thirty five years of its life. *International journal of humanoid robotics*, 1(01):157–173, 2004. 20

M. Vukobratović and D. Juričić. Contribution to the synthesis of biped gait. *IEEE Transactions on Biomedical Engineering*, BME-16(1):1–6, 1969. 20

M. Vukobratović and J. Stepanenko. On the stability of anthropomorphic systems. *Mathematical biosciences*, 15(1-2):1–37, 1972. 20

P.-B. Wieber. Viability and predictive control for safe locomotion. In *Intelligent Robots and Systems, 2008. IROS 2008. IEEE/RSJ International Conference on*, pages 1103–1108. IEEE, 2008. 44

A. Yamaguchi and C. G. Atkeson. Combining finger vision and optical tactile sensing: Reducing and handling errors while cutting vegetables. In *Humanoid Robots (Humanoids), 2016 IEEE-RAS 16th International Conference on*, pages 1045–1051. IEEE, 2016. 46

S.-J. Yi, B.-T. Zhang, D. Hong, and D. D. Lee. Learning full body push recovery control for small humanoid robots. In *Robotics and Automation (ICRA), 2011 IEEE International Conference on*, pages 2047–2052. IEEE, 2011a. 42, 69

S.-J. Yi, B.-T. Zhang, D. Hong, and D. D. Lee. Online learning of a full body push recovery controller for omnidirectional walking. In *Humanoid Robots (Humanoids), 2011 11th IEEE-RAS International Conference on*, pages 1–6. IEEE, 2011b. 48

T. Zhang, J. Wang, L. Xu, and P. Liu. Fall detection by wearable sensor and one-class SVM algorithm. In *Intelligent computing in signal processing and pattern recognition*, pages 858–863. Springer, 2006. 44

Y. Zigel, D. Litvak, and I. Gannot. A method for automatic fall detection of elderly people using floor vibrations and sound — Proof of concept on human mimicking doll falls. *IEEE Transactions on Biomedical Engineering*, 56(12):2858–2867, 2009. 42, 43

KARLSRUHE SERIES ON HUMANOID ROBOTICS

Karlsruhe Institute of Technology (KIT) | ISSN 2512-0875

Edited by Prof. Dr.-Ing. Tamim Asfour

Band 1 **MANFRED KRÖHNERT**
A Contribution to Resource-Aware Architectures
for Humanoid Robots. 2017
ISBN 3-937300-56-2

Band 2 **CHRISTIAN MANDERY**
Organisation, Repräsentation und Analyse menschlicher
Ganzkörperbewegung für die datengetriebene
Bewegungsgenerierung bei humanoiden Robotern. 2017
ISBN 978-3-7315-0729-1

Band 3 **MIRKO WÄCHTER**
Learning and Execution of Object Manipulation
Tasks on Humanoid Robots. 2018
ISBN 978-3-7315-0749-9

Band 4 **PETER KAISER**
Whole-Body Affordances for Humanoid Robots:
A Computational Approach. 2018
ISBN 978-3-7315-0798-7

Band 5 **LUKAS SEBASTIAN KAUL**
Human-Inspired Balancing and Recovery Stepping
for Humanoid Robots. 2019
ISBN 978-3-7315-0903-5